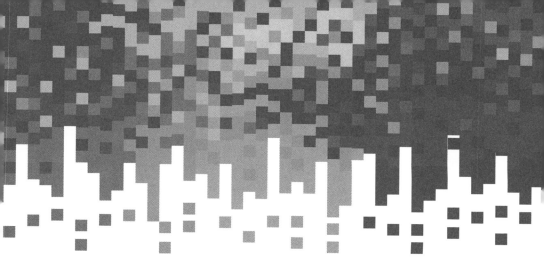

It's Their
WORLD
Teens, Screens, and the Science of Adolescence

Erin Walsh

free spirit
PUBLISHING®

Library of Congress Cataloging-in-Publication Data
Names: Walsh, Erin, 1981- author.
Title: It's their world : teens, screens, and the science of adolescence / Erin Walsh.
Other titles: It is their world
Description: Minneapolis, MN : Free Spirit Publishing, an imprint of Teacher
    Created Materials, [2025] | Includes bibliographical references and index.
Identifiers: LCCN 2024039521 (print) | LCCN 2024039522 (ebook) | ISBN
    9798885547949 (paperback) | ISBN 9798885547956 (ebook) | ISBN
    9798885547963 (epub)
Subjects: LCSH: Child rearing. | Parent and teenager. | Computers and children. |
    Internet and teenagers.
Classification: LCC HQ769 .W196 2025 (print) | LCC HQ769 (ebook) | DDC
    649/.1--dc23/eng/20241223
LC record available at https://lccn.loc.gov/2024039521
LC ebook record available at https://lccn.loc.gov/2024039522

Edited by Christine Zuchora-Walske
Cover and interior design by Colleen Pidel

Printed by: 68348
Printed in: USA
PO#: 16635

Free Spirit Publishing
An imprint of Teacher Created Materials
9850 51st Avenue North, Suite 100
Minneapolis, MN 55442
(612) 338-2068
help4kids@freespirit.com
freespirit.com

FSC
www.fsc.org
MIX
Paper | Supporting
responsible forestry
FSC® C005010

"*It's Their World* is a thoughtful, thorough, and above all actionable resource for any parent striving to understand what research says about teens and tech. Erin Walsh is deeply dedicated to helping parents support their kids. She is a steady, reassuring guide through the big issues of adolescence in a digital world. Parents who want to choose connection over conflict will find pages and pages of ideas to try today."—**Dr. Emily Weinstein**, researcher and co-founder, Center for Digital Thriving at the Harvard Graduate School of Education; and coauthor of *Behind Their Screens: What Teens Are Facing (And Adults Are Missing)*. For over a decade, her work has focused on understanding teens' experiences with new technologies and creating resources to help adults meet the moment.

"Erin Walsh joyfully explains the science behind how social technologies impact children and families, intermixing accessible expert perspectives with down-to-earth guidance, thought exercises, and activities to try with your own kids. Throughout the book, Walsh is keenly aware that a one-size-fits-all and purely protectionist approach is not always the most helpful. A true highlight in this work is how much youth voice and storytelling are honored and embraced—a key ingredient in unlocking the puzzle of parenting an adolescent in the ever-present digital developmental discovery hub."—**Linda Charmaraman**, Ph.D., senior research scientist at the Wellesley Centers for Women, founder and director of the Youth, Media & Wellbeing Research Lab at Wellesley College, co-author of the 2023/2024 American Psychological Association's health advisory on social media use in adolescence

"In *It's Their World*, Erin Walsh offers an empathetic, research-based exploration of adolescence in our tech-saturated era. Combining the latest science with practical wisdom, this book is an invaluable resource for parents who want to help their teens navigate the complexities of a technology-mediated life. Walsh reframes technology from a source of alarm to a powerful opportunity for growth—when guided by understanding and connection."—**Katie Davis**, author of *Technology's Child: Digital Media's Role in the Ages and Stages of Growing Up*, professor of digital youth and co-founder and co-director of the Digital Youth Lab, University of Washington

"Amazing! This is an essential guide for every parent navigating the minefield of today's digital world—practical, insightful, and packed with really concrete strategies and language to help you tackle it alongside your kids. It also illuminates how young people's developing brains shape their choices, offering wonderful insight to create a smoother path to healthy screen habits for both parent and child."—**Danielle Feinberg**, visual effects supervisor at Pixar Animation Studios, including for Disney and Pixar's *Turning Red*; advocate for girls in STEM; artist; and mom of twins

"The title of this wonderful new book exploring the vast, complex world of media (specifically social media) in the lives of teens—*It's Their World*—says it all. Teens and those of us who care deeply about their well-being will come to understand the influence of media through a developmental lens. Erin Walsh combines compelling scientific knowledge, her own wisdom and experience as a parent, and her years of work in the field of media advocacy and education to offer us this scholarly yet easy-to-read book. I appreciate the positive tone (teens aren't always easy!), the incorporation of the words of teens themselves, and especially the insightful interweaving of science and common sense. Erin Walsh's winning approach to guiding teens (and adults) to use and enjoy media wisely and intentionally will serve us well."—**Dr. Marjorie Hogan**, MD, FAAP, and former member of the American Academy of Pediatrics Council on Communications and Media

"*It's Their World* is a gift to parents and teachers, simultaneously an optimistic confidence-builder for the adults in the lives of adolescents and a constant reminder that it *is* their world. This is an evidence-based guide to being present for teens (and for soon-to-be teens) rather than restricting them so they always have us as a lighthouse, encouraging their curiosity and imagination as they build the world they want to live in."—**Michael Rich**, MD, MPH, author of *The Mediatrician's Guide: A Joyful Approach to Raising Healthy, Smart, Kind Kids in a Screen-Saturated World*, director of Digital Wellness Lab and Clinic for Interactive Media and Internet Disorders, Boston Children's Hospital, associate professor of pediatrics, Harvard Medical School, and associate professor of social and behavioral health, Harvard T. H. Chan School of Public Health

For Katie, Miles, and Emmett.
The world is changing quickly, and so are we.
I am grateful we get to figure it out together.

■ ■ ■ CONTENTS ■

Introduction 1

Part 1: "What Am I Capable Of?"

Chapter 1: Built for Discovery 10

Chapter 2: Primed for Rewards 26

Chapter 3: Sensitive to Stress 47

Part 2: "Who Am I?"

Chapter 4: Separation and Connection 76

Chapter 5: Independence and Exploration 92

Chapter 6: Online Self-Expression 114

Chapter 7: Love, Relationships, and Sexual Identity 128

Part 3: "Where Do I Belong?"

Chapter 8: Belonging with Friends 146

Chapter 9: Self-Worth 168

Part 4: "How Can I Contribute?"

Chapter 10: The Power of Purpose 188

Chapter 11: The Power of Voice 200

Afterword 211

Acknowledgments 218

Recommended Resources 219

Notes 224

Index 247

Reading Guide 254

About the Author 256

"You mean we can just leave?" I joked with the nurse as we prepared to check out from the hospital. Despite being in the ninety-ninth percentile for length, our newborn baby looked small and exceedingly vulnerable. I felt the same way. The humming machines and bright lights in the labor and delivery area that had been annoying just hours before now felt oddly soothing. I resisted the urge to invite the entire team of nurses and midwives to come home with us. "At least people here know what they are doing," I thought.

"You have everything you need," our nurse assured us. "Remember, you are a team," she said, gesturing toward the baby, who also appeared at ease. I was grateful for her vote of confidence. "I like that idea," I said to my wife. "We are a team."

Several hours later, I was feeling less confident in our team dynamics. Our first night at home felt chaotic and overwhelming. My search history between 1:00 and 4:00 a.m. illustrated my apprehension. I Googled, "Is it normal for a newborn to not pee for hours?" Hours later, after a diaper change, I typed, "Is it okay to get infant pee in your mouth?" Shockingly, the internet did not provide the reassurance I craved. When the sun rose, I was so grateful for my newborn's grasp reflex. I benefited enormously from holding my baby's hand.

Welcoming a child was a life-changing experience for us, as it is for all parents. At first, it felt like there were a thousand ways we could get things wrong. In the months that followed, we relaxed and learned to adapt to the reality that change is constant in parenthood. Extraordinary stress can shift quickly to extraordinary love—and back and forth and back again. You probably hear a lot about the rewards of parenting. But the strain is important to acknowledge too. According to Dr. Lisa Damour, one of the cardinal rules of psychology is that change equals stress. She explains, "The more change a life event requires, the more taxing it will be."[1] Raising children is a life event that requires a *lot* of change.

For years, it was hard to imagine ever encountering another transformation as seismic as becoming a parent was. Then adolescence happened, and the earth shifted under our feet again. Suddenly there were changing bodies, feelings, and friends. Technology accelerated the tremors and exposed new fault lines. My children are no longer babies. They are both still in the ninety-ninth percentile for height, and they no longer look small and vulnerable. My older kid is now taller than me. Together with their friends, my kids tap, play, scroll, text, consume, and create. One day my middle schooler sent me a link to a hilarious video followed by "Love you. Be home later." Compared to the hands-on, sleep-deprived days of early childhood, at moments like this, I think, "We have arrived!" Other times, emotional storms rip through the house, leaving all of us shaken. Our late-night Google searches reveal a new level of vulnerability. Like many parents of adolescents, sometimes I worry about my team, and I wonder, "What do we do when our kids no longer want to hold our hands?" I have spent my career studying screens and adolescent development. I am convinced that understanding adolescence can make the parenting journey a bit easier. Yet, even equipped with this knowledge, I find that the real-life moments of parenting teenagers can still be bewildering. The perennial gap between theory and practice is a reminder that parenting is as much an art as a science.

My Expertise—and Yours

I wear multiple hats when I write and speak about teens and screens. These intersecting identities shape my story in important ways.

I am a writer and a translator. My professional work is to dig into the research and comb through the data on adolescent development and digital media use. I am not a clinician or primary researcher. Instead, I bring more than two decades of experience translating the latest science into easy-to-understand language for parents, educators, and young people.

I got into this field when my dad started one of the first nonprofits in the country dedicated to studying media's impact on child health and development. Starting when I was young, my dad asked me to think about the power of screens in my own life. These conversations planted seeds that later took root in my professional life. After we navigated my adolescence together, my dad and I figured we'd gotten through the hardest part and would make a good professional team. Now, we write and work together.

I am also a speaker and facilitator. I have had the opportunity to meet people across the country, from big urban centers to small rural communities. I have listened to their experiences, hopes, fears, and worries. The stories in this book reflect my best recollection of these interactions, though I have changed many of the names and identifying characteristics to protect privacy. Through these conversations, I have learned more about the complexity of the role that digital technologies play in human lives than through any other source.

Perhaps most importantly, I am a parent. As I write this book, one child is quickly approaching adolescence, and one is already in it. With their permission, they show up here and there in the upcoming pages. This isn't a family memoir, though. I started with recollections of my first days of parenthood because I want to ground this research-packed book in the intense vulnerability, exhaustion, joy, humor, and agony of parenthood. I hope this book supports you in this space.

The first major professional talk I delivered happened by accident. My dad was scheduled to give a keynote address in a northern Minnesota community to a large audience of early childhood professionals. When he spiked a fever the day before the talk, it was clear that he was not going to make it onto that stage. He called the host organization to apologize and outline their options: they could cancel, reschedule, or hire his twenty-four-year-old daughter instead. To my excitement and dread, they opted for the backup Walsh.

The keynote topic was the impact of screen time on young children. To say I was nervous is an understatement. I had been hired to speak in communities before, but a major conference keynote was an entirely different matter. I armored up with a power suit and spent the entire night in a hotel poring over my dad's slide deck. I kicked off the morning by acknowledging the elephant in the room: "I know you are probably disappointed because I am not the Walsh you were expecting. But the good news is that I have some of his genes and, even better, I have his slides. So let's get going." Everyone laughed. I relaxed, and the talk went just fine. But looking back, it was clear that I wanted to be perceived as an expert who was competent to take the stage. To rise to the occasion, I crammed as much data, research, and "how-to-do-this-right" into my talk as I could.

Since then, I have delivered many keynote addresses to even larger audiences. I have also learned a lot about the kind of expertise that's needed to figure out how to live, teach, and parent well in a world dominated by screens. I am still passionate about the role of data, research, and evidence. At its best, research reflects lived experiences, helps people better understand problems and possibilities, and points to practical strategies. I have seen firsthand that understanding what is going on *inside* kids can help parents show up for them better. That's a big reason why I wrote this book.

Now that I am a parent, however, I am always a bit uncomfortable when I am introduced on a big stage as a "parenting expert." I am profoundly aware that parenting is a vocation in which no one can claim to be a universal expert. The science is clear on this point: There is no single recipe for raising thriving kids. Technology is constantly changing. Kids are too. All of us parents are trying to do our best for our children. Each parent is both expert and novice in every moment. We are expert in that we know our kids, cultures, and contexts. We see our kid's strengths, skills, and vulnerabilities. We are novices in that change is constant, and we are wonderfully and maddeningly human.

A NOTE ON TERMINOLOGY

The term *adolescence* is often misunderstood. Many associate it only with the teenage years. In reality, it spans a broader age range. From a neurological perspective, adolescence extends from age ten to twenty-five.[2] This may provide some measure of comfort to those of you who feel like signs of adolescence are emerging earlier than you prepared for. If you are parenting a young adult, it's a reminder that your kids are still growing and developing in significant ways.

Throughout this book, I use the terms *adolescents*, *teens*, *kids*, and *children* somewhat interchangeably when speaking generally. However, when discussing specific developmental stages, I'll use more precise language. For example, I will use the term *early adolescence* to describe the late elementary and middle school years, spanning roughly from ages ten to thirteen. I will use the term *older adolescence* to refer to the high school years and beyond.

I use the word *parent* throughout this book to mean any adult who is bringing up and caring for teens. A strong network of rooted relationships helps teens thrive. This includes primary caregivers of all kinds. And because I'm a parent, I will also use the inclusive *we* at times in the text. This risks creating some confusion—who exactly am I referring to?—but I choose to use *we, us,* and *ours* occasionally to communicate something important: I am not writing this book from some removed place of enlightenment. We are all in this together.

There Are Many Ways to Get It Right

"I missed your workshop last night!" a parent remarked as we both walked our kids into school. It was an oddly warm winter day in Minnesota. In place of the sharp cold that tends to bring brilliant sunshine, the air felt gray and heavy.

"Listen," I responded. "Winter is long, life is busy, and it's a gray week. It's a miracle we can get out the door at all some days." We both laughed.

"I really needed it, though," the parent responded. "I just feel like there are a million ways to get this wrong right now! It's exhausting."

"What do you mean?" I asked.

"My kid just got a phone, and I feel like it unleashes a million new things. There are so many overwhelming headlines, so many parental controls to try to figure out, apps that I don't know the names of, and a lot of advice I want to give my kid that she doesn't seem at all interested in. Things are changing so quickly. I just can't keep up," she replied.

"I hear you," I replied. "It's a wild time to be a parent and a wild time to grow up."

We both quieted, dissatisfied with this underwhelming summary.

Then I shared some reassurance: "I have to say, though, I am comforted by the research. It reminds me that we know a lot about what teens need from us—even as technology keeps changing. It also reminds me that there are so many ways to get it right."

I often repeat this to myself when I'm feeling overwhelmed. The dizzying pace of technological change makes it easy to throw up my hands, convinced that I can't possibly keep up. As I write this book, artificial intelligence (AI) is upending the world. By the time you read these pages, there will be new apps, new technologies, new opportunities, and new risks. Things change in a blink. This is what it means to be alive during the digital revolution.

It's my job to stay on top of these changes and to understand the way they shape the dynamics of adolescence. But this book is not organized by tech innovations or digital risks, and here's why: Chasing ominous headlines, the latest AI innovations, or trending topics *out of context* can contribute to the feeling of we-will-never-keep-up-and-we-are-never-enough. It does little to ease the stress and strain that inevitably come with changing technology and changing children. Instead, this book is organized around the core developmental tasks of adolescence. Each part invites you to consider how your kid is exploring an important developmental question, and the chapters in each part describe how teens try to answer these questions:

1. "What am I capable of?"
2. "Who am I?"
3. "Where do I belong?"
4. "How can I contribute?"

Young people are exploring these questions both offline and online—with time spent online ever increasing. The average thirteen- to eighteen-year-old in this country uses entertainment screen media for eight and a half hours a day.[3] For today's teenagers, the digital world *is* their world. It is no doubt different from the one you grew up in. This is the nature of raising teens; each generation navigates new risks and opportunities. But one thing remains the same: As young people's worlds expand during adolescence, they benefit tremendously from the curiosity and support of caring adults.

I hope this book shifts the conversation away from the framing question "Is technology good or bad for teens?" The research indicates that for any individual young person, the evidence-based answer is unsatisfying: "It depends." A more nuanced set of questions is needed. This book invites you to ask, "How can I support healthy development across online and offline contexts?" This question in turn inspires other questions, such as "When does technology help kids build a sense of belonging?" and "What supports and boundaries do kids need as they explore their identities?" Individual answers to these questions differ. The answers are shaped by a kid's specific strengths and vulnerabilities, by their digital activities, and by culture and context.

Many parents I talk to feel trapped in a cycle of conflict over technology, caught between constant worry and endless power struggles. The biggest casualty in these cycles is often the very thing that young people need most in a digitally connected world: a collaborative relationship with you. Asking a more nuanced set of questions isn't just interesting. It can change your perspective, your parenting strategies, and your connection with your kid.

You are reading this book because you care about your teenager. You want to do more than just protect them from harm. You want to prepare them to live a whole, connected, and meaningful life. As you will learn in the pages ahead, the adolescent years are a time of profound growth and opportunity to shape these kinds of positive futures. They can also be a baffling, overwhelming, and sometimes scary part of the parenting journey. Knowledge of what's going on *inside* your kids as they grow up—online and offline—can bring real comfort and reassurance when you need it most. It also equips you with strategies to navigate this critical period and offers supports grounded in what your teen needs to thrive.

This book tackles important and challenging topics such as sexting, cyberbullying, and online pornography. It explores parental monitoring, boundaries, and youth mental health. It approaches these topics *in the context* of adolescent development, so I recommend reading it from front to back if possible. Reading a full book from cover to cover is a big lift, but a worthwhile one, because understanding your kid's big changes and how they fit together may help you see them and the long arc of their development more clearly.

That said, I know that parenting challenges often feel specific and urgent. In those moments, certainly page ahead to sections or topics that feel particularly relevant. Then, when you have a little more bandwidth, I invite you to return to the text in its entirety.

Sprinkled throughout the book, you will find special features called Inside Insights. These scenarios are meant to spark curiosity and model how developmental insights can help parents slow down, build empathy for challenging behaviors, and respond in ways that are more likely to meet adolescents' needs instead of escalate conflict.

You'll also find tools for reflection and action throughout this book. These features are called Reflect and In Action. The prompts in these sections are designed to help you situate the research within your own lived experience, family system, and goals. Some will feel relevant and useful immediately. Others, not so much.

A NOTE ON SCREEN TIME RESEARCH

In this book, I draw on research that spans a range of disciplines, including clinical and developmental psychology, pediatrics, communications, neuroscience, youth studies, family social science, and media studies.[4] This collection of evidence tells us a lot about young people's digital activities and the impacts of those activities. There are, of course, limitations to the current research. Here are a few such limitations:

- Screen time is tough to measure accurately. Studies vary in their focus (time spent, specific activities) and measurement methods (self-reports, device tracking).

- Sample selection varies. Some studies use nationally representative samples, while others rely on more accessible groups or target specific subgroups.

- Technology evolves rapidly, often outpacing research, and long-term studies following young people into adulthood are scarce.

- Historically, much research has focused on North American, White, and college-age samples.[5]

To address these limitations, I prioritize insights from meta-analyses and umbrella reviews when possible. These "studies of studies" help identify important patterns and explain variation across studies. I also highlight research on underrecognized subgroups such as neurodivergent adolescents, adolescents of color, LGBTQ+ teens, and early adolescents. As you make meaning of the research, remember that you, your teen, and your context are unique.

I hope this book gives you a supportive developmental framework that holds up no matter what challenges you face or what tech innovations appear in future headlines. I invite you to bring this framework into your world and into conversations with your loved ones. I hope it helps you support healthy development by powering up relationships, skills, and opportunities—not just powering down devices.

As our kids move through online and offline spaces, they are engaging in the biggest and most important developmental task of all: growing up. Having a caring adult on their team matters much more than the latest app, chatbot, or platform. You have everything you need. Let's get started.

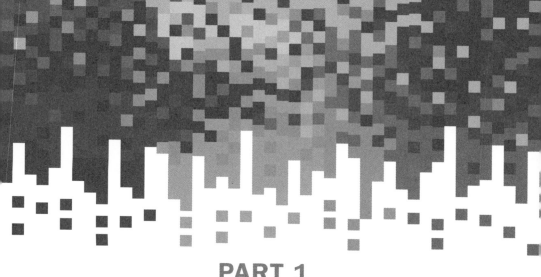

PART 1

"What Am I Capable Of?"

CHAPTER 1

Built for Discovery

"Isn't it odd, we can only see our outsides, but nearly everything happens on the inside."
—CHARLIE MACKESY, THE BOY, THE MOLE, THE FOX AND THE HORSE

When I have conversations with adolescents about technology, I often start by asking, "What do you love most about technology?" and "What's not working for you?" I like asking these questions for two reasons. First, I always learn something new. Young people are observant, insightful, and adept at figuring out innovative ways to make tech work for them. Second, I am constantly reminded that adolescents and adults have many of the same concerns. There are plenty of things teens wish adults understood better, but the idea that adults are hand-wringing while young people cling thoughtlessly to their devices is mistaken. Many of their concerns are related to how adults use technology. It turns out that adults and adolescents are in this together, trying to figure out answers to the same question: "How do we live well in a world dominated by screens?" Young people have a lot to contribute to this conversation.

■ The Adolescent Brain Is Not Broken

I had just finished setting up my computer for a student presentation at a large middle school in the Midwest. The auditorium was cavernous and quiet. To be honest, giant auditoriums are not my favorite settings for engaging with students. They don't lend themselves to conversations that fuel learning and reflection. But the principal had made a compelling case for bringing information about technology and the brain to the entire student body and promised that classroom teachers would follow up with more interaction.

Soon students started to trickle in. While most were happily immersed in conversation, one student approached me. I welcomed him, grateful to be able to talk one-on-one with an audience member before standing on a stage in front of hundreds of tweens and teens. As we exchanged greetings, I learned he was a seventh grader.

"Are you the speaker who is going to talk to us about our brains and technology?" he asked.

"That's right," I replied.

"So, is it true then that our brains are broken in middle school?" he wondered.

"Oh, no. I'm so sorry," I responded.

"What do you mean?" he replied.

"Your brain is so far from broken. But I'm not surprised you've heard something like that. Not only is that story unfair, it's also untrue."

By that point, students were filling the auditorium. The seventh grader gave me a polite but skeptical look, clearly eager to rejoin his friends. He pushed back the hair falling over his forehead. "Listen," I said before he left, "I'll give you the short answer now, but I'd love to talk more after this workshop. Your brain isn't broken; it's transforming. And it's built for discovery."

I didn't need to ask this middle schooler where he got the idea that his brain might be broken. References to vulnerable and out-of-control adolescents are everywhere. They show up in news headlines like "Watch Out! Teens Online Are Risky Business." They also creep frequently into parents' nervous conversations as their kids stand at the precipice of adolescence. Dr. Ellen Galinsky, author of *The Breakthrough Years*, surveyed parents about words they would use to describe the teen or adolescent brain. Sadly, only 14 percent of parents used clearly positive words.[1] When popular media discusses the science of the teenage brain, it often tells a simple story that blames the brain for all the teen behaviors adults find challenging—especially risk-taking online and offline.

The tween and teen years *are* rocky, and risky behaviors *are* part of the picture. Adolescent brain science does help explain and normalize some of the ground-shifting changes and behaviors that confuse teens and parents alike. For example, we know that the prefrontal cortex is the brain's "orchestra conductor." The prefrontal cortex coordinates competing information and impulses from across the brain and helps people regulate their emotions. It is the brain's thoughtful decision-maker that helps humans engage in goal-directed behavior. And during adolescence, it is also the site of major construction and renovation. But the teenage brain isn't broken, compromised, or injured. Instead, changes in the adolescent brain prime young people for learning and discovery.

Adolescence Is a Window of Opportunity

When I do workshops with young people, I often ask, "Is being a teenager really that different from being a little kid? Everyone wants to talk about adolescence, but is it really that different from being seven or eight years old?" Nearly all nod their heads up and down emphatically. I often follow up with, "How is it different? What feels different?"

"It's way harder," some say. Others report, "It's way better," "There's more pressure," or "There's more drama."

Every human takes a unique path from childhood to adulthood. But the words and experiences that young people share about this journey tend to be similar. It is an emotionally intense time full of contradictory feelings and impulses. On the one hand, adolescents are ready for independence. On the other hand, they are nervous about it. They feel confident and prepared. They also feel unsure and overwhelmed.

These descriptions make sense considering what is going on inside the brain during adolescence. The human brain develops in fits and starts—not in an even, steady, uniform way. That's because the brain is modular, meaning certain brain circuits and structures govern specific brain functions. As children grow up, certain areas have periods of intense activity and development, while others remain relatively quiet. Then the quiet structures begin to develop rapidly, while the previously active ones reach the end of their growth spurts.

Although growth spurts happen at every phase of development, early childhood and adolescence are two critical periods of rapid change across the brain. During the first few years of my children's lives, I could practically *see* my kids' brains growing. Going from totally dependent to walking and talking felt like a miracle. Spend any amount of time with a toddler or preschooler, and it's clear that their brains are constantly learning and changing.

Kids certainly learn and grow a lot in elementary school, but neurologically speaking, it's a relatively quiet period. That changes as they reach middle school. Just like the rapid change in early childhood, throughout adolescence the brain undergoes an extensive "overhaul and upgrade."[2] It is a series of major construction zones. These construction zones are shaped by a few key developmental processes: blossoming, pruning, and myelination.

The first two developmental processes are paired. At the onset of a neural growth spurt, the area of the brain ready for intense growth starts to overproduce dendrites. Dendrites are the branches at the ends of the neurons (brain cells). During a growth spurt, these branches go through hypergrowth. This is called **blossoming**. After this overproduction of dendrites, experiences take over the process. Experiences cause certain neurons to fire, and as they fire, the branch connections bridging one neuron to another get stronger. The branches that don't fire shrink, wither, and eventually disappear. This is called **pruning**. Experience, therefore, prunes or sculpts the circuits of the brain. Experiences during neural growth spurts, more than at any other time, shape the brain's neural networks and have a huge impact on the brain's wiring.

The third developmental process is called **myelination**. Myelin is a fatty substance coating the axon (cable) of each neuron. Myelinated axons transmit chemical electrical signals quickly and efficiently. Signals sent along axons that are not insulated with myelin are slower and more susceptible to electrical interference. The contrast is stark. An electrical charge travels one hundred times faster on a myelinated neuron than on an unmyelinated one.

These developmental processes drive dramatic changes in the brain from age ten to twenty-five. Through myelination, the adolescent brain is getting faster and more efficient as neurons in the brain become more effective at communicating with each other. Meanwhile, accelerated blossoming and pruning help overhaul key brain regions. This is why many neuroscientists refer to adolescence as both a window of sensitivity and a window of opportunity. During this time, young people explore and learn from the world around them. They form a sense of identity, purpose, and contribution. They learn essential skills for adulthood, including healthy decision-making, emotional management, and relationship building. Changes in the brain prime young people for these essential tasks.

As the brain begins to undergo renovation during adolescence, changes don't always unfold evenly. Here's the catch: the emotional center of the brain goes under construction first, followed by the prefrontal cortex. The prefrontal cortex is responsible for planning, keeping goals and information in mind, managing big feelings, assessing risk, and making decisions. This means that newly supercharged emotions can sometimes outpace the more deliberative and thoughtful prefrontal cortex. This is especially true during emotionally intense or stressful situations. Researchers often distinguish between so-called "hot" (high-stakes) and "cool" (low-stakes) executive function skills. Hot executive function skills often lag behind their cooler counterparts. This helps explain why young people are often more capable of thoughtful decision-making in lower-stakes environments than in emotionally charged ones.[3]

The order of brain renovation also accounts for some of the intense and bewildering behaviors associated with adolescence when emotions are running high. Parents often ask their kids, "What were you thinking?" to try to make sense of their actions. It's just as common for kids to stare back blankly, unable to explain their thought process. They *are* capable of thoughtful and reflective action. They *aren't* trying to be difficult. But they are still learning how to regulate their behavior in hot situations. This can be as confusing for them as it is for their parents.

The intensity of adolescent emotions can be overwhelming to teens and to the adults around them, but these emotions are not a liability. Dr. Galinsky explains that these strong emotional reactions have unique benefits. During this stage, kids are moving out into the world, where they will need to navigate complicated social dynamics without constant help from adults. This means that they need to be "highly sensitive to social and emotional situations."[4] According to Galinksy, strong emotional reactions position them to be the "emotional detectors" that they need to be to explore the world.

The Brain Gets Good at What It Does a Lot

The adolescent brain is primed for developmental leaps and growth, but too often adolescents' environments don't set them up for success. Teens today spend as much time online as they do offline. Eight and a half hours *a day* with entertainment media[5] is a lot of time. It's the equivalent of a full-time job.

Given how the brain grows and develops as shaped by experiences, it makes sense to pay attention to how adolescents' tech habits and activities shape their experiences while their brains are growing. What they're doing is reinforcing brain wiring for those activities. Conversely, what they're *not* doing is weakening other circuits. This is true of all experiences young people have during this window of opportunity.

Experience is not the only driver of brain development. Genetics matter as well. If you have children who are biological siblings, you can see firsthand how kids who share a lot of DNA can differ from one another. For example, my first child slept like an angel. As a naive first-time parent, I assumed this was due to my exceptional parenting. My second child slept like a rabid raccoon—in other words, not at all. I learned quickly that kids' behaviors and personalities are shaped by a lot more than just the experiences they have. There is a lot of natural variation, or neurodiversity, in how kids' brains develop, function, and experience the world. Being a parent means embracing neurodiversity and all the ways it shows up in ourselves and our kids.

For example, a teenager with attention deficit hyperactivity disorder (ADHD) might find it a lot more challenging to focus their attention amidst digital distractions. That's partly due to their genetics, or hard wiring. That same teenager might also use tools to help them stay organized, turn off their phone while they do homework, and take activity breaks to improve attention and focus. These strategies and experiences are called their soft wiring. It's important not to over-attribute teens' behavior in either direction. Chalking up a challenge to genetics and a growing brain robs them of agency and opportunities for skill building. Likewise, overemphasizing experiences contributes to the harmful fallacy that all brain variations can or should be "fixed" with the right kind of practice. Adults should try to remember that a constant interplay between kids' genetics and experiences shapes how they show up in the world.

Nevertheless, environments and experiences are worth paying attention to. Neuroscientists often say that "the neurons that fire together wire together." That is: the more often neurons pass on an electrical charge from one cell to another, the stronger the connections between those neurons become. This is especially true while the brain is undergoing a growth spurt. A middle schooler playing a brand-new video game may frequently lose lives and strength. But after a few weeks, the moves feel automatic, and it is easier to advance through the game. Whether it is video games, math facts, music, empathy, managing feelings, impulse control, social communication, or sports, the brain gets good at what it does a lot.

Adolescents Aren't Unwise; They Are Developing Skills

Poor online decisions can be baffling to parents who have discussed internet safety tips with their kids. Many adults consistently share advice like "Think before you post," "Be aware of your digital footprint," and "Be kind online." Indeed, most young people can recite these phrases quickly and confidently. Many add an eye roll for emphasis.

Young people do get it. Today's adolescents have been raised with frequent warnings from parents and teachers about the risks they might encounter online and reminders of the long-term consequences of online missteps. Many could write a persuasive essay about online ethics and responsibility. Most young people use a variety of creative strategies to manage their online information and privacy.[6] But they are still learning.

Hamza, parent of an eighth grader, pulled me aside before a workshop at his daughter's school. "I just don't get it," he said. "We've talked about this over and over. She knows better!" He shared that his daughter had gotten pulled into an online conflict in a large group chat. The group chat started with light banter about an upcoming basketball game. It quickly devolved into hostility. A few kids left the chat, but many stayed on, including Hamza's daughter. It became increasingly hurtful and ended late at night with promises of a physical altercation the next day at school. Hamza found out about it when school staff reached out to address the conflict that was now playing out in the hallways.

Hamza's frustration may resonate with you. It's helpful to remember that challenges like this are less about kids knowing what to do and more about kids managing feelings and building the skills needed to navigate complicated social dynamics.

The Teenage Brain Is Built for Discovery

Risk-taking isn't a "bug" in development. It is an adaptive feature. And honestly, it's necessary. Increased motivation to explore and try new things—to take risks—positions teens to tackle the risky challenge of growing up.

If kids' brains were built to hang back, consider all worst-case scenarios, and wait for total certainty before trying something, they might never leave home. Leaning into risk is key to positive development. While parents tend to associate risk-taking with negative outcomes, the UCLA Center for the Developing Adolescent simply defines risk as doing something when the outcome is uncertain.[7] Risk-taking looks like and leads to many and varied things. For a young person, standing up in front of class to screen a short film on relationship violence and pointing out racism in a Discord server are risky moves. They are also filled with potential for learning and growth.

Growing up is full of uncertainty. The combination of a prefrontal cortex under construction and emotions in overdrive means that on balance, young people are motivated to forge ahead anyway. Indeed, research shows that teenagers do have a higher tolerance for ambiguity than adults have.[8] The brain is built for discovery—even in the face of uncertainty. The good news is that the brain also learns from its experiences.

INSIDE INSIGHTS

Hamza's daughter likely didn't engage in the group text because she analyzed it, weighed the pros and cons, and thoughtfully decided to participate. Intense and stressful situations like this put a lot of demand on hot executive function skills. The part of Hamza's daughter's brain that helps her slow things down and consider alternative actions is still developing. Strong emotions can quickly override the more thoughtful and deliberative prefrontal cortex in higher-stakes scenarios. With more practice, she will get better at managing her feelings and accessing her prefrontal cortex during situations like this. Once things cooled down, Hamza's daughter was probably able to identify helpful response strategies such as leaving the chat, changing the topic, or talking with an adult about physical threats. With adult support and opportunities for reflection, such challenging experiences are exactly where young people build the skills they need to navigate future dilemmas.

"I will never forget what that felt like," a tenth grader named Liam shared with me.

"What *what* felt like?" I asked. I could tell that it wasn't a positive memory.

"It wasn't a huge deal," Liam went on. "But when I was in seventh grade, someone took a video of a kid crying in our class and shared it online."

"Of you?" I asked, trying to clarify.

"No. Not of me. But sort of a friend. A class friend, anyway. It was free time, and everyone was just messing around, and things got rowdy. This kid stumbled into the edge of a table, and I think he for real hurt his leg. He went back to his table to get it together, but it was clear he was messed up about it. Instead of asking if he was okay, everyone just kinda laughed. I didn't do anything. I just sat there and let it happen."

"It makes sense that that isn't a pleasant memory," I agreed.

Liam said, "After school, I ended up talking it through with my dad. I eventually apologized to my friend for just sitting there. It ended up being fine overall, and the video didn't go far. But it was a while ago now, and I still feel awful every time I think of it."

I wouldn't wish the emotional intensity of that memory or the suffering of the crying classmate on anyone. But the clarity with which Liam recalled this incident illustrates how teenagers often learn powerful lessons through experience. With help from a caring adult to make sense of what happened and plan for next steps, the painful episode turned into a site of reflection and repair.

The teenage brain remembers such experiences more intensely than an adult's brain does. In the teen brain, there is more communication between the striatum (the reward center) and the hippocampus (the memory center). Elevated sensitivity to rewards also helps teens attend to new information. (More about this in chapter 2.) All this together means that adolescents are likely to form strong and specific memories as they get out and explore the world—even when they fail. Neuroscientist Dr. Laurence Steinberg argues that learning is more likely to stick during this developmental window.[9]

During adolescence, increased independence and exploration bring missteps and mistakes. These don't always have to be painful. Successes and failures alike give teens valuable information about themselves and how they want to show up in the world. This information ranges from more benign things, like what online influencers they want to follow, to more significant things, like whom they want to be in a relationship with. Avoiding missteps entirely isn't possible. But learning from them, something the teenage brain is good at, is key to healthy development.

Approaching Screen Time with the Adolescent Brain in Mind

The latest science supports the idea that adolescence is a time for exploration, learning, and discovery. This idea challenges the dominant model of adolescence as a time to be endured, policed, protected, and monitored as young people move through dangerous minefields. Wall-to-wall talk of online risk fills news coverage of teens and tech. It suggests that a vulnerable brain should not be let loose on the internet. That's why it's so tempting to respond to adolescents with a fear-based approach that shuts them out or locks them down. As parents, we've all had days when we are tempted to walk around our homes powering down devices and tossing phones, earbuds, and controllers out the window.

This approach isn't the worst idea—for babies. There is little evidence showing that babies under eighteen months benefit from screens (except for video chatting with loved ones).[10] As children get a little older, adults can easily protect them from risky content by creating safe and contained "digital playgrounds" for them. Time limits can be easier to draw for young children (though they're admittedly likely to spark tantrums) because the boundary between on and off is still relatively clear. Researchers call these kinds of time and content rules "restrictive mediation strategies."[11] Turning off the TV, approving only specific shows, or taking away the tablet can certainly reduce time on screens and thus risk exposure for younger children. That said, research indicates that young children benefit most when adults also use media *with* them and help them make sense of what they are viewing and doing.[12]

The need for an expanded parental toolkit intensifies during adolescence. The challenge is that parents are tempted to double down on restriction as their sense of control diminishes and digital risks escalate. But relying on restriction alone robs teens of the practice, learning, and discovery that their brains are built for. Here are a few reasons that restrictive strategies alone don't work well for tweens and teens.

Control Tends to Assume All Tech Is Toxic (It Isn't)

If technology only *harmed* young people, then relying more heavily on restriction would make more sense. Instead, as upcoming chapters explore, research shows that technology and gaming have divergent impacts on young people's mental health and well-being.[13] Depending on the teen and their tech habits, digital activities may be protective or detrimental. Even the most vulnerable adolescents appear to be more sensitive to the negative sides of social media *and* gain more than their peers from the positive experiences they have on social media.[14] Especially for older adolescents, overly restricting them from all platforms might cut them off from much-needed support.

Control Isn't a Good Fit for the Teenage Brain

The teen brain is built to explore, engage, and learn. Clinging solely to restrictive strategies puts parents on a collision course with these developmental drives. It also doesn't work well. A review of the research demonstrates that the effectiveness of restrictive strategies declines with age and tends to backfire with older adolescents.[15] This doesn't mean that parents should hand kids a phone at age ten and say, "Good luck out there!" Setting clear and purposeful boundaries while gradually providing more opportunities for the independence and exploration adolescents crave is a better fit for their brains.

Control Doesn't Promote Skill Development

Finally, evidence shows that restriction alone can inadvertently make young people more vulnerable to the very risks adults are trying to protect them from. Even if parents hold off on phones or social media, young people *will* encounter online risks and challenges at some point. The question is whether they will have developed the skills to navigate them. In other words, how will they be able to deal effectively with online risks if they haven't had any practice?

Additionally, online interactions and challenges are often inextricably linked with offline ones.[16] For example, simply deleting an app doesn't help kids practice the skills they need to navigate the social conflict unfolding in the hallways of school. Setting a digital curfew doesn't mean that teens automatically have other healthy ways to deal with the anxiety that rears up at bedtime.

The skills that young people need to navigate these online and offline dilemmas are still developing. Left entirely to their own devices, adolescents are more vulnerable. Without coaching related to the complex realities they are negotiating, they lose opportunities to discover what they are capable of. Remember, the brain gets good at what it does a lot.

From Control to Connection

Given all of this, it makes sense that teens need adults to be more than just the on-off regulators of screen time. Purposeful boundaries really matter. This book dedicates a lot of time to the importance of screen-free time and spaces. But even if you hold off on phones and social media for as long as possible, teens still need you to engage, connect, coach, and communicate about their screen use.

A study of nearly four thousand adolescents and parents offers good information about what actually works when it comes to teens and screens.[17] Researchers used an online survey tool to recruit a national sample of English-speaking thirteen- to eighteen-year-olds similar in racial and ethnic makeup to the US adult population. This study was unique in a couple of ways. First, rather than looking only for *commonalities* among the participants in the study, the researchers also looked for key *differences* between subgroups of teens. This is helpful because a lot of screen-time research lumps all subjects together, which can mask important granular differences between groups.

In addition, instead of looking only for harms, the researchers were interested in the risks and benefits of technology use. In other words, they wanted not only to identify what was going *wrong* in the lives of some digitally connected youth; they also wanted to know what was going *right*. This is no small thing. When researchers focus on population averages and risk factors, they can overlook important insights about the strengths, skills, and protective factors that help teens thrive. Asking "What is going right?" in the lives of teens is just as important as asking "What is going wrong?"

What did this team of researchers find? The good news is that almost two-thirds of the teens in this study were doing well. This subset, called the "family engaged" group, had better health outcomes and higher well-being indicators. You might expect that this subgroup had limited screen time or strict rules. But that wasn't necessarily the case. Instead, when it came to parental involvement, here's what these teens tended to have in common:

- screen-time rules based on content and purpose, not just time
- positive parent-teen communication
- family devices and co-using media with parents
- lower parental social media use

The remaining one-third of young people in the study were not faring well in their health outcomes and well-being indicators. Their parents were heavy social media users and enforced few or no boundaries around screen use. Other studies have shown that parental screen use is a strong predictor of teens' screen use.[18] Teens seem to do better when their parents balance meaningful restrictions with healthy modeling and opportunities for communication, skill building, and shared decision-making. The wisdom emerging from a broad collection of studies on this topic says that active engagement in young people's media use as well as using media together helps protect kids from media-related risks.[19]

Discovery Takes Time, Patience, and Practice

"This weekend was amazing!" a colleague shared with me. "Last weekend? Not so much. It's a roller coaster."

"What do you mean?" I asked.

"My teen and I went to an event on Saturday with their favorite cosplay YouTubers. I wasn't sure if I would be doing more than playing chauffeur, but we ended up walking around together, and I was so blown away. There was so much creativity and community! I had no idea."

"And the weekend before?" I prompted.

"A living nightmare," she replied. "My kid was outraged that their digital curfew still stands for tenth grade and spent the entire weekend telling me what an awful parent I am."

"What a ride," I offered empathetically. "I've been there."

We've likely all been there! Finding the right balance of limits, connection, and coaching sounds good on paper. In practice, it can feel messy, foggy, and bumpy. During a negotiation over video games or a discussion about influencers and body image, it is easy to wonder, "Is this going to turn out okay?" It is especially overwhelming when teens hit major bumps on the road. Is it our job to protect them? Prepare them? The answer to these questions is a little frustrating: "It depends" and "Yes, both." For example, when it comes to cyberbullying or exposure to online hate content, parents should step in and work to protect young people. On the other hand, adolescents do need to learn how to navigate conflict with friends and how to solve digital dilemmas. Swooping in to rescue them in these scenarios inadvertently makes them more vulnerable. This book walks through such complicated issues and unpacks the risks and opportunities of growing up in a world dominated by screens.

Tell Your Teen: We Are on the Same Team

"What is wrong with me?"

I asked myself this question often when I was a teenager. Some of my behavior was perplexing. During my adolescence, happiness sometimes turned to complete despair in a matter of seconds. These were abrupt changes, to say the least. They were likely disorienting to my parents on the outside—and they were confusing to me on the inside as well.

My mom's consistent, gentle response meant the world to me: "There is nothing wrong with you. We will figure this out together."

At the time, I didn't dry my tears and give my mom a warm and loving "Thank you." Instead, I often responded with a wail followed by an indignant "You don't understand!"

Yet on some deeper level, her quiet confidence was bedrock during a time of great upheaval. Growing up was exhilarating. It was also hard. I needed grown-ups around me who believed we could do hard things together, especially when I doubted myself.

Communicating to our teens that we are on the same team is an essential part of parenting in the digital age. Being on the same team doesn't mean being best online friends. It also doesn't mean taking over the role of their prefrontal cortex through control and restriction. Instead, it means stepping into their digital lives with care, connection, and coaching. We can set boundaries so our teens experience safety and support. We can also expand opportunities, build skills, and walk with our teens through mistakes. Perhaps most importantly, we can assure them that there is nothing wrong with them. Their brains aren't broken. Their brains are transforming. There is a lot to discover on the path ahead. Good thing their brains are built for it.

◀ REFLECT WHAT IS MY PARENTING STYLE?

When it comes to digital media, parenting styles tend toward three main approaches: restrictive, balanced, and hands-off. To identify your style, choose the statements below that fit you best.

Overall:
- A. I don't think anything good can come from technology.
- B. I think there is a lot to learn and discover with technology—both positive and negative.
- C. I am skeptical that anything that bad can happen online.

I think that:
- A. The more time my teen spends away from technology, the better.
- B. I want my teen to be able to balance technology use with other life experiences.
- C. It's up to my kid to decide what they do online. I don't or can't get involved.

I believe:
- A. Teens should be protected from digital media.
- B. Many opportunities my teen can access online are valuable.
- C. The risks and rewards of teen digital media use aren't important.

In our family:
- A. Only my opinion about technology counts.
- B. I ask questions, listen to my teen's opinions, and enjoy exploring technology together.
- C. I defer to my teen's opinions and desires when it comes to their tech use.

In our home:
- A. I've set rigid rules and strict enforcement with my teen around their tech use.
- B. We have purposeful tech boundaries, consistent enforcement, and meaningful negotiation.
- C. My kid is pretty much in charge of their tech use.

Review your choices and take note of patterns. Were most of your responses A's, B's, or C's? (A=restrictive, B=balanced, C=hands-off.) This exercise isn't meant to assign you a parenting style or judge your answers. It is designed to help you reflect on where you are and where you want to go as you consider moving toward a balanced approach to screen time.

Now, pause and think about these three questions: What did you learn or notice about yourself from this set of questions? What do you want to continue doing? What do you want to change?

IN ACTION: DIGITAL DECISION-MAKING

Scenario: Your middle schooler asks to create an online account for a new video game all their friends are playing. How should you respond?

Response: Teens do better when their parents balance meaningful restrictions with healthy modeling and opportunities for communication, skill building, and shared decision-making:

1. You are not comfortable with games that have explicit first-person violence, sexual violence, or racial or cultural stereotypes. Your middle schooler knows this because you have talked to them about why you think those stories and messages are harmful. You've agreed that these games are off-limits in your family. When your kid approaches you with a game request, remind them of the agreement and ask if there is anything you need to know about the game.

2. Ask your kid to take the lead on researching the game. Ask them to consider a few questions:
   - What is the game about?
   - Why do they want to play it?
   - Who will they play it with?
   - How do Common Sense Media and other sources review the game?
   - How would they stay safe while playing the game?
   - If it costs money, how would they contribute to or pay for it?

3. Keep a close eye on gameplay in the first two weeks. After that, watch your kid play now and then. Consider playing together, if your kid will have you! Ask who they are playing with, what they like about the game, and how they are getting better.

CHAPTER 2

Primed for Rewards

"It's cool to get on the computer, but don't let the computer get on you. It's cool to use the computer; don't let the computer use you."
—PRINCE, 1999 SPEECH AT YAHOO! ONLINE MUSIC AWARDS

"**I** am decidedly *not* as brave as my daughter is," a parent shared during a small workshop on teens and screens for high school parents. I was grateful that she spoke up. Initially, the group had been dead quiet, scattered across the school media center. For parents of very young children, chatter about sleep and eating and other common concerns tends to bubble up easily. But parents of teens can feel vulnerable, and their kids need more privacy.

"What do you mean?" another parent asked gently.

"Well, I have autism. And my daughter is autistic as well. She just sees things so differently than I do." She described a social media campaign that her seventeen-year-old daughter and a group of classmates had participated in with the public library in their community. "You know the #RepresentationMatters conversation that's happening across social media platforms? My daughter had the opportunity to explore and test different ways to contribute to the conversation. These kids ended up working on all kinds of creative projects inspired by their own experiences, from writing to film to spoken word, and they joined in the public conversation online."

"That is so powerful," another parent responded. Others were now leaning forward in their seats, turned toward each other.

"But it isn't just the act of sharing that I think is brave. It's what they chose to share," she said, and then paused. Encouraged by the warm attention of other parents, she went on. "When I was a kid, I was taught that I needed to change myself to fit into the world. But it's clear that my daughter and these other young people are telling our community that there is a lot in the *world* that needs to change to fit them. Maybe I was more bold as a teenager, but today I spend time changing myself to make other people more comfortable. And here goes my own kid sharing her superpowers for the world to see."

"Brave is right," I said. Everyone nodded in agreement.

I think about that conversation all the time. The story stays with me because of the parent's willingness to share something personal, positive, and vulnerable. Talking about adolescent brain development and technology doesn't always generate such strength-based stories. Parents can get so caught up in the long list of unhealthy risk-taking behaviors they hope their kids avoid that they forget about the positive risk-taking that helps kids learn and grow.

It wasn't lost on anyone in that room that this parent had demonstrated the value of positive risk-taking by sharing her own story. All parents have stories like this to share. We have watched our kids be brave. We've watched them explore and try new things even when they are overwhelmed or uncertain. They do this in small and big ways every day, in both the privacy of our homes and the wide world of the internet. We shouldn't ignore the potential for unhealthy online risk-taking during adolescence. Nor should we gloss over the confusing and concerning decisions that our kids make as they explore their digital world. But tuning into their strengths is important, because it reminds us that our job isn't to squash their desire to take risks. It is to help them channel this impulse into beneficial actions. And when our kids inevitably take risks that are perplexing, harmful, or worrisome, we need to help them learn from the experience.

Risk Versus Reward

I can still remember the conversation my older brother had with his friends at our kitchen table as they excitedly made plans for their afternoon together. My brother is four years older than me, and I idolized him. I had perfected the art of invisibility during his social gatherings to avoid being asked to leave. I withheld any questions and comments that might invite notice. After some discussion, the group reached a consensus.

"Let's go!" my brother said, and soon five teenagers raced out the front door with their skateboards. Five minutes later, they were skateboarding down Twenty-Fourth Street in Minneapolis, tethered by rope to a car. Luckily, there wasn't much traffic that afternoon, and they made it safely to our neighborhood park before letting go of the rope to skate across the asphalt playground.

My parents didn't know about the plan or its flawless execution. But our neighbors did. Shortly after my brother returned home with his friends, my parents called him into the next room. I overheard the question so many care-givers ask their teenagers: "What were you thinking?!" Their emotional intensity was a bit lower than I expected, perhaps because my brother was standing in front of them intact. But I could make out some follow-up discussion about the poten-tial for broken bones and concussions. I am not sure how my brother responded. But if I had to guess based on his excitement when he returned home, he probably rolled his eyes. My brother could easily have listed the risks he'd taken. But from his perspective, the reward was worth the risk.

This story reinforces the tired stereotype that teenagers are loose cannons who can't be trusted with anything. As chapter 1 discusses, the region of the brain that helps young people manage impulses, the prefrontal cortex, is still growing. Yet reckless impulsivity isn't a fair description of the complex processes that propel teens to take risks—positive or negative. Adolescents are capable of controlling their behaviors to achieve their goals. It's just that their goals aren't always aligned with adults' goals. Not only do they often have different priori-ties, they also move toward their goals with a different risk-reward calculus than adults do. This is a result of what is going on in their brains.

Reward Sensitivity and the Teenage Brain

Neurons aren't the only physical aspect of the brain undergoing significant change during adolescence. Brain chemistry is changing too. Adults have long loved chalking teen behavior up to "raging hormones." Hormones are a big deal during adolescence, yes—but they aren't the only chemicals at play. A stew of chemicals that fills the gaps (called synapses) between neurons is important during adolescence as well. These chemicals, neurotransmitters, are often called "molecules of emotion." That's because their levels affect feelings and moods.

The brain contains more than one hundred different neurotransmitters. One of them, dopamine, is the "happy" neurotransmitter. The more dopamine that circulates in a person's brain, the better they feel. The human brain releases more dopamine during adolescence than during childhood or adulthood.[1]

What does this have to do with risk-taking activities, like skateboarding at top speed down a city street tethered to a car, or vulnerably sharing a piece of creative work on social media? Elevated levels of dopamine and increased dopamine sensitivity in the teenage brain may contribute to these risk-taking choices by adolescents. Familiar experiences with predictable and enjoyable outcomes cause the brain to release dopamine—but the brain releases additional dopamine when you do something with an uncertain outcome. According to Dr. Adriana Galván, a psychologist at the University of California, Los Angeles, dopamine's primary role in the brain is to help the brain learn from the environment.[2] Dopamine alerts the brain that something important is about to happen. It cues attention and primes the brain to learn from whatever comes next. While engaging in an activity with uncertainty and risk, young people may experience a greater rush than most adults engaged in the same activity.

This reward sensitivity gives the teen brain a higher tolerance for ambiguity than the adult brain has.[3] This is why young people sometimes make risky choices that are confusing to adults. An adult's experienced prefrontal cortex takes full stock of the potential negative outcomes and won't experience nearly the same level of "happy" from the potential rewards. In contrast, young people are less experienced, more comfortable with the risks, and get more "happy" from the reward.

These facts contradict the idea that young people can't stop to think about the consequences of their choices or that they don't know any better. Most of the time, adolescents are aware of what might happen. They also understand correctly that, usually, the worst-case scenario isn't inevitable or even probable. Young people aren't irrational; they are making strategic choices between safer and more thrilling options. Adolescents are still gaining experience, and their cognitive controls are still developing. Yet most teenage decisions are not defined by impulsivity. Rather, young people often move toward adulthood by purposely seeking the emotional rewards of risk-taking.

As adolescents test out new experiences, they encounter all kinds of dopamine-producing activities. Life is full of them. Some activities, such as using alcohol, drugs, and nicotine, bring high potential costs to kids' health and well-being. Some activities are decidedly positive. Consider the possible benefits of trying out for a school play, submitting a poem to an online publication, standing up for a friend, or starting a club. Other activities are double-edged swords. Technology falls squarely in that category. Digital spaces are packed with opportunities to explore, take chances, and seek rewards. (Recall the young person described by her mother at the beginning of this chapter. Digital platforms made it possible for her to share her story in a way that benefited both her and her community.) On the other hand, social media can create reward loops for risky behavior. Constant digital exposure to unhealthy behaviors can normalize them, especially if friends portray these behaviors positively. A review of twenty-seven studies found a small correlation between social media use and engagement in risky behaviors during adolescence.[4]

Most of the platforms popular among young people aren't built with healthy risk-taking in mind. Kids can benefit from digital activities, but these benefits most often occur *despite* how platforms are designed, not *because* of how they're designed. Most platforms, especially the free ones, are built to maximize clicks, time, and profits. Current design encourages compulsive behavior, captures private data, and allows unknown users to contact kids and teens. The data companies collect on users drive algorithms that can place young people directly in harm's way.

Young people need equitable and safe spaces to learn, connect, explore, and grow,[5] but the current digital environment places the burden on the user to make these spaces safer for exploration. Many brilliant young people are trying to change this environment. For example, the Connected Learning Lab at the University of California, Irvine, highlights the ways young people are creating "spaces of refuge" that prioritize support and care in dominant social media platforms.[6] But these efforts are the exception, not the norm.

Teens are not mini-adults. They have developmental strengths and vulnerabilities that should be prioritized both online and offline. Yet most platforms aren't designed to do that. Even in the digital mental health field, development has focused on one-size-fits-all solutions for adults and dominant groups.[7] Few digital mental health solutions center young people or underserved populations in more than a superficial way.

It's the business model that creates this mismatch. As Amanda Lenhart and Kellie Owens, authors of the report *The Unseen Teen*, note, "[Tech] business models that incentivize exponential growth, product stickiness, and average user metrics also make it difficult to center adolescent well-being."[8] In other words, the central question asked by most social media and gaming companies is not "How can we design these platforms for healthy development?" Instead, the attention economy asks, "How do we get users to pay attention to this platform above all the others (growth)? How do we get them to stay longer (product stickiness)? How do we get them to keep coming back (user metrics)?"

Why Do They Keep Returning to the Screen?

Early in my career, a mental health collaborative in a Midwestern small town invited me to speak with a group of parents and their kids at a community center. An advisory group of adults and teens had chosen the topic: technology and mental health. When I arrived at the door, an enthusiastic tenth grader welcomed me and showed me into the large room where we would be gathering.

"This topic is so important," she said.

"Thank you so much for inviting me!" I responded before she dashed off to greet more participants. I welcomed her enthusiasm, knowing how unlikely it was to be shared by all the teenagers in the audience that night. Before long, the room was packed with young people and their adults. Seated in folding chairs, most parents were turning around to greet each other before the workshop started. Many of the kids at their sides were slouched low in their chairs. A few in the front row were saying clearly with their body language, "My parents made me come here."

I had planned a large-group workshop followed by breakout discussion groups. One of the questions we explored as a large group was "What does science say about why it is so hard to unplug?" Given the initial I-was-dragged-here vibe, I was encouraged when many young people sat up and engaged. Others remained guarded. At that point in my career, I was still young, and I was eager to be perceived as relevant by teens. Their varied levels of engagement made me nervous for the youth breakout session. But as soon as we circled up, one young person who had seemed completely checked out made it clear that he had indeed been listening and had some opinions to share. "I get that our phones are designed to hook us. But it's not like we have no control over them or that we don't choose to go online for good reasons," he protested.

My instinct was to get defensive and explain the research about reward pathways. But as I considered my response, I realized that I agreed with this teen. I too resented the narrative that young people flock to social media and gaming platforms simply because of some chemical reaction in their brains entirely beyond all conscious control. "I am so glad you are bringing this up," I responded. I turned toward the entire group. "Let's dig into that a little bit and hear from more of you: Do you feel like you are in control of when and why you go online?"

Their responses were real, earnest, and as diverse as the teens' identities and life experiences. They gave me a powerful reminder to talk less and listen more when I'm working with adolescents. One young person, whose parents had emigrated from Somalia, shared, "My parents are fluent in two languages, but not English. They are the smartest people I know, but they don't know a lot about technology. I'm online all the time helping them. That's also how we connect with family. I just need to chill at the end of the day looking at videos and stuff. But I don't think it is bad, because I get all my other stuff done too." I appreciated this teen's willingness to push back against the idea that kids are just going online for quick entertainment rewards. There are many purposeful reasons young people turn toward devices.

"Yeah, I hear you," one young woman shared after listening to her peers champion their digital habits. "But I definitely spend *way* more time than I would like to on Snap[chat], and I know I am not alone. There is a lot of toxic trash there, and I just keep checking anyway." Even those who had been quick to argue that they were in control of their digital lives nodded their heads in agreement.

Another young person quickly backed her up: "Yeah, I agree. I can't decide if TikTok is the best thing ever or a gigantic waste of my time. Probably both. Either way, I am probably addicted to it."

I didn't need to flood the conversation with research on the push and pull of social media. When young people are invited to say what's on their minds, they usually articulate these dynamics on their own. National surveys consistently reflect these kinds of conflicted feelings among teens. Young people report that they enjoy some of their most frequent online activities, like watching videos, "a lot."[9] Yet for other activities, there is a disconnect between where they spend time and what brings them happiness. For example, young people spend almost an hour and a half a day on social media platforms but report enjoying this activity less than they enjoy watching videos or playing video games.[10] This feedback is likely shaped by the tension between quick rewards that keep them scrolling and mixed feelings about their experiences there. Many young people report being exposed to extreme, inappropriate, or harmful content. Yet a third of adolescents say they use at least one of the top five social media platforms "almost constantly."[11] Nearly half of teen girls say they feel "addicted" to TikTok, and almost one in three who use Snapchat say they feel pressure to be available on the app every day.[12]

What's most important in this data isn't just the minutes and hours young people spend with their devices. It's whether they feel like they are in control. The young person who pushed back against the idea that teens have no control over their digital habits was cued in to a very important dynamic. Dr. Katie Davis, author of the book *Technology's Child* and codirector of the University of Washington's Digital Youth Lab, has spent nearly twenty years investigating the impacts of digital technologies on young people's development and well-being. When I asked her to summarize what she's learned about media experiences that benefit youth, she shared, "It comes down to asking yourself two questions. The first is: Is this experience self-directed? . . . The second piece is just as important: Is this experience community supported?"[13] She went on to explain that adolescents benefit most from self-directed media experiences that are initiated, sustained, and ended voluntarily. They also need the support of adults and friends to help them make sense of their online experiences. In contrast, media habits shaped by external rewards or punishments are less likely to support healthy development.[14]

Last year my older kid and a friend were perched at our dining room table with their school-issued Chromebooks open. "What are you two tackling first?" I asked them.

"Math," they replied in unison without looking up from their devices.

I wandered behind them and quickly saw that one of the tabs open was their math assignment. The problem? It was just one of ten tabs. I could barely break through their frenetic clicking to start a conversation about it. Despite their earnest attempts to dig into the assignment, it was clear that their attention was being pulled in ten different directions. And they had just gotten started.

My first instinct was to slow their fast-clicking fingers with my own, position myself in their field of vision, and tell them, "Pay attention!" I have learned through experience, though, that the say-it-louder-and-more-emphatically approach doesn't work very well. Plus, I knew that their brains were paying attention to their computers—just not to a single assignment. People tend to think of attention as something they are either doing or not doing. (For example, they are either paying attention or daydreaming. Or they are either working on math or watching YouTube.) The reality is a little more complicated. Human brains have various attention systems that help people prioritize some things over others. Attention is like a spotlight; the beam can widen or narrow depending upon what is happening inside and around someone.

To understand why it is challenging to focus amidst digital distractions, it is useful to distinguish between the attention system that helps us react quickly to things in our environment and the attention system that helps us focus on our goals. If you heard a loud noise behind you while reading this book, you wouldn't "decide" to pay attention to it. Instead, within milliseconds, and regardless of how engaged you were in reading, you would turn around to see what was happening. You can thank your reactive attention system for this speedy and efficient response. This "orienting response" is managed deep within your brain.[15] It is sometimes called "bottom-up" attention, because it is automatic and instinctual. It helps you shine the spotlight of your attention on things that are moving, jarring, novel, or unexpected. This is essential to your survival. To stay safe, you need to react quickly to potential threats.

Your focused attention system, on the other hand, is directed by your prefrontal cortex. It is called the "executive attention network" and helps you exert "top-down" control.[16] Focused attention helps you prioritize some content over other content *based on your goals*. This could include filtering out the distractions of TikTok to focus on writing a paper, or focusing on the face of a friend instead of maintaining a Snap streak. Unlike reactive attention, focused attention is not entirely hardwired. The strength of your focused attention depends upon two things: wiring and practice. Based on the brain you were born with, focused attention may take more or less effort. This is part of the neurodiversity that makes each person unique. Context matters as well. For example, neurodivergent and neurotypical teens alike often struggle to focus when they are stressed or tired. Well-rested and well-regulated teens likely find it easier to focus. Focused attention can get stronger with practice. This is because the brain gets good at whatever it does a lot.

A NOTE ON NEURODIVERSITY

Many teens are at the forefront of embracing neurodiversity. You might already use this language while advocating for your own neurodivergent teen. However, there's still a lot of confusion around these words, so it's worth clarifying their meaning. *Neurodiversity* describes the idea that there are many ways that the human brain can be wired. It respects the idea that these differences are not deficits and that variation doesn't indicate flaws or mental illness. Neurodiversity exists only in groups of people. *Neurodivergent* refers to someone with specific variations in their mental functioning. This term is often used in the context of autism spectrum disorder (ASD), ADHD, dysgraphia, Tourette syndrome, and other conditions.

Digital Design: Distract and Deliver Rewards

Unfortunately, most digital platforms aren't designed to support sustained focused attention or to encourage self-directed use. Instead, tech companies often hijack focus and direct users' attention based on *their* goals: exponential growth, product stickiness, and average user metrics. Designers and researchers call these features "dark patterns" when they benefit the tech companies more than users.[17] Dr. Jenny Radesky, a developmental behavioral pediatrician and media researcher, has demonstrated that "persuasive design" features show up in most interactive media—even media designed for very young children.[18] This means that by the time kids are teenagers, they have spent most of their lives with dark patterns.

Why are dark patterns so prevalent? Compelling content, good storytelling, meaningful connection, and engaging learning experiences can certainly hold people's attention. But the cheapest and easiest way to cut through the noise is to deliver a hook for reactive attention. This is why devices are loaded with push notifications, autoscroll, jump cuts, message alerts, pings, and buzzes. One study showed that adolescents receive a median number of 237 notifications on a typical day.[19] This barrage of notifications makes the pull of screens hard to resist. Devices are designed to grab and *hold* attention by tapping into the brain's reward systems.

Our brains reward us for doing things we enjoy. Smell of baking cookies? Mini dopamine dose. Hilarious YouTube video? Mini dopamine dose. What is more: our brains don't reward us only for *doing* things we enjoy. They also reward us for *seeking* things we enjoy. The search itself is rewarding. In fact, our seeking or wanting circuit delivers a stronger reward than our liking circuit.[20] Think about a young child pining after a new toy. The anticipation of playing with the toy is often more exciting than actually playing with it. This powerful drive fuels learning, curiosity, and motivation; it's important to survival. It propels us toward discovery. But the seeking brain on tech? Welcome to the rabbit hole.

Reactive attention plus the seeking brain helps explain why the middle schoolers in my dining room found themselves "doing homework" with ten unrelated tabs open. They likely didn't *decide* to scatter their attention across the internet. They knew they had to do their math homework. To do this task, they needed to open Google Docs. Once they were in Google Docs, they noticed that classmates had messaged them. One message contained a link to a hilarious video. After the first video finished, a second automatically played. Soon, a suggested video piqued their attention, and a notification of a new message arrived. And on and on.

This distraction chain is no accident. Persuasive design features like notifications, infinite scrolling, variable and unpredictable rewards, algorithmically personalized content, autoplay videos, and streaks ignite the seeker within each person. The reward loops in internet rabbit holes are so powerful that a reactive attention hook isn't even necessary to get you started. Even when you silence notifications, according to one review of the research that highlights several studies with undergraduate students, you are likely to self-interrupt to check your favorite platforms.[21] Switching to a higher-reward activity, such as watching YouTube videos, may be particularly tempting when the task in front of you, such as math homework, is challenging. One study found that the mere presence of phones is distracting during particularly demanding tasks.[22] As Adam Alter says in his book *Irresistible*, when it comes to technology, "proximity is destiny."[23] If your device is close by, you are likely to start scrolling.

Young people are growing up in a booming attention economy. Their time, focus, and data make the tech industry hum. A study by the Harvard School of Public Health estimated that the top five social media platforms generated nearly eleven billion dollars in advertising revenue from users under the age of eighteen in 2022.[24]

All this research evidence reinforces the importance of purposeful boundaries. Sending our kids into their rooms at night with the instruction "Don't use your phone!" as it charges next to their bed is a developmentally inappropriate expectation. Placing devices away from sleeping areas at night instead helps give a young person's brain and body the rest and recharge it desperately needs. The research also serves as a reminder that until platforms are safer *by design*, teens will continue to struggle to manage digital distractions and risks. But telling kids that they are helpless and pleading with them to stop using entertainment and social technologies altogether and forever is decidedly unhelpful. Helping them develop a critical lens for understanding how digital design undermines their agency and control? Much better.

A team of researchers explored the impacts of different messages on adolescents' motivation to control social media use.[25] Traditional messaging tends to emphasize the longer-term rewards of reducing use. Yet the more abstract benefits of adequate rest or fewer distractions pale in comparison to the immediate rewards on most social and gaming platforms. In other words, tapping, swiping, connecting, playing, discovering, and scrolling just feel "worth it." In contrast, these researchers found that teens who received "values-alignment" messaging were more motivated to reduce social media use and showed greater interest in self-regulation strategies. This approach taps into adolescents' core values, such as autonomy and social justice, and positions controlling social media use as a way to assert agency (the desire and ability of young people to shape their own experiences and futures) and work toward a better world. Values-aligned messaging emphasizes unfair industry practices that steal adolescent time and attention for profit. It says that reducing social media use is both an act of rebellion and a way to participate in a youth-led social movement—both of which feel good *now*, not just in the future.

Instead of saying, "Pay attention! It will feel better later, I promise!" louder and more emphatically, you might try, "Do you know why it is so hard to focus on what matters to you?" and, "Who benefits most when you don't focus on what matters to you? Let's find out." You can engage your kid in questions like these:

- "How do your favorite platforms make money? How much money do they make?"

- "How does the business model rely on you? Your attention? Your participation?"

- "What design tricks keep you on this game or platform? How do they work?"

- "Do you feel like you in are control here? Why or why not?"

- "Do you think this design is fair to young people?"

- "What are other young people doing to try to take back control from tech companies?"

- "How might you participate in this movement for change?"

Tackling all these questions at once is not a good fit for teens. But you can touch on these themes over time. Including your own screen time as part of the conversation can help. For example, on the way home from your kid's soccer game, you might have a conversation like this:

Parent: "Ugh. I'm so bummed that I missed your goal."

Teen: "It's fine."

Parent: "It's not fine. I'm so sorry. I got a text and got lost in my phone."

Teen: "Yeah . . ." (looking out window, clearly disappointed)

Parent: "I should have put it in airplane mode or in my bag. Then my attention would have been on you and not my phone."

Teen: "Yeah, you are always telling me to do stuff like that."

Parent: "Exactly. It's something we are all working on."

Teen: "Can we talk about something else now?"

Parent: "Absolutely. How did it feel to score that goal?"

The Myth of Multitasking

I love fourth graders. They are good at and committed to matter-of-factly correcting adults. I have yet to work with a group of fourth graders in which one hasn't politely informed me that they can indeed multitask. With even-keeled assuredness, a fourth grader will inevitably stand up and start simultaneously patting their head and rubbing their belly with a big smile on their face.

While I hate to rob kids of a good gotcha moment, I am always grateful for this demonstration. It is a great example of how the human brain works. Yes, with practice, you can probably pat your head and rub your belly at the same time. You can chew gum while driving. You can walk and carry on a conversation. But what happens on your walk if you get lost and must figure out where you are? The talking stops. If you perform two or more tasks simultaneously, one of the tasks must be familiar. You can perform a routine task on autopilot while paying attention to something else. If both tasks require focused attention, you're in trouble. Remember, your focused attention is like a spotlight: It can shine on only one thing at a time.[26]

This is why humans aren't great multitaskers. Frequent or chronic task switching comes at a cost.[27] Let's return to the middle schoolers trying to complete their math homework. When they switch back from YouTube to a math problem, they are unlikely to pick up right where they left off. They need to reorient their brains to the problem. This takes time and mental resources. If they switch their attention frequently enough, they are likely to skip some of that reorientation time and make more mistakes.[28]

Despite this research, most humans *feel* like they are good multitaskers. People certainly spend a lot of time doing it. On average, nearly a third of young people's screen time is spent juggling multiple media streams.[29] "Sludge videos," which use split screens to stream your clips alongside unrelated footage, are an extreme example.[30] But about one in five young people say they "often" use social media or have the TV on while doing homework. Most of those teens don't think this affects the quality of their work.[31] But rapid-fire processing and constant task switching come at a significant cost to both work quality and memory. When you multitask, your brain spends so much energy switching between tasks and responding to stimuli that you have fewer resources for comprehension and retention. If you're a heavy multitasker, you are also more likely to pay attention to irrelevant cues in your environment.[32] Frequent interruptions are likely to scatter your thoughts and erode your memories.

Many parents wonder about the relationship between screen time and attention over the long term. Studies do point to a small negative relationship between tech habits and distractibility.[33] However, the evidence relies on correlational and self-reported data. This makes it hard to say with certainty in which direction this relationship runs. Are more distractible teens drawn to media multitasking, or does media multitasking make teens more distractible? Or both? Do higher sensation–seeking teens seek out more stimulating and distracting digital environments than their peers? These are important questions. So far, it looks like heavy media use doesn't *cause* things like ADHD, which has a strong genetic component. That said, heavy media use may compound existing attention challenges. One thing is certain: focusing your attention requires more effort than ever in a world filled with digital distractions.

Taking charge of your attention in real time can be challenging, especially if you aren't used to it. Dr. Amishi Jha, a researcher at the University of Miami, says you can build this muscle through short daily mindfulness exercises. In her book *Peak Mind,* she suggests simple practices such as focusing attention on your breath, noticing when your attention is pulled away, and redirecting it back to your breath.[34] Dr. Jha notes that doing exercises like this for even twelve minutes a day can improve focus.

IN ACTION: PAY ATTENTION TO ATTENTION

Everyone needs to practice shifting from mindless scrolling to mindful tech use. Paying attention to your attention is a good way to start. Share this exercise with your teen if they are invested in strengthening their focus, or try it yourself.

1. **Notice.** Notice when your attention gets yanked away from your goal. No judgment. Just noticing.

2. **Reflect.** Did you decide to focus on this? Is it aligned with your goals?

3. **Redirect.** Take charge of your attention and bring it back to your goal.

How Much Is Too Much?

Remember the young person earlier in this chapter who said she was "probably addicted" to TikTok? She wasn't using the word *addicted* in a clinical sense. Instead, she was saying that she spends more time online than she would like to. For a small subset of adolescents, though, technology can and does tip into clinical addiction. One review of studies found that between 1 and 9 percent of the children and adolescents studied had an internet addiction called internet gaming disorder.[35] The range reflects significant disagreement among clinicians and researchers about how to identify, measure, and treat internet addiction. In 2013, the American Psychiatric Association (APA) decided that internet gaming disorder warranted further study but stopped short of including it as an official diagnosis. In contrast, the World Health Organization included the term *gaming disorder* in the International Classification of Diseases in 2019.[36] While researchers and clinicians continue to debate the problem, some teens are suffering and need help.

For these young people, technology use is interfering with their ability to function and thrive. Symptoms persist over time and tend to include a preoccupation with tech, loss of interest in offline activities, declines in personal hygiene, social withdrawal, and poor academic performance.[37] When confronted with these symptoms at home, parents tend to focus on getting technology use under control. Yet problematic overuse is usually just one part of a constellation of challenges.[38] For example, a teen who relies on gaming to cope with an undiagnosed social anxiety disorder is unlikely to respond well to tech limits alone. Reaching out to a primary care provider, school mental health professional, or therapist can help parents understand the full picture and choose appropriate treatments for their kids.

> **REFLECT** I'D RATHER INVENTORY
>
> Don't panic that your child is at risk of becoming addicted just because they spend a lot of time online or love playing video games. On the other hand, don't ignore signs of a real problem. This inventory created by Dr. David Walsh is not a diagnostic tool, but it can help you see if gaming, social media, or other internet activities are playing an outsize role in your child's life.

Invite your kid to check each of the following statements that they agree with. Explain that the phrase *being online* means whatever their favorite online activities are: gaming, social media, watching videos, or anything else.

- I'd rather be online than be with my friends.
- I'd rather be online than do after-school extracurricular activities.
- I'd rather be online than spend time with my family.
- I'd rather be online than eat.
- I'd rather be online than sleep.
- I'd rather be online than talk on the phone or text.
- I'd rather be online than go to school or work.
- I'd rather be online than go to a movie.
- I'd rather be online than take care of my body.
- I'd rather be online than keep up with my schoolwork.
- I'd rather be online than move my body.

Next, ask your kid to name three things they like as much as being online. If your child has trouble thinking of anything they would rather do than be online, or if online activities are taking priority over important life functions, this *may* be a sign of problematic overuse. (Remember, this inventory is *not* a diagnostic tool.) Internet overuse often occurs alongside other diagnoses, so be sure to follow up with a trusted professional for evaluation and support.

Tough for Adults, Even Tougher for Teens

"Get off your phone!" my middle schooler reminded me while we were streaming a show as a family.

My kids seemed unfazed by the stressful Marvel plot unfolding on the screen. My nervous system, on the other hand, was on high alert. Without thinking, I had picked up my phone for a little distraction. The irony was not lost on my kids.

"Isn't this what you do workshops about?" they pointed out.

"Ugh, you are right. Thanks for the reminder," I responded sheepishly, and put my phone down. Clearly it was time to take some deep breaths and soothe myself with the comforting reminder that "this is just a show."

My younger kid, an eager problem-solver, grabbed my phone and promised to find a "good hiding spot" so I could keep my word.

No one is immune to the pull of the screen. People pick up their devices to soothe themselves, connect, respond to notifications, seek information, and enjoy distractions. Sometimes this is helpful and aligned with personal goals. Often it isn't. This struggle is shared by kids and adults alike. Yet adolescents' biological sensitivity to social rewards and their developing impulse control can make them especially susceptible to persuasive design. Understanding this science can help us cultivate empathy for our kids and find strategies for building healthier media habits.

This science of adolescence also invites us to advocate for platform design that prioritizes self-directed media experiences. Young people deserve more choices than just the dominant platforms that profit off adolescents' time and attention, highly controlled little-kid versions of apps, or unplugging altogether. Kids shouldn't be an afterthought on the platforms where they spend so much of their lives. In response to this need, the National Scientific Council on Adolescence has outlined what a youth-centered internet could look like.[39] Developmentally appropriate digital spaces would feature the following:

- alternative business models that don't use and sell children's data for profit
- independent evaluation and ongoing research
- additional protections for safety and privacy
- equitable and accessible design

The internet will not be redesigned overnight. So, should parents just stand by as teens head off into the metaverse? Not exactly. Young people are capable of exercising agency on today's internet. Parents can encourage this by stepping meaningfully into kids' lives as digital mentors with modeling, connection, and coaching. This includes giving them plenty of opportunities for positive risk-taking—online and offline. It also includes setting clear and consistent boundaries to give teens' seeking brains a rest. (The coming chapters explore all of this.)

Everyone needs practice taking control of their digital life. Becoming aware of your attention, your evaluation of rewards, the design of digital platforms, and your media habits strengthens your sense of agency and control. This is called **metacognition**; it means "thinking about your thinking." Over time, metacognition can help you distinguish between the digital activities that deliver lasting rewards and those that deliver a quick boost but ultimately undermine your goals.

Of course, most teens are not eager to formally reflect on their digital habits with their parents. They are likely to sit begrudgingly by your side, making it clear that they don't want to be there. This isn't entirely avoidable. But skipping long lectures and rigid prescriptions can help. Instead, find creative ways to invite your kids to engage. Try to plant seeds, experiment, reflect, and ask curious questions. Practice purposefully picking up your devices and then purposefully putting them down.

There are a lot of distractions coming at us. Let's not forget to focus on the goal: raising a courageous, capable, and caring human. I can't imagine anything more brave and more rewarding than that.

REFLECT RISKS, REWARDS, AND DIGITAL-AGE PARENTING

Your teen's brain is primed for rewards. Use the statements below to reflect on how you currently tackle risks, rewards, and the pull of screens. For each statement, think about which response best represents where you are: "I hadn't thought of this," "I try," or "I got this." Then ask yourself: What are you most proud of? What do you want to work on? Write down the latter, share it with a friend, and give it a try.

- I talk to my teen about their brain and how reward sensitivity can fuel risk-taking and decision-making in both healthy and unhealthy ways.

- I provide healthy outlets for positive risk-taking, including "safe enough" opportunities online and offline for my teen to explore, make mistakes, and test their skills.

- I talk to my teen about attention and focus without delivering blame and shame. My teen understands that focused attention gets stronger with practice.

- I ask my teen's school if they are teaching media literacy, including teaching about the attention economy and persuasive design tricks that compromise digital agency. I talk about the attention economy at home.

- I encourage focus during learning at home and at school. This includes turning off entertainment and social media and putting it away unless it is part of the assignment.

- I understand that my teen's hard wiring may influence how much effort it takes them to focus. If focused attention is a struggle, I provide support, such as frequent movement breaks, using white noise, or breaking work into smaller chunks.

- I have explored apps, device settings, and tech solutions that might help my teen focus.

- I invite my teen to consider the difference between mindless scrolling and mindful use by slowing down and noticing where they are shining the spotlight of their attention. I model the same.

- I ask my teen to reflect on which digital activities bring lasting rewards and which deliver quick hits but ultimately get in the way of what they want or need to do.

IN ACTION: TRY A TECH EXPERIMENT

It turns out that parents have bodies and brains too. Everyone struggles to resist the pull of their devices. If you tell your teen one thing and do another, your words won't have much influence. Start by becoming aware of your own tech habits. Avoid lofty goals like "I will never check social media again!" Instead, start small and learn as you go. What a powerful model for your kid. You can use the following steps to get started.

Step 1. Make a Plan

Ask yourself the following questions:

- "What is my goal?" (Examples: "I want to feel more rested" or "I want to feel better about my body.")

- "How will it feel if I am successful?"

- "What small tech habit will I change to accomplish this goal?" (Focus on removing triggers for your reactive attention and seeking brain. For example: "I am going to set my device to 'downtime' an hour before bed for one week," "I am going to delete an app that makes me feel worse about myself for three days," or "I am going to curate my social media feed for positive content.")

Step 2: Do the Challenge

You got this!

Step 3: Reflect

Ask yourself the following questions:

- "What did I notice during this challenge? What felt good? What didn't?"

- "How challenging was this on a scale from 1 to 5?" (1 = no problem at all; 5 = impossible)

- "If I couldn't complete the challenge, what got in the way?"
- "Am I interested in sustaining this habit? If so, how will I address the roadblocks I encountered?" (Be specific. For example: "When I feel the urge to check social media before bed, then I will listen to soothing music instead.")

Step 4: Try This Bonus Challenge

Make this process visible to your teen. Invite them and others in your family to identify a challenge of their choosing. Brainstorm how you can support each other in these efforts.

■ ■ ■

CHAPTER 3

Sensitive to Stress

"In times of stress, the best thing we can do for each other is to listen with our ears and our hearts and to be assured that our questions are just as important as our answers."
—Fred Rogers, *The World According to Mister Rogers*

"I finally just deleted that app from my phone," an eleventh grader named Sonia told me. She pulled a phone plastered with stickers out of her back pocket and motioned toward its screen. I reflexively grabbed my phone too, wondering which apps I would be better off without. We had both just served on a panel at a community event on social media and mental health. Sonia had been reserved during the formal question-and-answer session with a large audience. Now that we were off the stage, she seemed eager to talk. "It was time to clean this thing up," she concluded.

"Why did you decide to delete the app?" I asked, curious about her decision-making process. I was impressed that she was able to follow through on something that many adults struggle with.

"I was *deep* into it last year. But this year, I guess I've realized it just isn't worth it."

"Did you spend too much time on it? Or something else?" I asked.

"It's the stress! It isn't worth the stress. I constantly think about posting, responding, and just being in there. And after a while, it stopped being fun."

"Sounds like a thoughtful move," I replied.

"I mean, I still use social media," she said, "I am just more selective. I tend to stress out, and that app activates my grind. I need to protect my calm." She tapped a sticker of a sloth on her phone that read, "Just breathe."

I looked down at my boring dark blue phone case and crowded home screen again. I wondered if I could benefit from borrowing Sonia's approach—both the sloth slogan and the thoughtful curation of digital experiences to "protect my calm."

Sonia is not alone in taking steps to manage the stress and overwhelm that accompany tech activities. Teens aren't reflexively singing the praises of technology while adults try to rip devices out of their hands. This image is too simplistic. Young people do often defend the benefits of their digital lives, but they feel ambivalent about technology too. They are aware of its stressors, but they feel ambivalent because they rely on social media to cope with *other* stressors.[1]

"I wish people would stop blaming *everything* on our phones," a student named Eli noted in a meeting I attended with a small group of student leaders who were organizing stigma-busting activities at their high school for mental health awareness month. The group was planning to do a "no-scroll" day as part of their campaign, and we were having a spirited and thoughtful discussion about the best way to talk about phones and digital well-being.

"I hear you. What about it doesn't feel fair?" I asked.

He explained, "I get that there is some really bad stuff online—especially on social media. But the whole *world* is rough. And honestly, sometimes being with my friends online is the only way I can just chill out for a little bit." He went on to describe the transphobia he encounters in the hallways and classrooms of his school. "My phone isn't always the source of my stress. Sometimes it's where I find relief."

Other students chimed in, saying that they too turn to the internet for support as they navigate life stressors. They go online for many things:

- mental health information and resources

- clinical help

- enjoyable distractions

- support from friends

The group ultimately agreed to complement the no-scroll day with a speaker on digital mental health tools and resources. Their conversation demonstrates the complicated relationship between technology and mental health. Tech is neither all good nor all bad for adolescent mental health. That said, many teens are suffering. Adolescents are experiencing high levels of emotional distress, and it's important to understand the role that technology may play in this.

The Kids Aren't All Right; Neither Are the Parents

As a parent today, you likely know someone who is struggling—perhaps it's you or a teen in your home. You're not alone in this. Things like anxiety and depression are not new; they have been on the rise for many years. Most of the nation's leading health organizations, including the American Academy of Pediatrics and the US Surgeon General's office, have sounded the alarm that adolescent mental health has reached a crisis point.[2] A flurry of announcements and advisories from these organizations put technical words and statistics to what so many families already experience as true: The kids aren't all right.

It is tempting to pin the uptick in depression and anxiety on the COVID-19 pandemic. After all, the pandemic placed major stressors on teens. Taking friends away from teenagers is like asking them to breathe with limited oxygen in the air—it's possible, but distressing. That said, depression and anxiety were on the rise well before COVID turned the world upside down. According to the US Centers for Disease Control and Prevention (CDC), the proportion of high school students reporting persistent feelings of sadness or hopelessness increased by 40 percent between 2009 and 2019.[3] More recent snapshots of youth mental health are also concerning. In 2021, the CDC reported that 42 percent of high school students, and almost 60 percent of girls, felt chronic sadness and hopelessness. An alarming 22 percent of LGBTQ+ students had attempted suicide in the prior year.[4] In 2022, at least half of youth of color reported experiencing moderate to severe depression and anxiety.[5] Depressive symptoms among young people have dropped from pandemic peaks but remain alarmingly high.[6]

It isn't just kids who are stressed. We parents are stressed too. And as Richard Weissbourd, family psychologist on the faculty of Harvard's Graduate School of Education, points out, "We can't really understand what's going on with teens if we don't understand what's happening in their families."[7] Noting in a *New York Times* op-ed that parents have been "pushed to the brink,"[8] US Surgeon General Vivek Murthy released an advisory on the mental health and well-being of parents in 2024.[9] Parenting without a strong social safety net, including affordable child care, health care, and sick time, is logistically and emotionally draining and rarely affords parents opportunities to take care of themselves or each other. Adults are struggling with the same issues that young people find challenging, including loneliness, political polarization, social media, and climate change. What is more, raising humans in any context already puts us on a regular collision course with our own anxieties, histories, hopes, and dreams. We worry about all kinds of things—including but not limited to the roles that social media, phones, and gaming play in our kids' lives. We even stress about our kids' stress.

Parental strain is a serious concern. Data collected in 2023 indicate that parents are suffering anxiety and depression at about the same rates as teens are.[10] This isn't lost on adolescents. About 40 percent of teens said they were at least "somewhat worried" about a parent's mental health. Caregivers living with anxiety or depression can certainly be deeply attuned to the emotional states of their kids. These struggles can make parents more aware of and empathetic to their kids' experiences. But mental illness can also reduce parents' capacity to support young people when they need it most. How young people are affected by depression and anxiety in the adults around them depends on many factors, including the severity and duration of the adults' symptoms, their coping skills, and their access to support networks.[11]

Stress and the Brain

Stress is not inherently problematic or pathological. It is a normal part of life. New experiences, transitions, real and perceived danger, deadlines, uncertainty, and pressure can all evoke feelings of anxiety and stress. How stress affects you depends on your genetics, your access to supports, the amount of stress you experience, and how well developed your coping skills are.

Too Much Stress

Your brain's most important job is to keep you alive. That's why it has a detection system that scans the environment for potential danger and responds instantaneously, without your conscious control. Imagine that you're walking down a busy sidewalk and you hear a loud screeching of wheels. Stress hormones rush into your bloodstream to coordinate your response. You've probably heard this response described as "fight or flight." Your stress response downshifts brain operations from your prefrontal cortex to the more reflexive and emotional parts of your brain.[12] Within seconds, once you realize that the screeching sound is coming from a nearby construction site and not an out-of-control car barreling toward you, your stress response subsides and your cortex reengages. Soon you can enjoy your walk again.

The good news: this stress response is why human beings are still around. The bad news: young people who are experiencing a stress response may have difficulty with executive functions that happen in the prefrontal cortex. Remember, the brain downshifts in the face of significant stress. If an adolescent is the target of intense cruelty online, they may struggle to regulate their emotions offline. Likewise, if a teen knows that a nude photo of them is circulating among their peers, they might have difficulty focusing on schoolwork.

Stress that is too big, that goes on for too long, or that is experienced with too little support is called "toxic stress."[13] Protecting children and teens from toxic stress is important for their health, development, and learning. Though stress hormones prepare us to respond to challenge in the short term, prolonged elevation of these hormones can negatively impact the immune system, digestive system, cardiovascular system, memory, and focus. In addition, under chronic stress the brain tends to produce less brain-derived neurotropic factor, or BDNF.[14] BDNF is considered "fertilizer" for the brain, because it grows and strengthens neural connections and enhances the brain's ability to cope with stress. Toxic stress leads to less BDNF, and less BDNF leads to reduced ability to respond to stress. Chronic and severe stress, in turn, can contribute to depression, anxiety, sleep difficulties, stomachaches, headaches, concentration problems, and other long-term health problems.

As parents, we want to protect our children from harm. But sometimes, our kids face challenges that can overwhelm their ability to cope. These challenges, which can lead to toxic stress, might include things like this:

- difficult experiences at home, such as abuse or losing a parent
- broader societal issues, such as racism, discrimination, or poverty[15]
- traumatic events or abusive interactions encountered online or offline

In recent years, we've seen more young people facing discrimination and traumatic experiences on the internet.[16] While it's important to teach our kids individual digital well-being strategies, that's only part of the solution. To really support our children's mental health, we also need to address bigger issues such as racism, bullying, and other threats to their well-being. Our kids *can* cope with and recover from toxic stress, especially when that strain is buffered by caring adults. But they shouldn't have to.

Too Little Stress

Parents and society should work to protect young people from toxic stress. However, it's equally important to ensure that our kids learn to navigate the positive and manageable stressors that come with exploring the world. As Dr. Bruce Perry, child psychiatrist and neuroscientist, and Maia Szalavitz, science journalist, write in their book *Born for Love*, "Just as you wouldn't build muscle by resting all week and then trying to lift a hundred pounds just one time every Friday morning, you can't build a healthy stress response system by complete protection from stress or occasional exposure to an overwhelming dose."[17]

This means that our job as parents is not to protect our kids from *all* stress. Part of growing up is learning the skills to navigate new challenges and responsibilities—many of which are bound to be stressful. A teenager's physiological response to challenge prepares them to meet it. In moderation, stress chemicals can fuel the focus and energy teens need to tackle hard but ultimately beneficial tasks. Research shows that helping teenagers understand that they develop skills through effort *and* that a physiological response to challenge can be an asset is protective for mental health.[18] Consider the positive stress that your kid might experience by auditioning for a school play, or the tolerable stress they might experience while having a difficult conversation with a friend after a conflict.

Learning how to handle negative emotions is a healthy and normal part of development. When your kid learns to deal with small challenges, they are better prepared to deal with bigger ones later.

The parental urge to protect kids from harm is understandable and natural. However, protection can be overdone. If kids are never disappointed, they don't learn how to deal with setbacks. If they never take responsibility for the harm they cause, they don't learn how to repair. If they never take on new challenges, they won't learn what they are capable of. If we overprotect our kids, we might inadvertently make them more vulnerable.

Coping with Stress

As chapter 1 explains, emotional regulation is centered in the prefrontal cortex, which develops throughout childhood. As kids grow up, they get better at managing their emotions and coping with stress. For example, when your child was two years old, they may have rolled around on the floor overcome by emotions when they hit a challenge. By now, when your child is an adolescent, they have probably developed a range of strategies to manage that kind of stress. You can thank a maturing and more experienced prefrontal cortex for sparing you the meltdown—or at least the writhing-on-the-floor part of it.

But emotions are intense in the teen years, and teens' skills for handling intense emotions are works in progress. So, many teens need extra practice managing big feelings, considering alternative perspectives, and adapting to new and sometimes overwhelming situations. Remember, the brain gets good at whatever it does a lot. The correct dosage of practice is critical, though. Too much stress shuts down the prefrontal cortex and disrupts the brain's developing architecture. Too little stress robs the brain of practice at meeting life's challenges.

It's Complicated

I met Essence a few months into her ninth grade year. She had just started a new school in a new city. In her previous school, she had enjoyed a tight-knit group of friends and a couple of trusted teachers. These positive experiences, and the help of a therapist, had helped her better manage the social anxiety that she had wrestled with during elementary school. Her dad noted that, by eighth grade, she had come "a long way" from the days of spending afternoons alone in her room.

"It's not that I didn't want to make friends," she shared. "I just got so over-whelmed when it was time to make those relationships real by hanging out outside of school. So I just didn't. That changed last year."

"It must feel like a big change to start high school," I noted. "How is school going so far?"

"It's . . . okay," she responded. Her dad was clearly eager to fill the silence, but he waited patiently for her to go on.

"I'm definitely in my room a lot again," she finally admitted. "I'm sure my dad wants me to ask you about whether you think gaming is part of it."

"Do *you* want to talk more about it?" I asked.

"I don't know. Maybe. But I don't think it is as bad as my dad thinks it is," she replied, glancing at her dad.

We chatted more about how ninth grade was going. It became clear that Essence's dad was worried that she was gaming to avoid the hard task of joining new activities or making new friends. Essence admitted that this was part of it. But she also wanted her dad to understand that gaming was the primary way she maintained close friendships from her old school, friendships that felt like a lifeline during an overwhelming transition.

"What do you think? Should she cut down, or should I lighten up?" her dad finally asked, half-joking, half-serious.

"Well, for starters, it sounds like the two of you are having good conversa-tions about this. That matters more than anything I might say. But for what it is worth, I'd say yes and yes. Both."

Wading into a parent-teen tech conflict is tricky, so I was relieved when they both laughed. We talked about the idea that how, when, and why people use technology matters. On one hand, Essence was gaming with close friends that mattered to her. This is a good thing. On the other hand, she had been holed up in her room more often partly because she was anxious about making new friends. She agreed to work with her therapist to examine her motivations for gaming.

Stress is tricky. If a healthy activity you want or need to do makes you anxious, avoidance will probably make you even more anxious. For Essence, gaming all afternoon to avoid making new friends provides short-term relief, but it does little to help her manage anxiety and forge lasting friendships. Essence's dad was right to be concerned about a pattern of avoidance, especially given her history. On the other hand, staying connected with close friends is important and protective. *Yes* and *yes*. *Both*.

I ran into Essence's dad later and asked how she was doing. "You know what?" he said. "She's doing well. Most of her middle school friends aren't really in her life anymore, but she's still in close touch with one of them. I have a feeling they are lifers," he reported.

"And how are things at her new school?"

"Much better. I gotta say, freshman year was rough. We got back in touch with her therapist, though, and figured out gaming in the context of anxiety. I just kept telling her to turn it off and get out of the house. But turns out she needed to re-up those skills on dealing with social anxiety too."

I was relieved to hear that Essence had made some new friends. I was also so impressed with her family's willingness to think about her technology use within the bigger picture of her mental health.

How Stress Shows Up

Essence was ready to name her feelings and find solutions. In doing so, she is a bit of an outlier. Most people don't respond to stress this way. Instead, as the brain downshifts, stress can show up for most of us as moods and behaviors such as those in the following list. This is true for kids and parents alike.

- **Fuzzy thinking:** Without the full power of the prefrontal cortex, it's harder to prioritize, filter out distractions, and take in information from the environment. This can result in feeling disorganized and foggy.

- **Not taking things seriously:** Sometimes people manage stress by downplaying its significance, making jokes, or pretending to blow it off. This is especially common among teens.

- **Anger and irritability:** Emotional regulation is harder under stress, which might result in flashes of rage or low-level but consistent annoyance, grumpiness, or prickliness.

- **Volatility:** A stress response can make for a wild emotional ride—euphoric one minute and raging the next, hopeful in the morning and despairing in the afternoon.

- **Perfectionism:** People often try to manage stress by controlling things. For example, a middle schooler might stay up late studying for an exam they are well prepared for, or they might fall apart when they can't figure out how to do an assignment exactly right.

INSIDE INSIGHTS

Remember, executive function skills—flexibility, emotional regulation, resisting distractions, perspective-taking, problem-solving, and others—all happen in the prefrontal cortex. The ways stress shows up make a lot of sense when you consider that in the face of overwhelming levels of stress, the brain shuts down from the top down. This means that in stressful situations, feelings can quickly hijack the "orchestra conductor" of the brain.

In the day-to-day of parenting, it is easy to misinterpret stress-induced moods and behaviors as willful actions and attitudes meant to drive us bananas. Once we've read the situation this way, our prefrontal cortex is likely to head out to lunch as well. Our response is likely not to offer empathy, set warm boundaries, or coach skills.

Understanding how stress shows up in moods and behaviors can help you access empathy and curiosity when you need it most. It also helps you avoid unnecessary battles and conflict. For example, instead of ignoring the situation or thinking "My kid is lazy" when they avoid their homework and game all night, you could consider what else might be going on—perhaps "My kid needs to practice communicating with teachers when they don't understand the assignment. How can I help them do this?" Instead of leaving your kid alone or thinking "My kid has a bad attitude," you could consider "My kid is feeling overwhelmed. What can I do to help?" The purpose of reframing situations in this way isn't to excuse poor behavior. It's to help you look for what is causing the behavior so you can help your kid regulate their emotions and consider healthy next steps.

Managing Emotions

You can probably identify with every one of the stress-induced moods and behaviors described above. And if you read through that list and thought, "My teen exhibits these intensely," you aren't imagining it. The renovation of the brain during the teenage years means that young people are especially prone to strong emotions and intense reactions. Researchers believe that neurological changes during adolescence not only dial up emotions but also increase young people's vulnerability to depression and anxiety compared to younger children.[19]

This does not, however, mean that adolescents are fragile. In her book *The Emotional Lives of Teenagers,* Dr. Lisa Damour says, "With teenagers, it's easy to mistake emotionality for fragility."[20] Intense emotions come with the territory. But they aren't necessarily an indication that teens are unwell. During an emotional storm, young people take cues from the adults around them. If adults treat intense adolescent emotions as scary, unmanageable, or even pathological, teens are more likely to experience them that way. This is true at home, in the classroom, and in the community. Adolescents need to know that some amount of anxiety, distress, anger, and worry are a normal part of growing up. So when your teen feels sad, you can say, "It makes sense that you feel this way. This is hard."

Young people learn formative lessons about emotions from adults, peers, videos, music, advertisements, and influencers. These lessons are powerful. For example, a friend of mine who identifies as a White cisgender man (his gender identity aligns with the sex he was assigned at birth) once told me, "I heard in one hundred different ways that my tears were not welcome in my house when I was growing up. No one ever had to say 'Boys don't cry' to be clear about the message. It was obvious." As a White parent, I know that my kids are likely learning different lessons than their friends of color. Shortly after the murder of George Floyd in my home city of Minneapolis, a Black friend shared with me, "My son learned quickly from some of his teachers that his anger is scary and has no place in school. I know he is still learning how to handle it—we all are. But honestly? How can he not be rageful right now? He needs space for those feelings."

From a young age, kids are taught in spoken and unspoken ways which feelings are welcome and which aren't. Having feelings isn't in itself a problem. How other people respond to feelings can be. For example, boys who show emotions or vulnerability are more likely to be the target of bullying.[21] Girls are often discouraged from expressing anger and know they pay a higher social price for getting mad.[22] This is especially true for Black girls, who are more likely to be punished for expressing their anger than White girls are.[23]

The goal of stress management and emotional regulation is not about teaching kids to be happy, quiet, and compliant. Rather, it is to raise teens who have strong emotional responses to things that are unsafe or unfair—and can handle these emotions in healthy ways. Consider the complicated and challenging skills young people must employ as they navigate online situations like these:

- intervening when a friend makes a racist comment on a Discord channel
- identifying and disrupting biased thinking as they search for information through filter bubbles (the information "bubbles" that algorithms create by making it more likely that we see online content that reinforces our existing beliefs)
- speaking up when their favorite YouTuber relies on sexist stereotypes for a laugh

Emotions can get intense in a conflict. When people haven't had practice noticing and managing their feelings during conflict, their brains are more likely to shut down "from the top down." Emotional regulation equips young people to *handle* conflict, big feelings, and challenges, not avoid them. The goal is not to make all distress and negative feelings go away. It is to help kids answer these questions:

- "What am I feeling?"
- "Where do these feelings come from?"
- "Who can I trust? Who is safe and/or appropriate to share my feelings with?"
- "How do I manage these feelings in ways that don't harm myself or others?"

Technology can both help and hurt here. Texting a friend, scrolling through videos, and listening to music are appropriate ways to manage distress. In contrast, flaming (posting hostile or offensive messages) on a Discord channel or putting emotional trust in a stranger online is risky and costly. Everyone must learn how and when to express and contain big feelings—online and offline. Teaching kids to do this means helping them know and name their feelings, understand the context, and settle their bodies enough to channel feelings into healthy and thoughtful actions.

IN ACTION: RESPONDING TO TEENAGERS' DISTRESS

When our kids experience the typical stressors that come with growing up, often they simply need us to acknowledge and accept their feelings. Other times, they need us by their sides advocating for them. Slowing down can help you access your prefrontal cortex and discern which approach is best. Try these three basic steps when your adolescent is in distress:

1. **Calm:** Remember, an activated nervous system is not in thinking, talking, and learning mode. This is the time to breathe, use mindfulness or body practices, take a break, drink some water, listen to music, or hum.

2. **Connect:** Connection is the primary way that young people manage distress. Try saying, "This is hard, isn't it? It makes sense that you are upset. I am here to listen if you want to talk." Sometimes connection is all young people need to move forward.

3. **Coach:** Coaching includes problem-solving, skill-building, reflecting, and advocating. Try saying, "Do you want to just sit with it for a little bit or do you want to problem-solve? What do you think the best next steps are?"

Dr. Elizabeth Englander, a leading researcher on online cruelty and cyberbullying, acknowledges that the parental impulse to rush to coaching, problem-solving, and fixing is understandable when teens are in distress. Yet, she notes, "One of the hardest things about being a parent, honestly, is that you often don't have a solution. What you have is the ability to teach [teens] how to think through a problem."[24] The good news is that when teens talk to adults, they often *aren't* seeking adult-generated solutions—they just want to be heard.

Take some time to reflect on the questions below. The point is not to find explanations for every behavior. Instead, use the science of stress as a lens to consider what might be happening on the *inside* of your teen when their *outside* behaviors are challenging. When it comes to coping with stress, resist the urge to categorize tech as all good or all bad. Instead, reflect on your teen's tech activities with an open mind.

- "How does my child react when they experience distress?"
- "What might be going on inside my child that helps explain these behaviors?"
- "What tech activities help my child cope with distress?"
- "What tech activities seem to get in the way of healthy coping?"

Now go through these questions again and answer for yourself:

- "How do I react when I experience distress?"
- "How do I react when my child experiences distress?"
- "How does the science of stress help me understand my reactions?"
- "What tech activities help me cope with distress?"
- "What tech activities seem to get in the way of healthy coping?"

Doesn't Social Media Cause Mental Health Issues?

In any given moment, your kid's technology use might help them express, manage, contain, or intensify distressing feelings. But what about the bigger picture? What is the relationship between social media use and mental health overall? The data show that the amount of time young people spend with personal devices and on social media has been rising in tandem with anxiety and depression. It's tempting to assume a direct causal link. News headlines often reinforce the idea that tech bears all the blame—case closed.

But such storylines haven't done a great job of translating the science. Though a few thought leaders have come down strongly on the side of causality,[25] most leading researchers point out that the best studies have produced mixed results.[26] The evidence overall does indicate a small but statistically significant association between increased time on social media and worsening mental health outcomes, especially among adolescent girls.[27] But research summaries by adolescent health and development organizations say there are also positive uses of social media among adolescents.[28]

A few important factors complicate the research picture and what that means for any individual teen. First, many different things happen on social media. Scrolling through self-harm content will almost certainly drive different outcomes than connecting with friends will. Second, the best studies continue to be correlational—meaning that these two things happen together but we don't know the cause. Do these studies indicate that social media causes anxiety? Or that young people living with anxiety are more likely to use social media? Or that other factors are driving the correlation? It is likely a combination of these things. Third, many studies rely on the average time kids spend on social media and then look at how it impacts *all* kids in the study group. Lumping all social media activities and all kids together masks a lot of variability among adolescents. While social media doesn't seem to have an outsize impact on some teens' mental health, for others it contributes significantly to suffering. For many young people, their online experiences are mixed. Researchers are working hard to untangle these complex dynamics.

This complexity should not blunt concern about social media. The American Psychological Association and the Office of the US Surgeon General released advisories in 2023 on social media and adolescent mental health.[29] Both advisories urge parents, policymakers, tech companies, and educators to take the potential negative mental health impacts of social media seriously. A team of researchers described how social media features intersect with adolescent developmental changes in ways that might increase adolescent vulnerability to mental illness.[30] Surgeon General Vivek Murthy acknowledges that despite the complexity of the issue, a "do no harm" approach is appropriate. Society has a track record of employing this approach in industries such as food safety, road safety, and consumer protection and can do so in the tech industry too. It's not necessary to prove that all platforms are toxic to all teens before demanding that tech companies prioritize engaging, safe, and developmentally appropriate design.

Endless debates about the exact mechanisms that drive mental health outcomes may feel far removed from your daily parenting life. You may yearn for clear solutions and concrete guidelines. Parents often say to me, "Just tell me how much screen time my kids should have!" I get it. Their risk-assessment capacity is fried, news headlines ignite their anxiety, and everyone could use some certainty right now. That's why I wince a bit when I deliver this evidence-based response: "Well, it depends."

Simple screen-time recommendations can be helpful at the extremes. Too much screen time? Not great for well-being. No screens at all? Not great either, at least for adolescents.[31] But the middle is messy. In the middle ground, outcomes are driven less by time and more by *what*, *when*, *why*, and *with whom*. For any individual teen, mental health outcomes are shaped by their vulnerabilities and strengths, their digital activities, the design of the platforms they spend time on, and their access to resources and supports.[32] As leading researcher Dr. Jacqueline Nesi shares succinctly, even the impact of social media on a child's mental health depends on "what they are doing on there and who they are."[33] To sum up: it's complicated.

■ Turn Toward Your Teenager

Some activists and policymakers argue that tech companies should be treated like Big Tobacco. This framing could galvanize public support for industry accountability and government policy change. It highlights the insidious tactics tech companies use to avoid consequences for online harms. But when it comes to parenting, this may not be the most useful analogy. Tobacco is harmful to adolescents no matter how or with whom it is used. Technology, on the other hand, can help or hurt depending upon the role that it plays in kids' lives. It's their world, and it benefits all of us to approach it with curiosity. The most powerful thing we parents can do for adolescent health and well-being is to turn toward the teens in our lives.

This is a good time to ask your adolescent questions such as these:

- "Where do you spend most of your time online? Why?"
- "What's going well for you?"
- "What isn't going well?"
- "When do you use that app/play that game/visit that website?"
- "How does it make you feel about yourself and others?"

- "How do people treat each other in this space?"
- "What could you be doing instead?"

The answers to these questions will tell you a lot more than tracking minutes of screen time will. Young people's experiences in digital spaces matter. Their reasons matter. When you ask questions, you may, for example, find that your kid feels connected and creative in their online community and lonely at school. That kind of information is important to know.

Don't expect to address all your questions in one long, emotionally available conversation. Don't be surprised if your kid answers some questions with very little detail or a dismissive eye roll. That's not a sign to give up; it's an invitation to get more creative. You can start small conversations while you're driving, watching a show, listening to a podcast, walking, or hanging out. For example, let's say you just finished watching a show with your teen and you are ready to sleep. Your teen, however, is ready to talk. You notice this and decide to take the opportunity.

Parent: "I can't believe it. Our favorite character's crush started dating someone else and they found out online."

Teen: "The worst."

Parent: "Do you or your friends ever find out stuff about each other that way?"

Teen: "Sometimes."

Parent: (waiting)

Teen: "Last year my friend found out they got broken up with at the same time we all did because their ex posted about it. It was so messed up."

Parent: "That must have felt awful."

Teen: "Snap has so much drama."

Parent: "Sounds like it. What kind?"

Teen: "I don't know. Mostly just kids joking around and being crazy."

Parent: "How do you manage it?"

Teen: "I don't know."

Parent: (waiting)

Parent: "If you ever want to talk more about it or if you feel stuck, I'm here for you."

Teen: "I know. Can we talk about something else?"

Parent: "For sure."

Parent: (loops back around a couple of days later)

Short, frequent conversations like this can help you get a more accurate picture of your own kid, including areas of strength and concern. When it comes to technology use and your kid's mental health, look for answers to the following questions.

How emotionally invested are they in online feedback? Most young people are highly attuned to the social metrics of peer approval online. (Chapter 8 takes a deeper dive into this subject.) Research shows that some young people may have more emotional investment in social media "likes" and "shares." In other words, their entire sense of self-worth rises and falls with online feedback. Other kids are more resilient to the emotional peaks and valleys. Being more emotionally invested may put kids at higher risk for anxiety and depression.[34]

What are the vulnerabilities of their age and stage? There are plenty of reasons to delay social media use, in particular, beyond early adolescence. One impressive study indicates that there are specific windows of developmental sensitivity where our kids may be more vulnerable to online harms.[35] If you have a child between the ages of ten and fifteen, you might consider holding off on social media. (The study found that the window of sensitivity occurs at ages ten to thirteen for girls and fourteen to fifteen for boys.) You might use similar logic to delay use of certain video games or messaging platforms. That said, kids mature at different rates, and there isn't a magic age where every kid is suddenly unaffected by online harms.

What kind of relationships and connections do they have online? Adolescence is all about finding your place and your people. Supportive interactions in online communities can be protective for mental health. This is especially true for LGBTQ+ teens, youth of color, immigrant youth, and youth living with specific mental health or medical diagnoses.[36] Conversely, young people whose online interactions and relationships are toxic or cruel are more

dynamics to keep in mind when navigating the barrage of mental health content on social media:

- **Misleading and inaccurate information:** While licensed mental health providers do use TikTok to share clinically sound information, many creators draw solely on personal experience. Without formal training or clinical experience, creators may inadvertently share inaccurate or even harmful advice. A recent review found high prevalence of health misinformation on social media.[47] More research is needed, but it's fair to say that misleading and inaccurate information is common and that algorithms can quickly lead to harmful content.

- **Self-diagnosis:** Some teens aren't just using social media for connection and conversation. They are using it to self-diagnose and sometimes self-treat. Content creators may encourage this practice by directing their audiences toward online quizzes or self-published books instead of toward clinical evaluation or support. Knowing the major symptoms of common mental health disorders is an important new literacy for a generation of kids committed to normalizing mental health. But jumping to quick conclusions or self-diagnosing online can backfire or delay appropriate treatment.

- **The Barnum effect:** In her research-based Substack *Techno Sapiens,* Jacqueline Nesi says the Barnum effect can easily come into play in these online spaces.[48] According to Dr. Nesi, the Barnum effect "refers to our strong tendency to believe that generic information or statements, which could apply to anyone, are specifically about us." In other words, short online videos can be a bit like horoscopes. It's easy for anyone to make them fit their individual experiences.

Let's not write off our teens' positive experiences in these spaces. They have real value for many young people. If we brush off legitimate concerns with comments like "It's just a phase" or "You are looking for attention," we may contribute to mental health stigma. Let's also avoid comments like "You just think that because of TikTok or YouTube." Instead, let's approach this content as a starting place for a meaningful conversation about mental health and well-being.

Instead of: "I can't stand that platform."
Try: "Which creators are you drawn to on this platform? Why? What do you already know about the algorithms that drive who and what you see here?"

Instead of: "There is no way that person knows what they are talking about."
Try: "How do you evaluate what you are seeing or hearing? Are they sharing or selling medical advice or diagnosing people online?"

Instead of: "You just think that because of social media."
Try: "It sounds like you have some concerns about your attention. Can you tell me more about what's happening?"

Instead of: "I don't think that person has any clue what you need."
Try: "Let's make sure you know who you can talk to about your concerns." (Share names and resources and give options.)

Both/And Parenting

I had the opportunity to do a workshop at a small community college. A campus wellness team invited me to talk about practical strategies for digital well-being. While the workshop wasn't part of a class, psychology students received extra credit for attending. My initial plan had been to ask the students to interview each other about their current digital habits. But as I observed the level of scrolling in the room, I decided my plan would come across as public shaming instead of an invitation for reflection.

I pivoted to a strategy that often works well with high school students: focusing on younger versions of themselves instead of the more vulnerable present. I invited students to follow me to a common space outside the classroom. I said, "Find someone on your way out and share your thoughts on this topic: Think back to middle or high school. Share a boundary, a practice, or a habit around technology that a friend, teacher, or parent encouraged. Choose one that you resented at the time but are grateful for now. What was it, and why are you grateful?"

I started up the stairs and hoped the students would follow me. Just moving out of the room shook up the scroll-and-avoid-eye-contact dynamic. Soon, students had paired up and were sharing stories. We extended the planned four minutes to ten before circling up for a group discussion. One student said they were grateful for a teacher who had done a podcasting challenge on mental health in class. Another said they were glad that their parents made them go outside every day. A student named Daniel courageously took the conversation in a more personal direction.

"I guess I should call my grandma and thank her!" he started. "I was *not* grateful at the time. I got a cell phone in fifth grade, so I got used to having it. Then, my freshman year of high school, my grandma took my phone from me at night."

"Grandmas always know," another student commented. Everyone laughed.

"Yeah," he went on, "we were just talking about that." Daniel gestured to his conversation partner, who apparently had a powerhouse grandma as well. "I didn't see this as a positive thing at the time. But what mattered is that she didn't just take my phone away. She also hooked me up with my school social worker. Looking back, I don't think one would have worked without the other. I was a mess. I was acting out but also really struggling with anxiety and didn't know how to talk about it," he said.

"What do you mean, 'I don't think one would have worked without the other?'" I prompted gently.

"I mean I *needed* to get away from the drama on that phone. But I also really needed help to work through some stuff. At first, I was just an anxious, sleepless mess. But eventually it got way better." Another student added that she couldn't sleep without her phone until she learned "replacement habits" for late-night anxiety. Instead of scrolling into the night, breathing and mindfulness tools eventually helped ease her into rest.

We returned to the lecture hall and kept talking as a group about how one-size-fits-all "practical strategies for digital well-being" can be tricky. One student bravely noted that he often uses his phone to "shut out the noise" in a home filled with younger siblings, a sensory experience that quickly overwhelms him. Researcher Kristen Harrison has a formal term for this. She calls it "media sensory curation," a practice that is more common among neurodivergent teens.[49] Another student noted that she is tethered to her phone because her friends lean on her for emotional support. Dr. Emily Weinstein, cofounder of the Center for Digital Thriving at the Harvard School of Education and coauthor of the book *Behind Their Screens: What Teens Are Facing (And Adults Are Missing)*, calls this the "social support burden" that comes with growing up during a mental health crisis in the digital age.[50] Young people are often faced with late-night decisions about whether to support a friend in distress or prioritize sleep and self-care. These aren't simple choices. The students and I ultimately agreed that it isn't always as simple as just turning off our phones. We also agreed that taking breaks from our phones is essential.

These students' experiences are common. Online struggles are often inextricably linked to offline ones. Struggling teens need adults to channel Daniel's grandmother and practice both/and parenting. You can set a digital curfew *and* practice replacement habits. You can be wary of social media self-diagnosis *and* acknowledge the importance of mental health conversations online. You can delay use of social media *and* enjoy technology with your kid. You can hold tech companies accountable *and* recognize how young people use today's platforms to cope and connect. You can do your very best to protect and support your kid *and* have a child who is in deep pain and struggling. You can be on the road to healing *and* acknowledge that the road is uncertain and long. *Both. And.*

Good mental health is not a thing that can be powered up or powered down with a swipe of the fingertips. Young people need adults to acknowledge the complexity of this moment. The teenage brain is sensitive to stress. But it is also sensitive to support and built for resilience. When it comes to social media and mental health, the path we need to take as parents is going to be messy, complicated, and specific to the young people in our lives. But the clear message from a complex field of research is that our kids benefit most when we are on the path with them.

REFLECT DIGITAL STRESS CHECK-IN

Read each statement and think about which response best describes where you are: "I hadn't thought of this," "I try," or "I got this." Then ask yourself: What are you most proud of? What do you want to work on? Write down the latter, share it with a friend, and give it a try.

- I ask questions about my teen's digital life in open, curious, and nonjudgmental ways.

- When my teen is in distress, I try to manage my own feelings so I can be a steady presence.

- I can let my teen feel sad, mad, disappointed, or frustrated without trying to fix it right away.

- I communicate to my teen that intense feelings and stress are a normal part of adolescence.

- I communicate to my teen that when stress becomes unmanageable, I am here to support them.

- I am open to the idea that technology can *both* help my teen cope with stress *and* get in the way of healthy coping.

- When I hear about an online experience or incident that sounds harmful or stressful, I don't ignore it.

- I can identify some of the basic signs and symptoms of mental illness.

- If I find signs or expressions of distress on my child's device or platforms, I talk to them directly about my concerns.

- I consider delaying my teen's use of social media until after early adolescence and set boundaries around technology with mental health in mind.

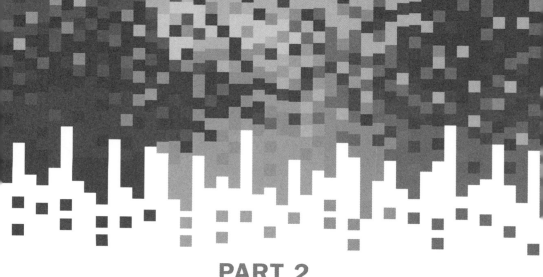

PART 2

"Who Am I?"

CHAPTER 4

Separation and Connection

"Eventually, we all make it home, and we each make an individual path by any means."
—JOY HARJO, CATCHING THE LIGHT

Wren I was in eighth grade, the teen TV drama *My So-Called Life* was in its first (and only) season. My friend Gretchen and I were enthralled by the complicated, tender, and honest picture of adolescents just two years older than us. We were committed to watching every episode. This required some planning, because in the olden times, TV shows were available by appointment only. Luckily, on Thursdays, the night our show aired, we had hockey practice together and could go straight to Gretchen's house afterward to watch.

This was convenient for me, because I preferred to spend every waking moment with friends. It was less convenient for my dad, who needed to pick me up late on a busy weeknight and then navigate an emotional minefield on the way home. I was eager to go over the details of every episode with Gretchen, but I was decidedly *not* as interested in debriefing them with my dad. He found this out the hard way.

"Why do you care so much about this?" I asked him when he questioned me about the show. You might think, given my vehement response, that he had lectured me about the show's mature themes as soon as I'd climbed into the car. No—his offense had been asking the benign question "What happened in today's episode?"

I went on, "You *really* are the only one who cares so much about this stuff." I knew I was being unfair, but I felt inexplicably annoyed by my dad's presence. He just listened. We sat in silence for a bit, then I turned on the radio and was relieved to be distracted by a Boyz II Men song. By the time it finished, I had already moved on. "I need to get my skates sharpened," I said to break the silence. Soon I was chatting happily about hockey practice. And yes, I filled in my dad on the episode.

I never imagined that one day I would encourage parents to ask their teens the same kinds of open-ended and curious questions my dad asked me. I also never guessed that I would focus my career on digital media and storytelling. I knew it was an option. My dad cared more about media than the average parent at that point. As the founder of one of the first media education and advocacy organizations, he was expert at asking thoughtful questions about the media content I consumed. As an adolescent, I was equally expert at rejecting his bids for conversation.

But I was listening. Toward the end of college, I got a job with a student organization facilitating workshops on body image and the media. As I developed my workshops, I soon realized that one of my best resources was a call home. My dad and I were both surprised the first time I reached out to brainstorm some ideas with him. His life work and conversation starters were suddenly highly relevant and interesting to me.

As parents, we can never be sure how the seeds we plant during adolescence will take root and grow. Our teens may end up being a lot like us—or they may not. Their developmental task as teens isn't to have measured and thoughtful discussions about where their interests align with and diverge from ours. It's to figure out who they are becoming.

Separation-Individuation

On a chilly October evening, I took a walk with a childhood friend. We hadn't seen each other in a while, so we started the conversation by catching up on our kids' ages, activities, and interests. Her youngest had just entered high school, and my older kid was in middle school. During a pause in this checklist-style conversation, we looked at each other and started laughing. "How are things *actually* going?" I asked her.

"It's just a big time, isn't it?" she said with a sigh. Her words hung in the air. We both knew she wasn't just talking about the physical size of our growing kids. She quickly added, "I mean, I know I want to raise independent kids who eventually go off into the world. I've done it before," she shared. "But I don't always enjoy this in-between part."

"What part is that?" I asked.

"Oh, the part where they wrench themselves away from our family, bury themselves in their phones, and treat me like an unwanted roommate," she replied.

"Oh, yeah. Let's talk about that part. That part is *not* easy," I said, laughing.

We both acknowledged that at this point in parenting, there is a fine line between laughing and crying. We ended up doing a little of both during our walk.

The words my friend used to describe this part of growing up, of kids wrenching themselves away from the family, are an accurate description of a key phase in adolescent development. Psychologists have a more technical and emotionally neutral term for it. They call it "separation-individuation."[1]

One of an adolescent's main jobs is to form an identity that is separate from those of their primary caregivers. This process can involve trying new things, exploring alternate opinions, and experimenting with different forms of expression. When your kid is young, you decide so many things for them: where they live, what school they attend, what time they go to bed, what they eat, and on and on. As your kid leaves childhood, they start making their own decisions. Pulling away from you is how they begin to exercise their own judgment. This space allows them to explore and define what is "theirs."

Finding your way to a new relationship with your kid will likely be a push-pull experience that ranges from disorienting to painful. Young people navigate this shift from dependence to independence in different ways. Some charge forward, and others dip their toes in and out of independence over time.

Many teenagers are more reluctant than younger children are to go places or do things with their parents. When I was a teenager, there were times when just the sound of my mom's voice annoyed me. It didn't even matter what she said. Having since spoken with hundreds of parents of adolescents across the United States, I know that such annoyance is common. The teen list of annoying things parents do includes the way parents text, dress, chew, sing, make jokes, pronounce words, and move through space.

Separation-individuation isn't easy on either side of the relationship. But here's the good news: your kid's annoyance with you is a sign that they are figuring out who they are and how they want to show up in the world. Even better: this process doesn't last forever. Once your kid has developed a more rooted sense of who they are, they probably won't feel that they need to express such disdain for who *you* are.

Hardwired to Connect

I teach an online class about adolescent development. I love teaching this class, because as a parent myself, I benefit from every conversation. In one session, a caregiver named James lingered after everyone else had logged off. I was grateful that James was a part of the class. He was high-energy, hilarious, and always encouraged other parents. Perhaps being a grandparent in a multigenerational home helped him access a little more perspective than the rest of us could. In this moment, though, he looked rather pensive. "James!" I said. "Glad you stayed on. Something on your mind?"

"Yeah. I just got stuck on something here at the end of class. I realize that we've really gotten away from family time this past year," he shared. In class, we had just spent an hour exploring creative ways to stay connected to teenagers. James explained, "We've raised Aster since she was a little kid, and we've *always* tried to eat meals together. A shared meal is important to us, and I'm proud and grateful that we've been able to make it happen."

"Until lately?" I asked.

"Until lately," he responded. "We are all going in different directions now that Aster's older. I mean, we still have meals together sometimes. But it doesn't feel like it used to. She doesn't talk. And all she wants to do is be on her phone."

"I bet that is pretty different from when she was younger," I empathized.

"Oh, yes. When she was little, I could barely get a word in edgewise. She wanted to tell us *everything*. It's not just that she is quiet. I'm quiet too! I get it.

But it seems like she doesn't want to be there. We tried to put our phones aside during meals for a while, but it didn't go well."

"What do you mean?" I asked.

"Well, it just wasn't the same as it used to be. It was awkward. It was such a relief to hear today that other families are experiencing the same thing."

I was grateful for James's vulnerability. "That's half the help of any kind of class or workshop—to learn that you aren't alone," I responded.

"Yeah. What a relief. Anyway, I think we are going to try again. I'm not sure if it will be dinner, because her schedule is getting so busy. But we are going to figure it out. If everyone else is spending awkward time together without phones, we can do it too."

"Let me know how it goes," I replied. "Sounds like you have a good plan."

I've had many conversations with caregivers who noted that device-free dinners weren't working. Like James, these parents wanted to continue to prioritize dinnertime together when possible. But their bubbly and expressive elementary-age kid had been replaced by a more reluctant and sometimes resentful teenager, and that made it harder. If you're in the same boat, remember that it is normal for an adolescent to seek separation from the family. This is not a sign that you are doing something wrong; rather, it's an indication that your family is growing up. Raising a teenager is all about figuring out the delicate balance between giving your kid the space they need to figure out who they are and staying connected with them as they do so. They'll often ask for the former. The latter, not so much. Your capacity to stay connected to your young person as their digital world expands is a major protective factor for healthy development.

Humans are born hardwired to connect. As Dr. Bruce Perry and journalist Maia Szalavitz write in their book *Born for Love*, "Connections are written into the architecture of our nervous system."[2] A baby's need for connection is obvious. I can still conjure the feeling of holding my kids close to my chest while soothing their cries with bouncing and back rubs. This wasn't always easy, but it was clear that they needed me. Babies have immature prefrontal cortexes and automatically look to adults to organize their experiences and soothe their nervous systems.

As kids get older and their brains mature, they develop a range of strategies to cope with intense feelings. This means that the parental support role must evolve too. When a middle schooler is struggling to navigate a conflict playing out in a group chat, scooping them up, wrapping them in a blanket, and rocking them side to side isn't helpful. But they still rely on supportive connection to cope with distress. Teens do need to learn how to manage their feelings. But human beings are never entirely self-regulated. From childhood through adolescence and adulthood, people rely on relationships as the primary way to manage stress and cope with adverse events.[3] This comes as a great surprise to many parents who are living through the wrenching process of separation-individuation. You kid may not know how to ask for connection or thank you for it, but they still need it.

For years, researchers studied only what went *wrong* in the lives of teenagers. In the last few decades, the focus has also turned to what goes *right*. What are the internal and external strengths that enable some teens to experience significant challenges during adolescence yet continue to learn, grow, and even thrive? Unsurprisingly, youth thriving has a lot to do with access to health-promoting resources, systems, and experiences.[4] These range from safe housing to high-quality after-school programming to mental health care. Another powerful protective variable is connectedness. Connectedness shields teens from risk and helps them build on their strengths.[5] Adolescents who feel connected to their parents are more likely to delay sexual initiation, report lower levels of substance use, and are less likely to engage in violence. This doesn't mean that an individual struggling adolescent isn't connected to their caregiver. It does mean that connectedness can help kids cope with adversity and unleash the power of their prefrontal cortex to learn and grow from their mistakes.

Teens Need Warmth and Structure

When you hear advice like "stay connected to your teen," it may conjure up a stock image of a parent enveloping their teen in a hug while bathed in warm light. You may have a general sense of connection as intuitive, warm, friendly, and fun. That's why it can be disorienting when your adolescent resists your attempts to connect or you spend a device-free dinner in awkward silence. There is, of course, plenty of fun to be had with teenagers. For example, no one makes me laugh harder than my middle schooler. I think teenagers are thoughtful, hilarious, adventurous, and compassionate. But measuring the strength of connection by enjoyment alone isn't realistic. It also isn't backed up by scientific evidence.

Decades of research on connectedness at home and in the classroom show that warmth alone isn't enough to meet kids' developmental needs. Lisa Delpit, MacArthur Fellow and multi-award-winning educator and author, writes about the powerful positive influence of teachers who are "warm demanders" in the classroom. She says these educators "expect a great deal of their students, convince them of their own brilliance, and help them to reach their potential in a disciplined and structured environment."[6]

This concept applies at home too. Dr. Lisa Damour puts it in simpler terms: "There are two things that teens need more than anything else: warmth and structure."[7] We don't have to choose between connection and limits. Kids thrive when we provide both. Young people need to know that we are in their corner *and* that we care about them enough to create and negotiate meaningful boundaries. The next chapter explores where tech limits matter most.

All of this sounds wonderful on paper. But in practice, this delicate mix of warmth and structure may feel hard to achieve. This is especially true as our kids start to separate, push against limits, and turn toward friends and phones.

Technoference

"Hmm," I said, vaguely attending to my nine-year-old's treatise on what features he would add to a Minecraft realm if given full coding control. My attention was split between his never-ending description and a news story a friend had texted me. I hadn't made a conscious choice to pick up my phone. But as chapter 2 explains: when it comes to technology, "proximity is destiny."

Adults lament how often teens are on their phones when spending time together—or that teens would rather be scrolling than talking to their parents. Yet I know that I am not the only parent who has struggled to prioritize the personal connections in front of me over the allure of my phone. In fact, a national survey in 2015 revealed that 89 percent of adult cell phone owners used their phones during their most recent social interactions.[8]

Phones are always on and always near, so people frequently shift attention between each other and their screens. Researchers have coined the term *technoference* to describe the purposeful or inadvertent use of technology to withdraw from a social interaction. A review of the research confirms that technoference may harm connection.[9] In the studies reviewed, parental technoference was associated with lower relationship quality and worse adolescent self-reported mental health concerns. Association is not causation, so it's unclear whether phone use or another factor caused poor relationship quality. Research has not yet produced robust evidence of long-term harms from technoference, but it has shown short-term effects on stress and behavior. For example, research with younger children shows that parental absorption in devices leads to less conversation and more behaviors like tantrums and withdrawal.[10] The more absorbed we are in our phones, the more kids escalate to get our attention, and the more annoyed we are when we finally turn toward our kids. Not great news.

The better news is that the presence of phones doesn't *have to* lead to technoference. Let's think about the different ways that my Minecraft conversation with my son might play out:

- **Scenario 1:** My son is eager to share his ideas about Minecraft, and I am only partially paying attention while scrolling through news headlines. I pretend to tune in by saying "hmm" occasionally. After several attempts to talk, my kid gets frustrated and shouts, "Never mind!" before retreating to his headphones. I look up and raise my voice in return, frustrated by the disruption and his attitude.

- **Scenario 2:** My son is eager to share his ideas about Minecraft. I know that I cannot listen to deep dives about Minecraft in perpetuity. I say, "I'm happy to listen, but I'm on my phone right now texting with my friend. I'll let you know when I am done. How does that sound?"

- **Scenario 3:** My son is eager to share his ideas about Minecraft. I say, "I'm having a hard time focusing on what you're saying while I am getting texts. I'm going to turn off text notifications for ten minutes. Now let's open the Minecraft app on my phone so you can show me what you're talking about."

The first scenario illustrates how technoference can escalate conflict and hinder connection, at least in the short term. The second and third scenarios show that avoiding technoference doesn't necessarily mean sustaining meaningful phone-free eye contact from dawn to dusk. Phones play a role in all three scenarios. Yet each has a unique interaction pattern.

As kids grow up and get their own devices, it is more likely that parents and kids alike will struggle to put down the devices and turn toward each other. That's why it's important to be aware of technoference. As your kid's bids for your attention become rarer, you'll want to be able to catch opportunities to connect when they arise. Indeed, I am already wistful for my nine-year-old's long-winded Minecraft manifestos. Many parents of teens would pay good money for such a comprehensive window into their kids' digital interests.

The trap of parental blame and shame about technoference is easy to fall into. But it is utterly unhelpful, and it doesn't reflect what is happening in the real world. Tech choices don't occur in a vacuum. Just like teen tech use, parents' digital habits are shaped by their strengths, vulnerabilities, and contexts. At the beginning of the COVID pandemic, lack of child care, stress, and limited access to critical support shifted parents' approach to technology overnight. But the pandemic isn't the only factor at play. A group of researchers studying the forces that shape parental decision-making have documented the diverse reasons that parents of young children use their phones. Parents turn to their devices for much-needed breaks from parenting demands.[11] They check their phones to attend to time-sensitive work and family obligations. They scroll through social platforms to cope with challenging emotions or sensory overwhelm. They reach for phones when they are overwhelmed by their kids' behaviors or needs. They log on to find resources, support, and information.

This is not a list of justifications for mindless scrolling. It's an invitation to reflect on our habits and patterns by asking, "How does my behavior get in the way of the kind of relationship I want with my kid?" It's an encouragement to prioritize screen-free spaces and create family norms that include turning off devices sometimes. Acknowledging the complexity of our choices can help us move beyond shame and blame. Building awareness of our context, constraints, and choices can help us communicate our priorities. What a powerful model for our kids.

Getting Creative with Connection

Creating space every day to interact without the possibility of technoference can strengthen the connective fabric of our families. That doesn't mean it will always be pretty. The key to sustaining this practice is to set realistic expectations. If you're expecting an idealized version of connection, then you'll be less likely to try again when your kid rebuffs your overtures. Instead, focus on creating regular screen-free "containers" for connection. Prioritize *opportunities* for warmth, conversation, and connection. For example, the container might be a screen-free meal, a car or bus ride, a time between work shifts, or the pre-bedtime hour. Some days the container will fill with raucous laughter. Other days, connected chatter. Still others, stony silence. But stick with it. If you stick with it, your kid will come to expect it. You won't have to renegotiate the terms every day or engage in fresh attempts to reduce technoference. Perhaps most importantly, your kid won't have to create the container. They'll know that if they need you, there'll be a time each day when they won't have to compete with the internet for your attention.

Maintaining other rituals and traditions communicates a similar message. Maybe you watch a favorite show together, make a special recipe, or follow a special cultural tradition or ritual. For example, some friends of ours used to have regular family board game nights. When the kids were little, they were enthusiastic. This faded a bit when the kids hit middle school. Instead of forcing it with board games, the family brainstormed an alternative. They decided each kid could invite one friend over for a family-and-friends Mario Kart tournament. The parents provided snacks—and extra entertainment, as they clumsily launched their cars off the track.

Remember James and his granddaughter, Aster? I recently got an email from James, and we hopped on Zoom to reconnect. I had the chance to ask him how screen-free time was going for his family. "Honestly, on any given day, results are all over the board," he said, laughing.

"I appreciate the real talk," I said. "Last night our dinner ended with my younger kid crying, my older kid in sullen silence, and my dog pawing into my lap. Not ideal," I added, joining in his laughter.

"Yeah. That's real," James said. "The good news is that overall, we are doing way better. Seems like we just pushed through some of that awkwardness. I am sure we will hit it again, but it feels all right today, anyway. We text a lot, and Aster makes me laugh so hard. I've been helping her edit some videos because of my experience in production. I get to help, and she gets to teach me new stuff. She thinks it's hilarious how old I am."

"Nice!" I responded. "I'm inspired."

Rituals, traditions, and screen-free containers for connection can serve as anchors in a stormy sea. They communicate to your kids that things are "the same but different." That you keep going, even in the face of awkwardness or resistance. You also flex, change, and adapt. While I was sleep deprived at the time, I have fond memories now of taking early morning walks with my little kids when they woke up with the sun. Those walks were filled with observations and conversations. Since I am a morning person, we were perfectly synchronized. That has changed as my kids have grown. For most teens, early mornings are not the ideal time to create positive memories. Now I work to keep my eyes open later at night when my middle schooler gets chatty and more playful.

Mistimed invitations can feel intrusive or annoying to adolescents. Instead, young people are often more likely to open up on their own schedule and on their own terms. When we invest a little time, patience, and creativity into offering containers for connection, teens will take small opportunities to start the conversations that they want or need to have. It might be well after our bedtimes, or as they are walking out the door. It could be while we are editing videos together, texting, or watching a show. It could be in the car after a Boyz II Men song comes on the radio. All we can do is create the container and keep inviting our kids in.

REFLECT CONTAINERS FOR CONNECTION

Connecting in online spaces can be valuable for adolescents, but they need reliable screen-free containers for connection too. This isn't because screens are bad, but because face-to-face time is good. The following questions can help you assess your family's opportunities for connection and incorporate more screen-free time if you like:

- Do you have screen-free time as a family now?
- If you do have screen-free time: How, where, and when do you spend time together without devices?
- What do you know about your teen that you don't think you would know without screen-free time?
- If you don't have screen-free time: What gets in the way?
- What is one time, space, or situation in which you might try spending time together without devices?
- How will you navigate the barriers that get in the way?

IN ACTION: CONNECTING THROUGH TECH

Sustained screen-free eye contact isn't the only way to connect meaningfully with your teen. Enjoying technology *with* your kid is a great way to stay connected and learn more about their digital interests. In the following list, note the things that you are already doing and choose two things that you would like to do more of—or come up with your own ideas.

- Text each other.
- Game together.
- Watch shows and movies together.
- Watch videos together.
- Make shared playlists.
- Create videos together.
- Code together.
- Make stop-motion animation videos together.
- Watch your kid play their favorite games.

- Video chat.
- Interact on social media.
- Share podcasts.
- Take and edit photos together.

Rooted in Relationships

"I don't know how to feel right now," a parent shared when we bumped into each other on the way out of our kids' school conferences.

"Want to say more?" I asked.

"I just chatted with the coach of the Lego robotics club, and she went on and on about how open and engaged my kid has been this fall."

"That makes sense," I responded. "That's my experience of him too!"

"Totally. And I know that he is wonderful. *And* it feels just kind of wild because we haven't seen that version of him at home much lately," she shared.

"Yeah, I get that," I said.

"He's just been so stormy. On one hand, I love hearing about how he is doing in robotics. On the other, it makes me kind of miss him," she concluded.

"Sounds like he feels safe enough to fall apart more at home. It's normal—but not easy," I gently reminded her. "I hope you can take in the coach's feedback though."

"Yeah, I can. And I am so grateful for this coach. Xavier loves coding and loves the coach. It makes sense that robotics is a place he can shine."

It's hard not to take it personally when other adults see versions of your kid that you don't see at home. Here's why that happens. The start of family time in the evening is often the finish line for an adolescent's prefrontal cortex. After a long day of managing emotions at school, it's common for a teen to fall apart at home. Plus, it's developmentally appropriate for them to push adults away. Finding educators, coaches, mentors, guides, or family members who can give you windows into how your kid is showing up in the world can be very powerful and helpful—if you can take it in.

Adults like Xavier's Lego robotics coach do more than provide windows, though. They are the "roots of thriving" in youth development.[12] Search Institute has been studying what young people need to thrive for decades. It uses the metaphor of a gingko tree to represent this rich body of research. The gingko tree can grow in diverse conditions and has deep roots that protect it from harsh weather. Its visible leaves and branches represent positive outcomes for young people. Its root system represents what Search Institute calls "developmental relationships."[13] Adults who form developmental relationships with young people express care, expand possibilities, challenge growth, and share power. They provide warmth *and* structure. Like the gingko tree, which does not have a single taproot, young people don't have just one important relationship with adults. Parents don't bear sole responsibility for connecting with adolescents. Cultivating a diverse web of relationships—including teachers, coaches, neighbors, supervisors, mentors, and extended family—provides much-needed stability during times of big change.

The Same but Different

A parent shared with me, "I think the hardest part is not knowing if the conversations we are having make any difference. I have been talking to my daughter about body image and mental health and privacy and on and on. But she is not a talker, and I seem to annoy her a lot right now, so it is just impossible to know how she is really doing. She is just in her own orbit."

"It's so disorienting, isn't it?" I replied. "We have fewer windows into their world as they get older. Remember, just because your daughter isn't talkative doesn't mean she isn't listening or doesn't care."

When kids are young, their world is small, and parents are at the center. It is both exhausting and delightful. As kids grow up, their world expands, changes shape, and starts orbiting around different centers of gravity. These include friends, school, and phones. They separate from parents to find themselves.

The push and pull of new orbits make relationships with teens feel volatile and unpredictable. Sometimes you might feel positive, stable, and connected with your kid. Other times your relationship may feel awkward, off-kilter, and distant. Don't rely on your kid's feedback to know whether you are on track. Even on your finest days, your teen is unlikely to turn to you and say, "Thank you so much for being a warm demander in my life! The combination of warmth and structure is so helpful. You are really nailing that balance. I especially love the digital curfew at night."

Instead, your kid may deliver an exasperated, "Why do you care so much about this?" In moments like this, it is helpful to remember that your kid's exasperation isn't personal; it's developmental. Their job is to push you away to figure out who they are. Your job is to loosen your grasp without letting go.

Ever since my kids were little, I've shared "special things" with them at bedtime. It is a comforting ritual I borrowed from a friend. Among other things, I remind them that I love them no matter what. When my kids were young, they would ask for this ritual, sinking back into their beds as they listened attentively to my words. They are much older now, and bedtime is vastly different. One month, I was traveling a lot for work and was away several nights in a row. Now that my kids are self-sufficient, this isn't as big a deal as it would have been years ago. But when I got home, my wife told me to head to their room. I knocked on my kids' door and quietly let myself into their darkened room. "Oh good, you're home," my middle schooler said. "You can say our special things now."

I'm not sure how many more direct acknowledgments I will get to tell me that this family ritual still matters. How I share my kids' "special things" will likely need to change and grow in the years ahead. But I know that continuing to do the things that hold us together is often just what kids need as they figure out who they are apart from us.

◀ **REFLECT** **KEEPING A CONNECTION MINDSET**

Read each statement and think about which response best describes where you are: "I hadn't thought of this," "I try," or "I got this." Then ask yourself: What are you most proud of? What do you want to work on? Write down the latter, share it with a friend, and give it a try. Keep going.

- I understand that rejection is not always personal; it's developmental.

- I am willing to give my teen a fresh start to move our interactions in a more positive direction.

- I make sure my teen knows that I enjoy their company. Part of how I communicate this is by putting down my phone sometimes to be present with them.

- I am willing to reflect on whether my phone consistently causes technoference in my family relationships.

- I make a point of looking for and naming my teen's strengths—online and offline—especially when we are stuck in a pattern of negative interactions.

- I can identify other adults outside our home who enjoy and connect with my teen.

- I remind my teen that they can be annoyed with or embarrassed by me, but I draw the line at rude or disrespectful behavior.

- I reach out to friends or other adult family members to process my teen's separation instead of asking my teen to make me feel better about it.

CHAPTER 5

Independence and Exploration

"Crucial to finding the way is this . . .
You must make your own map."
—Joy Harjo, "A Map to the Next World"

A large group of parents braved the cold, snowy weather one evening to gather in a middle school media center and learn about the latest research on technology and teens. Traveling on unplowed Minnesota roads during a storm is no small feat. Then again, neither is raising a kid. You typically don't leave home in a snowstorm to hear a speaker unless their topic is at the top of your list of concerns. Parents streamed into the room, stomping the snow from their boots and discussing the road conditions. Poor visibility and unexpected slick spots seemed like a good metaphor for parenting.

Once we got started, I invited parents to put aside their worries for a moment and share the ways their families benefited from technology use. Some parents stared blankly as they tried to recall positive experiences. But a parent in the front row had no trouble finding one. "Tracking them!" she said. The person sitting next to her quickly agreed, "Now that they are so independent, I like being able to see exactly where they are." Other heads nodded in agreement. Someone in the back followed up, "Especially on a night like tonight."

"How many use tracking apps and appreciate being able to know your kids' whereabouts?" I asked. Nearly half the parents raised their hands. Their reasons for tracking ranged from safety to convenience to proof that their kids were where they said they would be. We talked about other benefits of technology too, but nothing inspired the same enthusiasm that tracking did.

Many parents seemed relieved when I finally turned to their concerns. I asked, "What worries you, or what do you find challenging?" Every hand shot up.

The list of concerns these parents shared was a familiar one. Across the United States, parents are worried about bullying, sexting, overuse, addiction, self-esteem, misinformation, mental health, and more. They are dismayed by their lack of control in digital spaces. Parents are angry at tech companies for failing to prioritize adolescent health and well-being. They are confused by conflicting headlines and shifting guidance.

Amidst these fears, it's no wonder that tracking kids' whereabouts reassures parents. During adolescence, parental visibility is low, and metaphorical slick spots are difficult to avoid. And if conditions are literally physically hazardous, watching kids move across a map provides a measure of comfort.

But parents don't track their kids just when conditions are dicey. They also don't track their kids just during the teen years. Devorah Heitner notes in her book *Growing Up in Public* that the geotracking app Life360 has more than fifty million active monthly users. She goes on to share the results of a survey of 695 college students. Nearly one-third of them were still being tracked by their parents using Apple's Find My app or Life360.[1] That's on par with the rate of parents tracking high school students. A Pew Research Center study found that while geotracking is less common than other forms of monitoring, such as checking browser history or looking at text messages, roughly one-third of caregivers track the location of their child.[2]

The parental impulse to track kids at any age is understandable. That impulse grows stronger when kids hit adolescence. Teens are more likely to be out in the world without direct supervision. As author Elizabeth Stone writes, "Making the decision to have a child—it is momentous. It is to decide forever to have your heart go walking around outside your body."[3] As your kid grows up, your heart starts walking farther away from you. Your list of concerns may be long. You may not always be there to protect your kid, but with today's technology, you can at least know where they are.

But does this keep them safer? And does it meet their developmental needs?

■ I Can Do It

"I do it!" my three-year-old insisted.

He pushed my helping hands away so he could see and wrestle with his coat zipper. Cue another epic morning of trying to leave the house with a little kid. I remember looking at the clock, noting how late we were, and then looking back at my tiny child fiercely committed to putting his jacket on all by himself. From my perspective, it was not a convenient time to work on his fine-motor and self-help skills. Then again, it often wasn't. I took a deep breath to quell my we-need-to-get-going energy and sat back to watch my son struggle. Several minutes later, he successfully zipped up and headed out the front door toward an icy set of steps. He preempted any forthcoming offers to help with another "I do it!" before sliding down the steps on his butt. I think he would have driven himself to preschool if I had let him.

Anyone who has raised or worked with toddlers knows that the push and pull of independence is not unique to adolescence. Three-year-olds love to assert that "I can do it!" one moment and run back into their parents' arms the next. Adolescents do the same thing. As chapter 4 explored, teenagers often push their parents away to answer the question "Who am I?" They don't answer this question overnight. But most are clear about one thing early on: "I am not a little kid. So don't treat me that way." Some take this further than others. When my brother Brian was in high school, he'd have liked to move into an apartment. I'm sure my parents were occasionally tempted to pack his bags and send me with him. But they knew better: The art of raising a teenager is figuring out how to loosen without letting go.

Some teens are ready to run into the world; they're eager for independence and ready to fall, fail, and try again. Other teens would rather stay right by their parents' sides. It's different for each family, based on priorities, culture, individual personalities and needs, and context. A stormy night might motivate you to track your kid's location. When the sky clears, you're more willing to trust that your kid will find their way home safely. As your young person grows more independent, they depend on you to be there when they need to fall back into your arms. They rely on you to set and hold purposeful boundaries. But within those boundaries, they need your encouragement and confidence that they can indeed do things themselves.

The Benefits of Exploring New Terrain

I try to resist the temptation to romanticize my childhood and my parents'. But some pre–cell phone experiences are worth noting. If you talk to people born before 1980, you'll notice that many tell stories about roaming, exploring, and playing beyond adult supervision. According to my parents, the adult guidance they received during the summer months consisted of "Come home when the street lights turn on." My mother-in-law and her sisters used to walk on their own to a beach seven miles from home. It took all day. Entire sibling battles were fought and resolved on that road. One of her sisters buried makeup in a plastic bag in the woods along the road so she could prepare for the beach on her own terms. The sisters skipped, ran, and made each other laugh to pass the time. I am sure that given the option, my mother-in-law would have agreed to drop a pin on a geotracking app in return for a ride to the beach. But she also has a lot to say about the benefits of those long walks with her sisters. "Oh, we loved them," she recalls. "It felt like we could do anything!"

Fast-forward to the 2010s. My mother-in-law was nervous when my wife and I left her first grandchild in the stroller outdoors to finish a nap. We were only ten feet away, on the other side of a screen door. I don't think she would currently let our kids out of her sight *at* the beach, much less send them on a seven-mile trek to one. So what gives? Has there been a real shift in independent activities, or does society have a selective memory?

According to a 2023 commentary in the journal *Pediatrics*, the memories of Gen Xers and older adults are not distorted.[4] Norms have changed significantly. Kids today do roam less than previous generations did. The authors cite a considerable body of research that documents declines in "children's independent mobility," meaning kids' ability to move freely around their communities without adults. They also analyzed hundreds of articles and advice columns since the early 1900s. They found a distinct shift over time from understanding children as competent, responsible, and resilient to focusing on their need for supervision and protection. In her book *How to Raise an Adult*, Julie Lythcott-Haims makes a similar observation in question form: "Why did parenting change from preparing our kids *for* life to protecting them *from* life?"[5]

Many people point to screens as the primary driver of this change. Devices certainly play a role, but independent childhood activities started declining long before the internet explosion. Other factors include increased time in school and on schoolwork, experiences and/or perceptions of community and traffic danger, economic pressures, and changes in free-time priorities. The cost of this decline isn't just nostalgic. It may be harming young people's mental health and well-being. According to the American Academy of Pediatrics, free play and free time are essential to healthy development.[6] They give children the chance to practice executive function skills such as these:

- developing and maintaining goals
- negotiating conflict and building social skills
- managing risk
- solving problems
- regulating feelings and behavior
- taking responsibility for self and others

Chapter 4 explores the importance of rooting adolescents' experiences in a strong web of relationships with caring adults. Organized activities with adult supervision certainly have a developmental benefit for youth, especially compared to too much unstructured time.[7] But kids also benefit from experiences apart from adults. Three core factors are key to child and adolescent well-being: autonomy, competence, and relatedness.[8] In other words, kids feel better when they have choice over their path, the skills they need for navigation, and when they don't travel alone.

There is evidence to back this up. A 2022 study looked at daily exploration among teenagers.[9] The researchers recorded the range of young people's movement throughout the day as well as how many new locations they visited during the tracking period. It found that highly exploratory teenagers reported larger social networks and better moods. A 2023 meta-analysis (a study of studies) found that physical activity among teenagers helped relieve depressive symptoms.[10] The effect was greater when the physical activity was unsupervised than when it was fully or partially supervised. The authors of the *Pediatrics* commentary explain, "If children are to grow up well-adjusted, they need ever-increasing opportunities for independent activity, including self-directed play and meaningful contributions to family and community life, which are signs that they are trusted, responsible, and capable."[11]

The inverse may be true as well. Adolescents who attend high-pressure schools suffer from anxiety and depression at higher rates than teens in lower-pressure schools do.[12] This could certainly be due to intense emphasis on achievement. It could also be related to the near elimination of unstructured free time for students with high academic and extracurricular demands. For most kids, regardless of where they attend school, homework time has increased while recess time has decreased.[13] And it's worth noting that healthy adolescent independence isn't about taking on adult responsibilities too soon. Many young people work multiple jobs outside of school or serve as caretakers for younger siblings. High-pressure early independence, often driven by poverty and an inadequate social safety net for families, can erode mental health instead of boosting it.

The simple statement "We should get kids off screens and let them play and roam more" doesn't account for the constraints many families face. Not all young people have access to high-quality organized activities and "safe-enough" independent activities. And the right to roam is not equitably distributed among adolescents. For example, White teens are more likely to be perceived as harmless while roaming the neighborhood, while teens of color are more likely to be perceived as threatening.[14] For some families, tracking their kids or keeping them close is a way to protect against worst-case scenarios, and preparing them *for* life's injustices early and often is necessary for safety.

Our parenting decisions are shaped by our histories, options, and context. Each of us knows what's right for our own family.

Is the Internet Built for Roaming?

Young people may be drawn to social media precisely because it offers accessible spaces to explore outside adults' direct control. Adolescents' tendency to leave a social platform when too many adults sign up is anecdotal evidence of this.

For some young people, time online is a rare opportunity to just be. In a Common Sense Media study, an eleventh grader shared this:

> Realistically when you're in school, you can't really use your phone. When you get home, especially if you're in middle school or high school, you're spending hours doing homework, and maybe after-school stuff . . . So I know a lot of people, especially my age, they will stay up late because they feel like that's really the only time that they can be on their phones or that they can really do anything outside of school.[15]

Unfortunately, many popular online platforms and games aren't ideal environments for the kind of independent activity teens need to thrive. As chapter 2 explored, the business priorities of tech companies are often at odds with young people's needs for autonomy (self-directed use), and they offer few protections to make their platforms safe-enough spaces to explore. Baroness Beeban Kidron, a longtime advocate for children's rights in the digital world, points out that the internet is "100 percent engineered. It can be anything you want it to be."[16] It isn't that the internet *can't* be a place for young people to experience autonomy, competence, and relatedness. It just isn't built that way.

This reality presents a challenge. On one hand, adolescents need to move out into the world. On the other hand, we need to be clear-eyed about the risks that come with online independence. How much do we delay, track, monitor, and set boundaries? When do we loosen our grip and let go? There are a lot of ways to get this "right." Keeping adolescents' needs for autonomy, competence, and relatedness in mind can help us decide when to step in and when to step back.

Ready for Independence, Ready for Phones?

Young people today are not marking their maturity with seven-mile walks to the beach. Instead, their first phone is a major milestone. Caregivers have mixed feelings about this rite of passage. On one hand, about half of US children have gotten their first smartphone by age eleven.[17] By age twelve, that number rises to about three-fourths of US kids. On the other hand, movements like Wait Until 8th urge parents to delay phone ownership until high school.[18]

No specific research pinpoints exactly when to introduce phones to kids. Some correlational data shows that young adults who got cell phones earlier reported worse mental health outcomes than those who got phones at later ages.[19] But this data doesn't say whether early phone ownership drove the outcomes.

On a practical level, having some kind of personal device may allow young people to roam and build the skills for independence. It's easier to bike home after school if you can text your parents about a flat tire or a change of plans. When parents do give their kids a device, they cite connection and safety as the major factors behind their decision.[20] However, phones can be a portal to social media and other online platforms that younger adolescents aren't ready for. There are plenty of compelling reasons to avoid handing a fully loaded smartphone to tweens and wishing them luck.

Each family has its own unique needs and priorities. Plenty of thirteen-year-olds do fine with devices, and plenty of seventeen-year-olds struggle. Turning toward your own teenager to assess readiness can be helpful.

REFLECT FIRST DEVICES

Reflect on the following questions as you consider getting your child their first device. This framework can help you move away from the idea that allowing any amount of technology is somehow failing as a parent. It also helps you slow down and think twice before delivering more technology to your child than is healthy or needed.

- What is the purpose of my child having a device?
- What is the *minimal amount* of technology that fulfills this purpose?
- Has my child demonstrated that they can be responsible for a device and the platforms/apps they will have access to? What shows me that my child is ready? What concerns me?
- Is my child willing to have a conversation about expectations and agreements?
- Am I willing to have conversations about things like porn, body image, privacy, and cyberbullying?

- Am I willing to model the kinds of behaviors I hope to nurture in my teen?
- Am I clear on which boundaries are negotiable and which are nonnegotiable?

Reflecting on the First Devices questions can help you get a better handle on timing and which device makes sense for your kid. If the purpose of the device is a safety net so they can roam the neighborhood, then a limited-feature smartwatch might be enough to start with. If your young person isn't willing to sit down and have a conversation about expectations and agreements, they may not be ready for a device.

No matter which route you choose, devices are not all-or-nothing propositions. You can take a gradual approach to first devices. Starting with the minimal functions and slowly expanding access allows a lot more time to practice, coach, and build skills as your kid gains independence. You can slowly work your way from simple texting to photos to social media access over time.

Just as most experts are reluctant to state a specific age for first devices, there isn't consensus on a safe age to start using social media. In a 2024 summary of the research, the American Psychological Association notes that "chronological age is not directly associated with social media readiness."[21] But emerging evidence suggests that delaying social media access beyond early adolescence is well worth considering. As chapter 2 explores, the design features of popular platforms are often at odds with the developmental needs of younger teens. One 2022 study found that children and preteens who started using Instagram and Snapchat before age thirteen exhibited more problematic digital behaviors than did young people who started using these platforms later.[22] And as noted in chapter 3, one well-designed study found that early adolescence may be a "developmental window of vulnerability" to social media harms.[23]

The same study showed that lower social media use in early adolescence and early adulthood predicted higher life satisfaction and higher use predicted lower life satisfaction.[24] It also showed that teens who estimated very low *or* very high social media use reported lower life satisfaction. These findings align with those of a 2017 study, whose authors concluded, "Overall, the evidence indicated that moderate use of digital technology is not intrinsically harmful and may be advantageous in a connected world."[25] "Not too much, not too little" may be a helpful guide for *older* adolescents.

Monitoring for Trust and Skill Building

Monitoring is an important resource in your tool kit, especially as kids get started with new platforms or tools. During childhood and early adolescence, stronger tech boundaries make a lot of sense. It's easier to loosen your rules than to clamp down on freedoms. And some scenarios warrant close monitoring. If your kid has been the target of online cruelty, or if you are concerned about self-harm or suicidality, then close monitoring could be an important part of your safety plan. Lighter monitoring can turn up harmful online content that you want to talk to your kid about. I can't outline every scenario in which monitoring makes sense. But I can suggest a few questions about monitoring that may help you figure out a good fit for your kid:

- "What is the purpose of this monitoring tool?"
- "How can I use this tool in a way that builds trust and centers my teen's need for autonomy?"
- "What are my kid's strengths and vulnerabilities as they navigate the internet and social media?"

Monitoring in a way that respects young people's growing independence and promotes communication is key. It doesn't work to install parental controls, close our eyes, cross our fingers, and hope for the best. No monitoring tool is going to ensure that teens always make healthy online decisions. A review of forty studies found "little support for advocating parental controls as a stand-alone strategy."[26] Instead, research shows that mentorship and conversations are far more powerful than any monitoring app.[27] If we use monitoring tools to covertly spy on our kids or to catch and punish their mistakes, we can inadvertently make them more vulnerable to the risks we are trying to protect them from. Setting up "gotcha" moments may shut down communication altogether or send our kids to more remote corners of the internet to avoid surveillance. And kids may experience intensive monitoring as an invasion of privacy, eroding trust and connection.

Remember, young people do better when they have some choice over their path, have the skills they need to navigate it, and don't travel alone. The point of monitoring isn't to catch kids being bad. Instead it can be a way to start conversations, encourage problem-solving, and practice new skills.

IN ACTION: MONITORING

Start with a conversation. Discuss why you have decided to use parental controls or monitoring tools. Emphasize skill building and safety instead of compliance and punishment.

Monitor in the context of media agreements. Media agreements can be especially helpful for first devices or new platforms. Chapter 11 talks more about this, and you can find links to agreement templates in the resources section at the back of the book.

Tell them first, then monitor. The goal of monitoring is to encourage safe and healthy choices, not to catch young people messing up. If you choose to monitor, be transparent about it from the start.

Assure your kid that you are not a spy. Explain to your kid that you will not be reading every text and post. Instead, explain the safety-related things you will be checking on.

Keep your word: don't be a spy. Avoid reading every line of your child's texts and posts.

Involve your kids. The best monitoring tools not only help *you* see tech behaviors but also help *your kid* see their habits. Involve your kid in reviewing screen time data or information.

How Will You Respond to What You See?

I met Sheena at a student leadership and health conference. One of the workshops, facilitated by an older high school student, started with the question "What do you wish adults knew about your digital life?" Sheena was my conversation partner. She said, "My dad saw something on my phone and just *lost it*. I just wish he had even *asked* me about what was going on before taking my phone away." She dropped her backpack on the floor by the side of her chair and ran both hands through her short hair as if ready to pull it out in frustration.

"That's tough. It's so tricky," I responded empathetically.

"I just don't think he understands what it's like. It is not as simple as he thinks it is, and he doesn't even know what he is looking at half the time," she concluded.

"He probably doesn't," I responded, "but not because he doesn't care to. I am sure he does. But I doubt any of us who aren't teenagers right now can fully understand what it's like."

Sheena and I didn't get into the details. She wasn't sharing her story because she wanted me to weigh in on the conflict between her and her dad. (And I wouldn't have.) She was trying to make an important point: Parents often don't understand the full picture. Her point is valid. I've also been in her dad's shoes, and I understand what it feels like to see a concerning snapshot of my kid's digital activities.

Whether you monitor directly or rely on conversation and co-use, you will inevitably run into something concerning. It is easy to underrespond or overrespond in these moments:

- Underresponding sounds like this: "I'm sure it's fine! Let's just let this blow over."

- Overresponding sounds like this: "What a nightmare. Time to incinerate the phone, like I've always wanted to."

These responses may seem like caricatures. But when you're stressed out, it's easy to go there. Even if your reaction is more measured, jumping to quick conclusions can result in unnecessary anxiety and conflict.

Sheena is right: The text messages and posts parents see are small snapshots of a much bigger landscape. They often lack critical context. Even when a kid's post is public, parents are usually not the intended audience.

In 2001, researcher danah boyd described the sudden internet-driven confluence of different social spheres as "collapsed contexts."[28] Later, this concept became known as *context collapse*. Context collapse happens when information intended for one audience is visible to unintended audiences, and the latter respond negatively because they don't understand the original context. For adolescents, unintended audiences may include teachers, strangers, parents, other friends, and even their future selves. Navigating context collapse is a huge cognitive and emotional lift for young people. Acknowledging this can foster open conversations about how public content might be perceived by different audiences.

Monitoring gives parents access to messages and interactions intended to be private. Of course, the internet is not a private domain. Anything sent or shared online can be captured and spread widely. And some private content is well worth flagging—from online drug sales to unwanted contact from strangers to interactions with hate or extremist groups. But parents should tread more carefully with other content. Developmentally appropriate conversations between friends can stir up parental anxiety. The temptation is strong to take over in situations that kids might eventually navigate well enough on their own. Barging in without context can make things worse.

The same goes for tracking. At the start of this chapter, I describe how reassuring it can be when you see your kid's blue dot dutifully traveling along a predicted route on a geotracking app. But let's count the ways this can go awry. Gaps in tracking or glitches in the software can deliver inaccurate location information. Also, apps aren't designed to deliver *reasons* for deviations from expected paths. I've talked to plenty of parents who lobbed accusations at their teens only to discover perfectly reasonable explanations. Finally, as Dr. Heitner notes, "That dot on the geo-tracking app doesn't tell us very much. Kids can be at the library studying with friends, or in the study room goofing off with friends, or *behind* the library vaping. The app will just show them at the library, not what they're doing there."[29] Tracking may be the reason a kid leaves their phone at a friend's house for cover instead of taking it to a party, where they might need it to call home if they feel unsafe.

The ambiguity of data offered by tracking and monitoring apps isn't a justification for *more* intel. Instead, it's best for us parents to proceed with as much care and curiosity as we can muster. We can slow our reactions when we see something concerning. We can start by taking a break, taking a breath, settling our bodies, or calling friends who can calm us down. When we do talk to our kids about what we've seen, we can ask for more context in a nonjudgmental way. For example:

Parent: "Is now a good time to talk to you briefly about something on your phone? Or do you want to wait until after dinner?"

Teen: "Let's just do it now."

Parent: "Okay, we both agreed that I would periodically check your new phone. I also agreed that I wouldn't jump to conclusions before we talk."

Teen: "Yeah, so?"

Parent: "I noticed that one of your friends shared a picture of some girls at school. It didn't look like they knew the photo was being taken. What else do you want me to know about this that I might be missing?"

Teen: "Nothing."

Parent: (waiting)

Teen: "I know. He always posts annoying stuff like that on the chat. But I am not even really good friends with him."

Parent: "What do you think of photos like that?"

Teen: "I mean, I understand that it isn't okay, if that's what you mean. But Marcus already basically told him to just stop doing that during advisory today."

Parent: "Do you think he will?"

Teen: "I don't know. Probably."

Parent: "Okay. If he doesn't, can we keep talking about it? We can brainstorm other things you might be able to do."

Teen: "Yeah, fine."

Parent: "Thanks for your willingness to talk this through. This stuff isn't easy."

It Comes Down to Respect

These conversations can be difficult, because parents' efforts to influence kids' behavior can be taken as a sign of disrespect. One day I was moving quickly through my home trying to get out the door for work. Cue another epic morning of trying to leave the house with a teenager.

"I need you to take off your headphones and get going!" I told my middle schooler. The reminder came at the end of my instructions about what to do next. My kid, more engaged in a podcast than my game plan, didn't budge. I considered increasing the volume, providing more information, or adding some exasperated sighs for emphasis. Before I could decide, my middle schooler made it clear in both body language and words that my help was not needed. Meanwhile, my eight-year-old overhead my instructions and realized that a couple of them were relevant to him. Without even being asked, he was off looking for his backpack.

Parents understand intuitively that feeling excluded, disrespected, or not taken seriously by peers feels awful during adolescence. We tend to be less sympathetic when our kids bring this same level of sensitivity into family interactions. It's maddening when we don't feel we are being disrespectful; we are just trying to get through the day. For young people, however, respect isn't just about tone or overtly disrespectful words. It is about autonomy, competence, and relatedness. They want to be treated as valued, capable members of their family.

This might explain why the effectiveness of school-based interventions to reduce "problem behaviors" like substance abuse, violence, and bullying tends to nosedive during adolescence.[31] Many traditional interventions are designed to deliver knowledge and advice for long-term health. The same messages that young children appear to accept willingly are met with reliable skepticism during the teenage years. This could be because traditional interventions often don't take near-term social dynamics seriously enough. It could also be because anything that comes off as adults delivering lectures flies in the face of young people's desire to be taken seriously as capable decision-makers.

> **INSIDE INSIGHTS**
>
> It would be easy to chalk up my kids' divergent responses to a bad attitude versus a good attitude. But adolescent resistance to parental control is driven by more than just mindset. It is a way of saying, "I am not a little kid." A combination of hormone and brain changes makes teens far more sensitive to social standing and status than younger children are.[30] This sensitivity primes teens to move toward new people and places and quickly assess social care or mistreatment.

Our kids often seek autonomy before we think they are ready for it. What we see as helpful guidance they might interpret as disrespect. The good news is that the perception gap tends to peak around eighth grade. The bad news is that if we aren't careful, this gap can set us up for escalating power struggles. Imagine the following scenario.

I approach my middle schooler and say, "I need you to stop playing video games and do your homework!" My middle schooler, feeling disrespected, rebuffs me. Because they are still developing emotional regulation skills, their response isn't a well-articulated statement of their needs. Instead, like many teens, they externalize their unpleasant feelings. Now I, as the parent, feel disrespected. My kid's "bad attitude" further cements my belief that they aren't ready for independence. I double down on commands. My teen doubles down on hurt-driven reactivity. It doesn't end well.

So, should parents just back out and leave kids in charge? No. Does it mean that rude behaviors are fair game? Also no. Young people may seek autonomy, but they still rely on guidance and boundaries as they learn how to set goals and move toward them. But *how* we set limits and give guidance matters. Our beliefs about our teens' capacities and goals matter too. We can reduce friction and attend to our kids' developmental needs by balancing structure with freedom and choice. Researchers call this "autonomy-supportive" parenting.[32]

Autonomy-supportive parenting doesn't mean sending kids out into the world solo. Research indicates that White parents are more likely than other racial groups to prioritize (and White teens are more likely to benefit from) an orientation toward independence that involves distancing from parents and embracing new roles.[33] In contrast, many families of color prioritize autonomy in the context of interdependence and family relationships. The focus is on living authentically in the context of close relationships rather than forging out on your own. One researcher also noted that "Latinx parents in the United States are raising their children in an environment characterized by racism and discrimination, as well as anti-immigrant sentiment. For these reasons, valuing interdependence may play a protective role."[34] How families negotiate independence within the home (for example, media choices) might be different from how they negotiate it outside the home (for example, issues related to safety). But across communities, adolescents seem to benefit from both autonomy *and* connectedness, warmth *and* structure. So, parents can be autonomy-supportive in a number of ways:

- Set meaningful boundaries and communicate the purpose of them.

- Provide expectations, guidance, and input when necessary.

- Encourage teens to share their thoughts, desires, beliefs, and values.

- Give plenty of room within family boundaries for agency, and respect teens' growing capacity to make decisions aligned with their values.

Instead of: "Stop with the video games! I need you to get outside and get your homework done today."
Try: "We both know you have homework and need to visit Grandma today. You also want to play video games. What is your plan for doing all of that today?"

Instead of: "Come over here right now so I can talk to you about what I saw on your phone."
Try: "I'd like to talk to you about something. Do you want to talk now or later tonight?"

Instead of: "You need to talk to your coach about what you posted online about the game. I can message her right now."
Try: "Your next challenge is to figure out who you need to talk with to make this right. What do you think are the best next steps? Would you like to hear my ideas?"

Instead of: "I would never start a YouTube channel if I were you. Let me tell you how this is going to end."
Try: "I am not ready yet to say yes or no about a YouTube channel right this moment. But I'm curious: What are you hoping to do with it? Why do you think it is a good choice for you?"

Your kid relies on you to set meaningful boundaries, but that doesn't mean they will be happy when you do so. Being clear about the purpose of your limits can help you tolerate your kid's distress as they push against those limits. Let's say your sixth grader is begging to open their own social media account. You know that they are finding ways to connect meaningfully with their friends outside of social media, and you have decided that they aren't ready for the risks that come with the platform they're interested in. You might have a conversation like this:

Sixth grader: "Can I *please* get an account? I am the only one without it."

Parent: "We've already talked about our boundary around social media for now. The answer is no. Here's why: That app isn't built for sixth graders, and it's my job as your parent to help you stay safe. Remember what we learned from looking at it together? The app doesn't have the safety features needed for users your age. But I do understand that it has some really cool parts. Can you help me understand why you want it so bad right now?"

Sixth grader: "You are the only parent who is like this. I just want it. It is *not* unsafe!"

Parent: "I understand that there are ways to make it *safer*, but the app was not designed for you. Does [best friend] have it?"

Sixth grader: "Well, no. But we are like the only ones."

Parent: "What are you hoping to do on it?"

Sixth grader: "I dunno. Watch videos."

Parent: "I am not going to change my mind about this app right now, but if you want, we can talk about other ways to make sure you are connecting with your friends and watching videos."

Sixth grader: "UGH. I hate this."

Parent: "You get to be mad at me. And it's my job to hold the boundaries I think are really important."

Sixth grader: "FINE. Can I get it next year?"

Loosen, But Don't Let Go: Setting Boundaries

Positioning yourself as the constant arbiter of your kid's technology requests is likely to result in endless power struggles. Consistent boundaries can reduce power struggles and give teens more room for independence within clear limits. But where do boundaries matter most when it comes to technology use?

Remember: except in the extremes, the *amount* of time your adolescent spends in front of screens is not the most important variable. Boundaries that prioritize your kid's health and well-being are more helpful. Dr. Jacqueline Nesi, researcher and psychologist, describes the various ways that families tackle tech boundaries.[35] Some create tech-free zones in the home (for example, no devices in the bedroom), some focus on timing (for example, no devices before school), and others protect certain activities (for example, no devices during time with elders). No matter your approach, boundaries that protect adolescent mental health are a good place to start. Prioritize connection, sleep, exercise and movement, green time, downtime, mindfulness, and mind wandering.

Prioritize Connection

Connection is so important that two whole chapters of this book talk about it. Head back to chapter 4 for reminders of how important family connections are.

Chapter 8 explores peer connections. Make sure technology brings you and your kid toward each other instead of enabling patterns of avoidance or isolation.

Prioritize Sleep

Devices deliver updates, music, friends, alarms, and more, so it is no surprise that so many people sleep with devices nearby. Plus, it seems fairly harmless to watch memes or connect with friends right before bed. But here's the problem: Research is clear that phones and sleep aren't a good mix.[36] Unfortunately, nearly one-third of adolescents sleep with a mobile device in bed.[37] Research also shows that 36 percent of teens wake up to check their device at least once during the night, and 5 percent of young people's 237 notifications a day arrive overnight on school nights.[38] A review of the evidence found that technology is related to sleep problems in at least two significant ways:[39]

- **Delays falling asleep:** Online activities keep you awake. Checking email, scrolling through social media, or sending something to a friend typically results in a chain of online activities that push sleep later.

- **Makes it harder to stay asleep:** Chimes, nudges, push notification, buzzes, and alerts wake you up at night. Once you are awake, your seeking brain immediately starts wondering, "I wonder what that was?" The urge to check is almost impossible to resist.

The influence of tech on poor sleep appears to run both ways. Tech use can negatively impact sleep, *and* teens who are already struggling with sleep tend to turn to their devices to cope. The stakes are high. Losing sleep doesn't just make your kid tired; it makes their brain less effective when they're awake. Sleepy teens are more likely to struggle with emotional regulation and find it difficult to focus their attention and be ready to learn. Sleep can be a powerful moderator in the relationship between tech use and poor mental health.[40]

It's worth brainstorming healthy on-ramps to sleep that work for your teen. For example, streaming relaxing music in the evening might be a better fit than a True Murder podcast. And when the time comes to sleep, consider charging devices away from sleep areas. An investigation of more than ten thousand teens found that those who left their phone ringers on overnight were more likely to experience trouble falling asleep and staying asleep compared to teens who turned their phones off overnight.[41]

Prioritize Exercise and Movement

You probably know that movement is important for physical health. It is just as important to mental health and cognition. Dr. John Ratey, a leading exercise researcher, argues that exercise is good medicine for the brain.[42] Exercise turns on your attention system and activates your prefrontal cortex. It also promotes the growth of neurons. Finally, you benefit from exercise-induced increases in dopamine (the happy chemical), serotonin (the mood stabilizer), and epinephrine (the energizer). In other words: movement is no small thing. If your kid is online at the expense of moving their body, then they're missing out on movement's many benefits.

Prioritize Green Time

When I was a teenager, I often spent summers waist-deep in muskeg (the northern Minnesota name for stinky swamp mud) with a wood-and-canvas canoe perched on my shoulders, while mosquitoes buzzed hungrily in my ears.

"Why do you do that to yourself?" one of my friends used to ask me. It was a fair question. Experiences like these were sometimes unpleasant. But they were worthwhile too. One of the main reasons I grabbed a paddle every summer was the overwhelming sense of calm and confidence I gained from the experience.

While the exact reasons aren't entirely clear, time spent in nature is associated with improved mental health among adolescents.[43] The good news is that you don't need to be waist-deep in muskeg to experience the benefits of green spaces. For those of us who live in cities, frequent exposure to urban green space is also likely to provide lasting improvements to mental health.[44] If we as a society want to replace screen time with green time, we should advocate for equitable access to nature for all teenagers—no matter where they live.

Prioritize Downtime, Mindfulness, and Mind Wandering

Kids and adults alike are constantly inundated with breaking news, hot takes, policy opinions, petitions, memes, misinformation, videos, and more. Checking our phones can open up a firehose of stimulation. Even though only our thumbs are moving, our nervous systems are in overdrive.

Research has revealed that the human brain has two different powerful brain networks: a looking-out network and a looking-in network.[45] Humans can't use both at once. Instead, we toggle back and forth between them. Here are some examples of using these networks:

- **Looking out:** We use this network when we check social media, compose a text to a friend, or watch news coverage.

- **Looking in:** We use this network when we rest, reflect, pray, meditate, remember, feel, or daydream.

Researchers Mary Helen Immordino-Yang and colleagues argue that "looking in" can help young people make meaning of the experiences that they have while "looking out."[46] It's challenging to look inward in a media-rich world, where our attention is so often directed outward toward digital content and tasks. Kids can learn a lot from what they swipe and scroll through, but processing the moral and emotional consequences of what they experience requires downtime and reflection. Far from being a waste of time, helping your kid find time to look inward is a key part of digital well-being and purpose.

REFLECT SCREEN TIME BOUNDARIES

- Teens thrive with purposeful boundaries and freedom within those limits. Identify three boundaries related to technology that matter most to you. You might consider zones, times, or activities that are device-free.

- What are the purposes of these boundaries? You might consider family time, focus on learning, sleep, movement, outdoor time, friendships, or downtime.

- Have you communicated to your adolescent the purpose of the technology boundaries you've set? If not, now's a great time to do so!

You Can Do It

Your adolescent is not a little kid anymore. They are growing up, roaming farther from home, and building skills for autonomy and independence. The boundaries you identified above can provide the structure that ultimately allows for more freedom. You will change your priorities based on your kid's age, growing skills, and changing world. But no matter how you approach tracking, monitoring, or boundaries, your kid will make mistakes. They will post something online that they later regret. They will fail to prioritize the "right" things. They will experience online conflict. These aren't signs that you should double down on control or start treating them like a little kid. It may mean that they need additional support or clearer limits. But it isn't evidence that your kid is incapable. It's evidence that they are growing up. They need you to grow and learn alongside them.

Your kid is capable of an endless list of things. All you need to do is step back long enough to let them try. It's one of the ways that you can communicate to them that they are a valued member of your family.

■ ■ ■

CHAPTER 6 ■■ ■ ■

Online Self-Expression

"I am out with lanterns, looking for myself."
—EMILY DICKINSON, 1855 LETTER TO HER FRIEND MRS. HOLLAND

"Yyyyeessss!" my brother and I cheered, standing up and pumping our fists in the air. Our favorite soccer team had just scored a goal to tie the game. My younger child, who'd been playing with his cousins in the other room, ran in to see what the excitement was about. He glanced briefly at the screen, then turned toward me and asked, "Which team are we rooting for?" He was eager to align his allegiance with mine. He joined the celebration as we watched replays together.

A few years later, he might have chosen to root for the other team simply because I wasn't. As chapter 4 explains, many young people temporarily push parents away so they can distinguish their own values from their parents'. Adolescents need space to answer the question "What does it mean to be me?" Renowned developmental psychologist Erik Erikson argued that answering this question is the core task of adolescence. He acknowledged that identity formation is a lifelong process but insisted that the teenage years are a particularly influential time for humans to figure out the kind of people they want to be.[1]

According to Erikson, young people engage in two ongoing processes that help them answer identity questions: exploration and introspection.[2] As they explore, young people are reflecting on questions like "What makes me feel most like me?" "What doesn't feel right?" and "What is most aligned with my beliefs and values?" This isn't just a personal process. It is a deeply interpersonal one.

As young people try out different expressions of their identities, they monitor how others respond. This personal and interpersonal reflection helps them make sense of the ways that they are—or are not—able to disclose various parts of themselves in various spaces. Identity exploration can be painful, playful, exciting, overwhelming, and gratifying.

Identity formation isn't a linear or predictable process. Nobody—including me—could've predicted that I'd cut my hair with the tiny scissors on a Swiss Army knife during a camping trip between sophomore and junior year of high school. But cut it I did, and I learned a lot about myself when I came out of the woods and had to reconcile Wilderness Erin with Back-to-High-School Erin. I was lucky to have parents who took experiments like mine in stride and friends who would cut their hair like mine if I needed them to. These relationships made all the difference. Psychologists have long noted that open and accepting relationships are key to facilitating healthy self-exploration.[3]

The journey of identity formation is long and winding. It's best for us parents to let young people explore without pointing out shortcuts, forcing detours, or paving the roads we prefer. Our kids are engaging in essential identity work related to their race, gender, class, sexuality, and other aspects of their identity, all while navigating the complexities of a rapidly changing digital landscape. They will experiment with their hair, their clothes, what and where they post online, what classes they take, whether they drink at a party, who they ask out, and on and on. Some of these identity experiments have higher stakes than others. When our kids stumble, they may turn to us for comfort and to reflect on what happened. Then they will quickly venture back out to their most trusted confidants: their friends. Our job is to support our kids, ask thoughtful questions, and serve as a safe home base when the journey gets overwhelming.

Online Playgrounds for Identity Exploration

"You look amazing," my son said.

"Thank you!" I responded proudly. I was grateful for his generous feedback on the Minecraft skin I was customizing before heading into a realm to play together with him. What I lacked in crafting and building skills, I was trying to make up with style. "Should I go with the long purple hair or a rainbow mohawk?" I asked.

"Definitely rainbow," he responded. I liked his confidence. Soon I was ready to head into the virtual world, commanding an avatar whose appearance did not remotely resemble my own.

There's often a gap between a person's offline and online personas. This gap is one of adults' main concerns as young people navigate identity exploration online. They worry that the internet creates opportunities for "teens gone wild" to express themselves in ways that are completely different from their offline personas. In the early days of the internet, when offline and online worlds were starkly separated, people had more opportunity for this kind of identity play than they have today—but it does still exist. Fantasy universes, virtual reality spaces, and games often encourage creative avatars and player skins. Anonymous apps may provide cover for activities that young people wouldn't consider doing if their names were attached. And of course, predators who use fake names and identities can lead to devastating outcomes.

For most teens today, however, their online activities and friendships are intertwined with their offline ones. Young people expect some degree of consistency across contexts. One eighth grader told me that if people aren't "being real" online, they are likely to get called out for it. Researchers Katie Davis and Emily Weinstein back this up when they note, "Existing friends expect their friends' online identity representations to be recognizable, familiar, and consistent with offline behaviors."[4] This expectation makes online self-expression both *new* (due to the design features of digital spaces) and *familiar*. Young people today are doing what every generation of adolescents has done before them: exploring who they are through self-expression, experimentation, and dialogue with friends.

So how is it different today? In the book *Behind Their Screens,* Carrie James and Emily Weinstein summarize how digital media transform the dynamics of adolescents' experiences and expressions.[5] They list eight things digital media design brings:

- **Constant connection:** Devices offer round-the-clock opportunities to connect.

- **Persistence:** Digital content, photos, posts, and comments stick around.

- **Searchability:** Search engines quickly and efficiently locate personal information.

- **Scalability:** With the tap of a finger, large audiences can access digital content.

- **Quantifiability:** Most apps log and display views, shares, likes, and follows in easily digestible formats.

- **Publicness:** The default settings on most platforms are set to broad audiences.

- **Absence of physical cues:** Most online exchanges don't contain visual facial cues or body language.

- **Reinforced filter bubbles:** Algorithms shape what users see and what they don't see online.

When I gave myself that killer wilderness haircut back in the analog days, I got to slowly take stock of how my family members and friends reacted as I saw people face-to-face. I also had time to get hair products before my school debut. My experience would probably play out differently today. Someone might snap a photo of me, post it to social media, and tag me with a critical comment that everyone could see. That photo and comment might persist in the digital landscape, continually adding salt to a painful social wound. It could make me feel like I need to work to control my reputation. Alternatively, I might share pics in a private story right away with a close group of friends to get support and reinforcement. My friends would probably tell me to skip the hair product and head straight to a stylist. But they would do it lovingly. They also might use photo filters to show their hair chopped off in solidarity. With the internet involved, I might feel more vulnerable—or I might feel stronger.

There is no single story of how technology shapes developmental processes. The design features of digital media sometimes strengthen and sometimes undercut kids' agency and confidence as they make the journey of identity formation. But there is no doubt that for kids today the journey is entirely different from that experienced by any generation before them.

Oversharing or Empowering?

"I just don't understand why she would share that so widely!" a parent named Sofia confided. "I don't mind her sharing other things, but this just seems so private. She says she's fine with it, but I worry about how people will respond." Sofia's daughter had recently come out as pansexual to her parents. They were surprised to learn that her friends had known "forever" and even more surprised later that day when she posted about it on social media.

INSIDE INSIGHTS

One of Sofia's daughter's main tasks in adolescence is to explore her identity, figure out what really matters to her, and connect with supportive people who can help her discover who she is. She feels that the benefits of expressing herself and exploring her identity semi-publicly outweigh the risks that come with personal sharing online. Sofia, like many parents, feels differently. Parents are more likely to overemphasize the risks of online expression while downplaying its potential rewards.

Today's online culture prioritizes and rewards the ideas of openness and authenticity. Kids see their favorite athletes, musicians, and actors not only on stages or big screens but also in their personal lives online. That's not to say that online influencers, creators, and pop stars are offering whole and healthy versions of themselves to their audiences. They generally present highly curated images and stories. Much of the content is professionally produced and often paid for.

But even though social media platforms tend to provide "highlights reels" rather than accurate depictions of real life, young people do benefit in some ways from pulling back the curtain of fame. As a young person, I would have loved to know that some of my heroes struggled with the same things that my friends and I did. Stories about mental health, experiences of racism, social struggle, or disordered eating and healing can help normalize these issues and make heroes more human. A tenth grader recently told me that she loved seeing that her favorite performing artist also struggles with anxiety. She shared, "It's just good to know that nobody is actually perfect."

This generational shift toward more sharing makes many parents uncomfortable. The persistence and publicness of images on the internet change the stakes of self-expression. As Devorah Heitner explains in her book

Growing Up in Public: Coming of Age in a Digital World, parents are worried that sharing personal things online will harm their kids' future opportunities and that their kids will be harmed by their peers' responses.[6] She references a Lurie Children's Hospital survey in which 52 percent of parents "at some point felt uncomfortable with the way their teen behaved or portrayed themself on social media. Of that group, the primary concern has been what the parents identify as a lack of privacy and tendency to 'overshare.'"[7]

Sharing online is a natural extension of self-expression for many kids—even about personal subjects such as gender and sexuality, mental health, political opinions, neurodivergence, or family or friend conflicts. That said, young people are still developing the skills to weigh long-term consequences against short-term rewards. Sharing too quickly, too widely, or in too much detail can lead to unanticipated challenges, and young people may underestimate the risks of social media disclosures.[8]

Still, it isn't fair for us parents to label all online expressions as impulsive. Let's also be open to the idea that sometimes, as Heitner says, "What we experience as discomfort, they experience as empowering."[9] Understanding and normalizing young people's motivations helps us focus on the goal. The goal is not to shut down exploration and reflection. It is to help kids get into the driver's seat of their digital identities. Following are five reasons adolescents may disclose information about themselves online.

1. To Discover and Connect with Their People

Identity formation is a deeply interpersonal process. Sharing online can help young people find and connect with like-minded and supportive friends. Dr. Mizuko (Mimi) Ito and her colleagues at the Connected Learning Alliance have long studied the positive influence of online affinity groups. She notes that the internet allows young people to build community with others who share similar interests or identities when a critical mass of these kids doesn't exist in their schools or neighborhoods.[10] This kind of connection doesn't happen just on dominant social media platforms. Researcher Meryl Alper has documented ways that autistic kids have built community and shared projects on Scratch, a kid-friendly computer programming website and online community developed by researchers at the Massachusetts Institute of Technology.[11] Whether it is connecting with other kids who love anime, who share identity, or who play *Dungeons & Dragons*, for adolescents, finding their people is an important part of growing up.

2. To Explore Emerging Aspects of Gender or Sexual Identity

From sharing a pride flag in their bio to sharing hashtags like #panpride, young people go online to explore and express their emerging identities. For many LGBTQ+ adolescents in particular, online communities can play an important role in identity development. They offer rare and much-needed refuge from the transphobia and homophobia many young people experience offline. For LGBTQ+ adolescents, online sharing is a double-edged sword. They are more likely than their straight or cisgender peers to rely on social media for positive, identity-affirming experiences. They are *also* more likely to be the target of bullying and harassment online.[12] Given this reality, online self-disclosure is both empowering and risky.

3. To Disrupt Stereotypes and Write Their Own Narratives

Much of the research on digital media and adolescence studies White teens. We need more research and resources dedicated to understanding how young people of color, who are the global majority, navigate identity in digital spaces. We do know that many young people who belong to underresearched groups go online to author their own stories and reclaim stigmatized parts of their identity. For example, a 2020 study explored how a Facebook group helped Asian Americans connect with others, engage in mutual care, and disrupt harmful stereotypes when anti-Asian racism spiked at the beginning of the COVID pandemic.[13] Black Twitter long served as a space where Black young people could not only come together to share experiences but also resist racism and marginalization.[14] Online communities can help young people gain new strategies for coping with and resisting things like racism, prejudice, and stereotypes.

4. To Build Pride in Their Racial and Ethnic Identities

Digital spaces not only offer protection from harm, but also cultivate pride and joy. The 2020 Native Youth Health Tech Survey found that American Indian and Native Alaskan young people listed Native identity and cultural pride as one of the most important health topics they accessed online.[15] More than 70 percent of teen girls of color who use TikTok or Instagram report that they encounter identity-affirming content related to race at least monthly.[16] This is no small thing. Dr. Joanna Lee Williams, member of the National Scientific Council on Adolescence from the UCLA Center for the Developing Adolescent, notes the protective power of Black laughter and joy: "I think there's a resurgence in this concept of Black joy, which is about 'despite all of the things that may be going on in our country, I still can look to my people as a source of joy.' And I think having those messages being prevalent for young people to have access to can also tremendously benefit them in terms of racial identity development."[17]

Pride-in-identity online experiences are important. Young people's online exposure to racial discrimination and traumatic events is on the rise.[18] But research shows that positive ethnic and racial identity can buffer against the negative mental health outcomes associated with online racial discrimination.[19] I recently spoke with Dr. Henry Willis, a clinical psychologist who studies the relationship between online and offline racial discrimination and mental health outcomes. He noted that positive racial identity beliefs make it more likely that "when youth of color see negative messages online, they don't automatically internalize it. They are able to identify it as something racism-related and that isn't true or valid."[20] While caregivers are the most important drivers of positive identity beliefs, young people also need to have identity-affirming experiences and interactions online.

5. To Share Political Opinions and Create Change

For most teens today, self-expression necessitates wading into politics. According to Weinstein and James, teens feel significant pressure to signal awareness of and support for or opposition to political issues. In their book *Behind Their Screens,* they explain, "Adults may consider social media a distinct domain, optional and 'extra credit' as a context for speaking up . . . A decade ago this might have been the case. But no such distinction exists for today's teens. Social media is a key venue for voice about all things. Silence on pressing issues can indeed feel like a betrayal."[21]

Exploring political identities and expressing political opinions online comes with countless pitfalls. These include getting it "wrong," seeming fake or performative, posting too much or too little, posting to echo chambers, or pandering to the "other side." Yet at the same time, teens report that the internet is where they are exposed to diverse viewpoints and learn about issues that are important to them. Seeing and engaging with other viewpoints is essential to identity exploration.

Choosing Channels for Expression

Years ago, I arrived at a high school prepared with what I thought was a great workshop on digital footprints and identity. I was looking forward to talking with a student leadership group about the ways that online posts combine to form a representation (or misrepresentation) of self. Despite my great intentions, I lost my small audience as I soon as I started. The term *digital footprint* in my lead slide turned off this group of tenth graders.

"You should be talking to the seventh graders, not us," a student named Chue offered within the first five minutes.

"Why do you say that?" I asked.

"Because I share way less than I used to. I can't believe the stuff I put up on YouTube in middle school. Kids share all kinds of cringy stuff. We know better now."

"I hear you," I said. I was a few steps behind my audience. By tenth grade, young people are used to hearing the warning to "think before you post." The conversation I'd planned about online representations of identity is certainly relevant to high schoolers. It is still relevant to adults. But the term *digital footprint* suggested that we were about to launch into well-worn online safety tips instead of the more mature discussion these tenth graders felt ready for.

"So what about online identity?" I asked. "Do you think people online see the real you?" I hoped they would let me restart the conversation.

I was lucky. The group seemed willing to pivot. A student named William jumped in right away and said, "My profiles aren't totally public, but otherwise what you see is what you get with me. I am not ashamed to just put it all out there."

Another student named Maeve was less sure. "Oh, my main feed is not a full representation. I keep that to my private stories." Turning toward Chue, she also offered a counterpoint to his assertion that all high schoolers have it together online. "I don't know, Chue, kids here still get themselves into all kinds of trouble for stuff they post."

Students went on to describe the numerous ways they partition audiences and curate content to control how, when, and where they express themselves. They were not all on the same page. No doubt some still needed reminders about internet safety. But none of them existed online in a state of total unconcerned transparency. Young people today don't have the freedom to leave behind old identities and explore new ones. This reality can be annoying, painful, mortifying, hilarious, risky, and nostalgic. Adolescents are constantly negotiating trade-offs among self-expression, connection, privacy, and safety. Their calculations might change based on age, content, and context.

A group of sophomores telling me to talk to the "kids" about digital footprint was a good reminder that tenth graders and seventh graders are worlds apart developmentally and navigate decisions differently. Research offers more examples. A study following up with a group of older adolescents who had posted frequently about politics two years earlier found that the majority of them had since quieted their civic expressions.[22] This behavior change could relate to developmental changes and/or the changing political and digital landscapes. Some teens in the study cited online toxicity and the permanence of their opinions as reasons for taking political talk offline. In another study, Asian American adolescents and emerging adults reported seeking mental health support in more private online channels as a way to avoid stigma around mental illness.[23]

Adults often wave off young people's attempts to manage privacy and navigate personal disclosure as misguided or even manipulative. When Instagram first hit the internet, parents worried a lot about the nefarious purposes of fake accounts (Finstas) or other secondary social media accounts. Yet some young people set up those accounts to be able to post more freely with a smaller group of friends rather than sharing things widely.[24] The strategy of using alternative channels to manage privacy is clear in Maeve's comment about her "main feed" and her "private stories."

Parents are eager to share with adolescents threatening reminders that the internet holds a permanent and public record of their activities. That's fair; privacy online is tenuous at best. But this is not breaking news, especially for older adolescents. If we recognize the agency and self-awareness that teens build over time, we're less likely to lose them before we can have important conversations.

Instead of: "I don't know why you would tell the whole internet about that."
Try: "How do you decide where and how much to share about yourself? Here are my concerns . . . How do those land with you?"

Instead of: "See! I told you that there's no safe way to post anything online."
Try: "Social media is so tricky, and it sounds like things did not go as you planned. Do you want to vent or brainstorm next steps?"

Instead of: "One wrong post, and your future might be ruined."
Try: "Managing your identity online is a challenge. What do you already know about settings and strategies around privacy, passwords, and location sharing?"

Instead of: "If you post that kind of stuff, potential employers will never hire you."
Try: "You are the one who is ultimately in charge of how you show up in the world. Do you think this post reflects the kind of person you are?"

Instead of: "I can't believe you did that! What were you thinking?"
Try: "Sounds like you wouldn't tag that person if you could do it over again. What can you do now to make it right with them?"

Instead of: "Nothing good can come of getting an account on that site."
Try: "My job as a parent is to watch out for your safety. I hear that you want to connect with friends. We are going to hold off on that particular platform for now because it isn't designed to be safe for people your age. That isn't up for negotiation. But how else can we make sure that you find your people?"

Instead of: "She really shouldn't be putting that out there. I am glad you know better than that."
Try: "It sounds like you are concerned about what your friend is posting. Do you know if she has an adult she can talk to?"

Instead of: "This really isn't something you should broadcast."
Try: "This is not a secret, and there is nothing to be ashamed of. But it sounds like this subject makes you feel vulnerable. Who do you think will take the care you deserve with this information and support you?"

IN ACTION: INTENTIONAL SHARING

Most teenagers are not eager to do reflective exercises with their parents. But you can plant seeds over time and prompt conversations about when, where, and with whom they want to disclose personal information. You can encourage them to slow down and consider questions like these:

- "Why do I want to post this here? What am I hoping for? What might go well? What could go wrong?"
- "Do I consider this sensitive information? Why or why not?"
- "Is this my story to share? Who do I need to check in with before I post it?"
- "Am I comfortable with this being shared widely, or do I want more control?"
- "How might people react to this? If I share this, how will I take care of myself if people respond poorly?"

Sharenting

"I felt awful about it," Susana shared. "I just wasn't thinking. He never used to mind when I shared pictures of him with my friends." She paused, then went on, "I guess I'm not sure if he minded . . . It's not like our friends overlapped."

Susana explained that she had posted pictures after a family birthday celebration. Without thinking much about it, she tagged the kids who had social media accounts, including her fifteen-year-old nephew. Within minutes of posting, her nephew removed himself from the post. She reached out to him, and he "politely but firmly asked that I don't tag him anymore."

"I immediately understood where he was coming from," Susana shared. "I felt so old. I just wasn't thinking about his context."

Young people aren't the only ones who sometimes overshare. I recently overheard an eighth grader mutter, "Maybe someone should talk to our parents about this too," during a conversation about digital footprints. For many kids, their online identities didn't begin when they got on social media. They began when their parents first shared the news about their impending arrival. Parents sharing information about their children online is so common that sharenting, a portmanteau of *parenting* and *sharing*, is now a topic of research.[25]

As parents, we share pictures of our kids for all kinds of reasons. Most of us aren't running accounts for child influencers at great risk to their health and safety.[26] Instead, we are posting to smaller personal circles or online parenting groups. We share to give and get parenting advice, receive affirmation and support, stay in touch with family and friends, express pride in our kids or our parenting, and document and collect memories.[27] This means that we are contributors to our kids' online identities. As our kids get older, the way we portray them is unlikely to align with the images they are trying to create. In one study, teens pointed out that parents should be more careful about sharenting once their kids become aware of online platforms.[28] Their advice for parents is remarkably similar to what we've been telling teens for years: Slow down, be more thoughtful, and ask for permission before we post.

If you've already created a full digital dossier of your kid's every move, there's still time to hand control over to them. Your adolescent may not have strong opinions about what you post. But checking in with them isn't just about gaining permission. It also models the kind of discernment and sensitivity you hope they bring to personal online expression. The catch is that you need to really listen to what they have to say and make good on your agreements. Teens say that their biggest frustration is when parents ignore their requests to take things down or when parents go back on their commitments. Setting expectations before you post is ideal. That said, it's never too late to say, "Now that I know better, I am going to try to do better. Let's talk about what, when, and where you feel comfortable with me posting online."

◀ REFLECT SHARENTING

Read each statement and think about which response best describes where you are right now: "I hadn't thought of this," "I try," or "I got this." Then ask yourself: What are you most proud of? What do you want to work on?

- I talk to my kid about the platforms I post on and who is there.
- I talk to my kid about general expectations related to posting pictures or stories about them.
- I visit my privacy settings often to make sure they are set how I want them to be.
- I check in with my kid before posting a picture or story to make sure they approve.
- I remove photos or posts that my kid is uncomfortable with.
- I apologize when I make a mistake related to sharing things online about my kid without their consent.
- I talk to my friends and family about my kid's wishes related to tagging and posting.

- I brainstorm alternative ways to share information and photos that my kid is comfortable with.

- I listen to my gut about the photos I am posting, even if my kid says they are fine with it.

You Can't Commission the Artwork

Your adolescent's emerging identity is like an ongoing mosaic project. When they were little, you had a good view of the whole picture. You got to see and even place a lot of the pieces. As your kid gets older, the picture evolves and grows, you can't see all the pieces, and you rarely get to place any. Young people keep most for themselves and give a few others away, usually to their friends and sometimes online. They have even more opportunities to be out in the world exploring and experimenting with the question "What feels most like me?" This is developmentally right on time.

When your kid returns to your side, resist the urge to inspect every detail of the mosaic all at once or to critique or paint over the image with your own design. Instead, you can ask for a peek at part of the picture and take note of what you see. What's missing? What's exciting? What's scary? What's inspiring? What skills, boundaries, or supports are needed? You can make sure other caring adults are keeping an eye out and asking questions too.

During adolescence, your kid is busily building a mosaic of their own design. It's a messy process. The internet mirrors, magnifies, and even transforms the possibilities and the pitfalls. There will be misplaced and cracked pieces. There will be mistakes and overshares. You can't commission the artwork. But you can ask questions, set boundaries, offer support, and make sure your kid knows that you love who they are becoming.

CHAPTER 7

Love, Relationships, and Sexual Identity

"We as a society are failing to prepare young people for perhaps the most important thing they will do in life—learn how to love."
—HARVARD UNIVERSITY'S MAKING CARING COMMON PROJECT

I came of age long before artificial intelligence was woven into the fabric of life online and before social media influencers existed. Still, I found ways to ask the internet some questions that felt too awkward or embarrassing to ask an adult. I remember the thrill of typing questions in a program called Dr. Sbaitso on my friend's desktop computer. Dr. Sbaitso was an early AI program that "conversed" with the user. Using it was meant to feel as if you were talking to a psychologist. Unlike a psychologist, however, Dr. Sbaitso had a robotic voice, and I don't recall it giving many satisfying answers to my questions. The program tended to respond with questions like "Why do you feel that way?" instead of dishing out critical information about crushes, puberty, and teenage social life.

Today, adolescents have countless sources of information and advice at their fingertips. They continue to turn to the internet and AI with questions like the following, which are among the top questions submitted in 2024 to an online teen health resource focused on bodies and sexuality:[1]

- "How do I come out to my best friend?"
- "Can I get pregnant after my partner washes their hands?"

- "Why is my left testicle hurting?"

Luckily, the questions I listed above were fielded by professional staff with oversight from clinical social workers, health educators, pediatricians, and other health professionals. Unfortunately, many questions kids type into search engines or AI do not land in such qualified hands. Instead, young people are trying to make sense of their emerging sexual identities in online environments that aren't built with healthy development in mind.

The adolescent quest to figure out "Who am I?" inevitably includes questions related to sex, love, and relationships. These are completely normal questions during a time of dizzying physical and emotional changes. Most teens have questions they are reluctant to ask in person. That is why so many young people turn to the internet with their vulnerable questions.[2] In a 2024 report, one teen noted that AI "can give you an outlet to talk about things you don't want anyone else to know."[3]

Sex, Relationships, and the Adolescent Brain

There is a common misperception among parents that if we talk to our kids about sex-related topics, it will spark their interest in sex—something most parents are eager to put off for as long as possible. The reality is that most teenagers are already interested in sex, whether we've talked to them about it or not. Developmental processes at work in adolescent brains and bodies accelerate interest in sex and initiate more intense curiosity about sexuality.[4] It's a healthy and normal part of growing up.

Around the age of ten, the human body starts producing more hormones called androgens. As androgens increase, young people may experience their first crush. Once puberty hits, a set of brain and hormone changes trigger romantic feelings and sexual thoughts and attractions. This attraction may be directed toward someone of a different sex or gender identity or toward someone with the same sex or gender identity.[5] During this time teens may also start to experience falling in love. When they do, it can be a wild ride. Falling in love is a powerful chemical experience: dopamine (a happy hormone), norepinephrine (an energy hormone), and serotonin (a mood-regulating hormone) are all in play. The prefrontal cortex, on the other hand, is relatively quiet. This explains the emotional roller coaster teenagers experience when they fall in and out of love. This isn't a process initiated by mentions of sex. It is what is going on in adolescent bodies and brains.

Of course, sexual identity is about more than hormones. It also involves feelings, values, culture, and experiences starting long before puberty. From a young age, kids absorb all kinds of information and messages that impact the romantic and sexual relationships they will have someday.

As Dr. Cara Natterson and Vanessa Kroll Bennett explain in their book *This Is So Awkward: Modern Puberty Explained*, "Talking about sex involves two sets of conversations: one about science and a parallel one about humanity. The subject cannot be limited to one or the other without serious consequences, physical and emotional."[6] Throughout adolescence, kids start grappling with serious questions about relationships. They may be feeling attraction while struggling to express this attraction respectfully. They know that consent is important but may not know how to ask for it or grant it. They may be intrigued by pleasure or intimacy while also navigating how to communicate their preferences and make healthy choices.

These are all normal aspects of adolescent development, but that development doesn't automatically unfold in safe and healthy ways. Young people today are indeed having less sex and delaying sex for longer than generations before; teen sex has dropped steadily since the early 1990s.[7] But having less sex is not the only goal of healthy sexual development. Most teenagers still lack good resources for understanding what healthy relationships and sexuality look like. For example, only half of young people in the United States are getting sex education that meets minimum standards as defined by the Future of Sex Education Initiative's National Sex Education Standards and UNESCO's International Technical Guidance on Sexuality Education.[8] Affirming and accurate sex education information is even less common for queer adolescents.[9] Many families don't make up for this dearth of education by talking often at home—especially about digital sexual topics like porn, sexting, and starting relationships online. One study found that only 7 percent of high school students had talked to their parents about all three.[10] There are a host of reasons parents avoid talking to kids more frequently about these topics. For starters, it's hard to believe our kids are ready for it. They were just in preschool! How can they be old enough to talk about sexuality, pleasure, relationships, and porn? These conversations can feel especially uncomfortable if we don't know what to say or if we learned from our families of origin or cultures that such topics are off-limits.

But if we don't get things started early on, our kids are much less likely to initiate conversations or ask questions when they really need help. This is especially true if they sense disapproval or judgment. They may feel safer and less awkward seeking answers from the internet or AI. One study found that LGBTQ+ young people were more likely to search for sexual health information online than their straight peers were.[11]

The good news is that going online for information isn't inherently problematic. Dr. Sbaitso didn't deliver much helpful information in the 1990s, but today's internet is full of evidence-based resources. More and more organizations are using technology to get young people the information they need to take care of themselves. And a review of the research indicated that formal technology-based interventions are effective in enhancing sexual and reproductive health knowledge and attitudes among teenagers.[12] As AI models improve, they can be trained to provide accurate information and to direct teens toward reliable resources. There are many promising possibilities for engaging young people in accurate and evidence-based sexual health information online—but first, this information must break through the unhelpful noise proliferating on the internet.

The bad news is that algorithms don't tend to lead kids toward high-quality resources, and the quality of AI chatbot advice ranges from wonderful to horrible. Aza Raskin, cofounder of the nonprofit Center for Humane Technology, had a very unsettling experience with a popular social media AI chatbot. Even though he told the AI that he was a thirteen-year-old girl considering having sex with a thirty-one-year-old she met online, the chatbot still engaged with questions about ways to "make her first time special."[13] The company quickly retrained its chatbot to avoid such interactions, but others are sure to pop up. Real humans on social media aren't necessarily more reliable. The internet is awash with nonexperts providing sexual health misinformation. A 2023 analysis showed that YouTube influencers are likely to share unhelpful or inaccurate information related to birth control.[14]

Rampant misinformation and bias in online information and AI tools amplify the cost of parental silence. Avoiding conversation about sex, dating, and relationships at home can inadvertently reinforce toxic dynamics that young people absorb from influencers, porn, and peers. According to a report called "The Talk" from the Harvard Graduate School of Education, a whopping 87 percent of survey respondents (ages eighteen to twenty-five) reported that they had been sexually harassed.[15] Sadly, 76 percent of respondents reported that they had never had a conversation with their parents about how to avoid sexually harassing others. Similar majorities had never had conversations with their parents about various forms of misogyny.

Dr. Emily Weinstein, codirector of the Center for Digital Thriving, and her colleague, Dr. Beck Tench, recommend that parents ask teens directly, "What kinds of questions feel easier to ask AI than a human?"[16] This directness creates opportunities to talk about the topics teens are pondering or to identify other resources teens can turn to for sound, nonjudgmental information. Having such conversations pays off. A review of three decades of research showed that parent-teen communication is associated with safer sex behaviors among teens.[17]

It's time to embrace the awkwardness. As parents, we need to talk early and often with our kids about sex-related topics. It's okay to talk directly about risks. But we must also remember that teens are hungry for conversations they aren't sure how to start. In our focus on sex, we often forget to talk with them about values and relationships. The authors of "The Talk" note that "most sex education is either focused narrowly on abstinence or is 'disaster prevention.'"[18] Conversations about sex, love, and relationships aren't just about protecting teens from harm or transmitting information. They are also important opportunities to communicate our expectations and values while giving teens space to start articulating their own.[19]

REFLECT THE STORIES WE'VE INHERITED ABOUT SEX AND RELATIONSHIPS

Talking to teens about sex and relationships is important. Depending upon the lessons you learned about sex early on, these conversations can also bring up discomfort and uncertainty. Use these questions to reflect on the stories you have inherited from family and culture:

- What stories or lessons about sex did you learn growing up?
- What stories or lessons about relationships did you learn growing up?

You will likely discover things that you want to keep, things you want to modify, and still others that you want to let go of. Take time to think about these two questions:

- Which of these stories or lessons do you want to continue and share with your teen?

- Which of these stories or lessons do you want to let go of and do differently with your teen?

IN ACTION: HAVING THE TALKS

Instead of: avoiding topics related to puberty, sex, sexuality, and relationships . . .
Try: looking for resources that help you feel prepared to talk early and often. Lots of little talks are far more effective—and easier—than one long conversation. They also allow you to adjust your language and information as your kid gets older.

Instead of: waiting for your teen to ask questions about specific topics or looking at their search history for signs of sexual curiosity . . .
Try: giving your teen accurate and evidence-based websites, books, and other resources they can refer to when questions inevitably arise.

Instead of: pretending that your teen isn't a sexual being . . .
Try: getting used to the idea that adolescence is a time when kids experience sexual curiosity, romantic feelings, pleasure, and attraction. Sexuality is a positive part of life and nothing to be ashamed of.

Instead of: using words like *good*, *bad*, and *naughty* . . .
Try: framing sexual decision-making in terms of health, safety, values, and expectations.

Instead of: focusing on disaster prevention and dire warnings . . .
Try: highlighting the joy, pleasure, and fulfillment that come with healthy relationships—sexual or otherwise.

Instead of: assuming you know your child's sexual orientation . . .
Try: using open and inclusive language so your child is more likely to open up to you as their sexuality evolves.

Instead of: assuming your teen knows what a healthy relationship looks like and feels like . . .
Try: talking to your teen about healthy relationships. Ask, "What do good friendships feel like?" "How do you know when someone isn't being a good friend?" Expand the conversation to include other kinds of relationships. Ask, "What do infatuation, care, attraction, and love feel like?" "What does it look like when these relationships become unhealthy?"

Instead of: telling your teen that they should never interact with anyone online that they haven't met in the real world . . .
Try: acknowledging that they are likely to meet new people and make friends online. Talk about what to do if someone asks them to keep a secret, promises gifts, is in touch too often, makes them feel uncomfortable, pressures them, or asks them to do something inappropriate.

Instead of: waiting to talk about consent until your teen is sexually active (or avoiding it altogether) . . .
Try: teaching consent early and often. Ask before you hug your kid, take a bite of their dinner, or post about them online. Asking for permission and getting consent is a skill that you both can practice in all areas of life.

Instead of: ignoring sexist or misogynist content by telling yourself it was "just a joke" or "We'll talk about it next time" . . .
Try: taking sexist, transphobic, and misogynist content seriously. Use media as an opportunity to step in, explain why you think the content is harmful, and have a conversation about why it matters.

Instead of: responding to your teen's feelings or behaviors with lectures or judgment . . .
Try: taking a deep breath. It's okay to say, "I don't quite know how to respond right now, but this is what I do know: I love you, and I am so grateful you shared this with me."

Don't Leave Sex Education to Online Pornography

"When did you start talking to your kids about online porn?" a friend with younger kids asked me, wincing a bit at the prospect of embarking on the conversation herself someday.

My face likely mirrored similarly tortured emotions as I responded, "Much earlier than I wanted to. But when I looked at the statistics, I saw that it's clear my kids needed me to talk about it before I felt ready."

Talking to kids about sex and sexuality is challenging. Talking to them about online porn is even harder. That's why so many parents delay these conversations—if we tackle them at all. This well-meaning procrastination is often fueled by equal parts dread, insecurity, and the belief that our kids are too young.

A 2023 report about teens and porn from Common Sense Media might provide the motivation we need to initiate conversations about pornography earlier and more often. The report, drawn from a nationally representative sample of US teens, makes it clear that most teens have seen porn, and their average first exposure is well before high school.[20] More specifically, nearly three-quarters of teens report that they have intentionally or unintentionally consumed pornography. Of these young people, more than half viewed it or were exposed to it in the last week. The average age of first exposure is twelve years old.

In other words, porn isn't hard to find. Young people search for it, stumble upon it, or are shown it by other kids. Nearly one-third of all teens report that they have been exposed to porn during the school day.[21] Porn is big business. Revenues from internet pornography register in the billions of dollars. Monetized streaming, texting, and photo channels abound. In addition to sites specifically dedicated to porn, popular social media platforms link to pornographic content even though it is technically banned.

It makes sense that viewing porn is so common among teens. Access through personal devices expands at the very time adolescents begin exploring their sexual identities. The internet is an obvious place to try to learn and experience more. According to the Common Sense Media report, teens have mixed feelings about porn as a teaching tool. Less than one-third agree that pornography shows sex accurately. Yet nearly half of them say that online pornography gives helpful information about it. Among teens who have viewed porn, more than 75 percent agree that they are learning "how to have sex," "about human bodies and anatomy," and "what types of behaviors are likely to feel pleasurable."[22] Despite acknowledging the inaccuracies, teens are taking cues about sex from porn. As the availability of AI-generated porn increases in the coming years, the accuracy gap will likely continue to grow.

I haven't yet met a parent who thinks porn is a great form of sex education. But many parents are unaware of just how extreme porn is today. The same algorithms that drive kids toward other kinds of extreme online content are likely to serve up the same when it comes to sex. This means more exposure to unrealistic, violent, degrading, and aggressive depictions of sex with plenty of gender and racial stereotypes.[23] I spoke with Dr. Megan K. Maas, an assistant professor in Human Development and Family Studies at Michigan State University, who studies media and sexual behaviors in adolescence. She noted that when it comes to today's porn, "What's at stake is not just unrealistic expectations of what should feel good or what bodies should feel like, but potentially agreeing to more aggressive behaviors when you don't want to or pressuring another person to engage in these more aggressive behaviors."[24] The data back up this claim. Depending on the teen and the kind of content they view, porn consumption may be related to increased sexual aggression and dangerous sexual behaviors.[25] Regardless of the content, half of teens also report feeling "guilty or ashamed" after watching online porn. Associating sexual pleasure or curiosity with shame is not a good mix for healthy sexuality and can get in the way of seeking support from parents instead of the internet.[26]

Teens want parents to talk to them about porn. But less than half of parents are doing so.[27] When they do, kids benefit. Among teens who have talked to a trusted adult about porn, 71 percent feel that "there are helpful resources other than pornography to explore sex or sexuality."[28] According to the evidence-based puberty and sex education organization AMAZE, here's when parents should start talking about porn:[29]

- a child uses a smartphone or has internet access without adult supervision

- a child attends school or has playdates outside the home where they experience varying levels of supervision

- a child has older siblings or friends that they regularly spend time with

- a child is asking lots of questions about bodies and sex

It's normal to feel nervous or unsure when talking to kids about online pornography. But even a nervous parent can have a conversation like this:

Parent: It's not always easy for me to talk with you about things like porn, because my family never talked about sex when I was growing up. I'm sorry we haven't talked more about this. But this is so important that I am going to do the best I can.

Teen: Can we NOT talk about this?

Parent: I know this is awkward. You don't have to look at me while we're talking. I'm just inviting you to hear me out. You deserve accurate information about porn so you can make safe and healthy choices.

Parent: (Chooses a few of the following talking points and tries to invite a two-way conversation with questions like "What do you think about that?")

- Curiosity is normal: "It's normal to be curious about sex and bodies and to be curious about pictures or images of naked people or sex."

- Feelings are normal: "You are likely to see porn at some point, and maybe you already have. If you see porn, you may experience a range of feelings from disgust to curiosity to pleasure to desire to fear to excitement. All of your feelings are okay."

- Porn is big business: "It's not your fault if you stumble upon porn or if someone shows you porn. Even though it isn't for young people, it is a huge industry, which makes it common online."

- Porn is not realistic: "Porn is a performance, for entertainment. Porn producers make sexual content that sells. Images in porn don't reflect what most people's bodies or sexual behaviors or relationships look like. Sometimes the images are just fake and unrealistic. Sometimes they are really harmful."

- Porn is not for kids: "Porn is content produced by adults for adults. It is not for kids or for teens. There are filters and tools we can use to block pornographic images on devices."

- Talk to trusted and caring adults: "If you have questions about sex or porn, please come to me or other trusted adults rather than hiding it, Googling your questions, or only asking friends. It might feel awkward to talk with me about it, but I can make sure you have the information you need."

Teen: (silence)

Teen: "Okay, okay."

Parent: "I understand this isn't your favorite topic to talk about with me. But thanks for listening anyway. I'll keep bringing this up occasionally so you have space to ask questions as they come to you."

Teen: "Okay."

As teens get older, parents need to be ready to ask more open-ended questions and engage with kids' complicated feelings about porn, sex, and relationships.

Teens report that they are frustrated with the "blurry notions of harm"[30] when adults say things like "porn is bad." To engage teens in conversations about how aggression, racism, stereotypes, misogyny, overuse, and other issues show up in porn, we can ask questions about these topics:

- Consent in sexual scripts: "Porn (and media overall) often portrays sex without showing sexual partners asking for consent. What do you think of that? What have you learned about consent?"

- Consent in production: "In mainstream porn sites, there is no way to know if the content was consensually shot or consensually uploaded. Did you know that the top free porn sites verify the age of the uploader but not the age of every person in the video? This means there is no way of knowing whether we are viewing someone else's trauma. How do you make sense of that reality?"

- Aggression and violence: "Porn sometimes contains aggressive and even violent depictions of sex, like choking. Do you think that porn is teaching teens to try to emulate things like this?"

- Bodies and stereotypes: "In real life, bodies come in all kinds of shapes, sizes, abilities, colors, and identities. Porn often shows bodies that are unrealistic because it is produced to entertain and sell, not to reflect real people and relationships. Do you think that impacts teens? Why or why not?"

- Overuse or addiction: "Sometimes people access porn because they are curious, but then have trouble managing it. They don't know how to stop or don't feel like they can stop. Have you ever heard of that happening? Usually, this is about more than just sex and porn. If you ever feel like that, you can talk to me or [other trusted adults' names] and we can help."

In our conversation, Dr. Maas gently reminded me that "in our media-saturated environment, we no longer have the luxury of silence."[31] But this doesn't mean that you must memorize every single talking point or be a certified sex educator to show up for your teen. One of the biggest gifts you can give your adolescent is your willingness to get the conversation started.

Nudes, Sexting, and Relationships

I was packing up my belongings after a middle school workshop focused on social media and mental health. I noticed that a caregiver was lingering by the door. As a parent, I appreciate that not all questions are comfortable to ask in a large group, so I asked the caregiver if she wanted to walk out together. As she and I walked down the empty hallway together, she said, "I still can't believe that this happened."

I waited patiently as she gathered the courage to say more. She went on, "We found out last week that our son had a couple of nude photos on his phone. At first, he claimed he didn't know how they got there, but he dropped that story pretty quickly. When we asked him what was going on, he said that other kids on the bus were sharing nudes and that he just did it too. He doesn't have a girlfriend that I know of, but what do I even know anymore?" Her words spilled on top of each other as she shared both the facts and her emotional response to them.

"We've already talked to the social worker here and are taking it seriously. I know you aren't a therapist, and I am not asking for advice," she assured me. "I just can't decide if I hope this kind of thing is common or uncommon. I hate the idea of this being a typical teenage activity. But I also hate the feeling that something is really wrong with my kid."

We both took a deep breath, and I thanked her for sharing. "This stuff is not easy. I am glad you and your son are getting the support you need. For what it's worth, your son's experience is not entirely outside the norm."

Sexting, or the sending of self-made nude or sexually explicit photos or texts, is not exactly rare among adolescents. According to a summary of studies, around one in seven teens has sent a sext. Nearly one in three has received sexts, and one in eight teens has forwarded someone's sexts to others.[32] This means that most teens don't ask for or send sexually explicit photos or messages. But some do—and if there is one issue that stokes parental fears about the long-term consequences of online expression, sexting is it. Sexting also forces us to grapple with our kids' emerging sexuality and the possible fallout if explicit images were to circulate widely. It's no surprise, then, that our dominant messaging to teens tends to emphasize worst-case scenarios. Common parental warnings include things like "One photo and you might go to jail" and "Never sext. It will ruin your reputation and create a serious legal nightmare." It's not that these warnings are wrong. The problem is that they don't seem to dissuade young people from exploring their sexuality through messages and photos.

It's hard for most parents to imagine that sexting can end in anything but disaster. But we need to consider the experiences of most teens. Most of the time, young people exchange nudes within consenting relationships.[33] When nudes are shared without pressure or coercion and stay with the intended recipient, they tend to result in . . . not much. Teens also report a variety of neutral or positive experiences associated with consensual sexting.[34] They certainly don't often see their friends getting hauled off to jail.

That said, the data show that sharing nudes is not a safe and low-risk alternative to having sex offline. A review of twenty-three studies found that adolescent sexting is associated with sexual activity and increased risk of psychological distress.[35] (This doesn't mean, however, that all teens who are sexting are having sex and all teens who are having sex are sexting.[36]) Also, young people experience sexting in a variety of ways. Pressured sexting or sexting shared beyond the intended recipient is associated with significant negative impacts on mental health.[37]

Teens need help navigating complex situations ranging from nudes shared among classmates to fake AI nudes and deepfake porn to worst-case scenarios like sextortion. Sextortion is a form of online blackmail in which someone threatens to share a nude photo or video of you unless you pay money or deliver additional sexual content or activities. Sexting carries serious risks, and every teenager should be aware of them. Yet focusing *solely* on dire warnings and worst-case legal scenarios can be counterproductive. Shame,

INSIDE INSIGHTS

Remember, the adolescent brain is especially sensitive to near-term rewards. Sharing nudes can deliver pleasure, social approval, or even relief by preventing conflict. And skills like communicating desires and needs, resisting pressure, and managing impulses are works in progress during adolescence. These skills, seated in the prefrontal cortex, can be especially difficult to access in high-stakes and emotionally activating situations. It's tempting for parents to focus on long-term consequences when talking to teens about sexting. But if we take the near-term rewards seriously, we can help young people navigate the dilemmas that inevitably arise when exploring sexuality online and offline.

secrecy, and fear of legal trouble do little to cultivate the honest and open conversations that protect against the worst outcomes.

Parental advice is more likely to be listened to and followed if we ground it in the realities of our kids' experiences. In their book *Behind Their Screens,* Emily Weinstein and Carrie James outline the myriad ways that sending nudes can play out among adolescents.[38] Sexting can be wanted and consensual or unwanted, pressured, or coerced. Sexts can stay with the intended recipient or be shared without permission. Some sexts contain identifying features and others do not. Sexting can be pleasurable and exciting or mortifying and unsafe. Sexting can be a demonstration of trust, a noncommittal form of flirting, or a way to show off. Weinstein and James also note the various roles teens play in these interactions. Telling a teen that "one photo will land you in legal trouble" focuses only on the creator of nudes while ignoring the other teens who may be involved in other ways:

- asking for nudes

- receiving unsolicited nudes

- threatening the creator of nudes

- pressuring others to send nudes

- sharing nudes with others

Kids' identities shape how they navigate this tricky terrain. Some queer youth, for example, might engage in sexting as a more private space to celebrate their sexuality and engage with potential partners. That said, one study showed that sexual minority youth are more likely to experience abusive sexting behaviors (but not to perpetrate them).[39] When it comes to sexting between cisgender boys and girls, research backs up what teens have been saying to anyone who will listen: A significant double standard is at play in all things sex-related. Author Devorah Heitner makes the stark observation that "girls usually pay a much higher social price when things go wrong."[40] One study found that girls report feeling more pressured to sext and experience more negative feelings related to sexting than boys do.[41] Even when girls try to opt out altogether, they don't always escape judgment. One early study noted that "girls were commonly judged harshly whether they sexted (e.g., 'slut') or not (e.g., 'prude'), whereas boys were virtually immune from criticism regardless."[42] Sexting is clearly a social minefield for most girls. But this double standard hurts everyone. Boys can experience social pressure to flex or celebrate even when they're feeling self-conscious, hurt, or overwhelmed.

There's reason for concern in any situation that combines emerging adolescent sexuality, developing impulse control, and digital environments that are public, searchable, and scalable. But just saying that "sexting will ruin your life" is insufficient guidance. In my entire career, I have been asked to do parent workshops on sexting and adolescent sexuality only a handful of times. Those events were all organized quickly in the wake of high-profile incidents among students. I don't blame schools or communities for starting conversations during high-emotion and high-intensity periods. But I think this pattern reflects how common the disaster-prevention approach is. I default to this approach too. Despite knowing how important sex-related conversations are to healthy development, I still have to remind myself to be brave and talk about these issues in "typical" workshops on adolescence. It's telling that when I do so, parents always seek me out afterward to talk. Just like kids, parents tend to be uncertain about how to start sex-related conversations without shame, fear, or embarrassment—and we are relieved when someone opens an affirming door. So let's do our best to start talking—before, during, and after critical incidents. As Fred Rogers says, "Anything that's human is mentionable, and anything that is mentionable can be more manageable."[43]

REFLECT TALKING ABOUT SEXTING AND NUDES

Talking to your teen about sexting and nudes isn't easy, but it is important. For each statement, think about which response best represents where you currently stand: "I hadn't thought of this," "I try," or "I got this." Then ask yourself: What are you most proud of? What do you want to work on? Write down the latter, share it with a friend, and give it a try. Feel awkward? Keep going.

- I ask my teen if they have ever asked for, received, or seen a nude. Is it common at their school? Do they think it is a big deal? Why or why not?
- I listen to my teen's thoughts and opinions on sexting.
- I share my values and expectations not just about creating sexts but also around forwarding and sharing sexts, receiving sexts, using AI to generate nudes, and asking or pressuring others.

- I talk about potential consequences without relying solely on catastrophic warnings.

- I talk to my teen about what sextortion is and assure them that if it happens to them, it isn't their fault.

- I know that both/and messages are okay. For example, "I expect that you prioritize your safety by not engaging in sexting. And let's talk about strategies for navigating sexting dynamics. If you find yourself in a tough spot, I am here for you."

- I tell my teen that there are things they can do to remove content from the internet if a sexually explicit photo has been shared.

- I talk about strategies for resisting pressure to send a sext or share a nude. For example, remind your teen that you are happy to be an excuse for them: "I can't do that. My parent(s) would kill me if they found out! And they always find out!"

- I don't let double standards, such as slut shaming or messages like "boys will be boys," slide.

- I nest conversations about sexting within conversations about relationship skills such as sexual decision-making, consent, self-worth, pleasure, and communication.

- My teen knows that they have at least one caring and trustworthy adult they can go to if they need to talk.

Keep Asking, Talking, and Listening

"Just guess!" I used to say to my bedroom wall, turned away from my mom, who was usually perched on the side of my bed.

"Honey," she often responded, "it's hard to just guess what you want to talk about."

I usually met her gentle resistance to this request with more crying and an insistence that she should just *know* what was on my mind or weighing on my heart. As a teenager, I hoped my "just guess" strategy would save me from having to start an embarrassing or difficult conversation. I hoped that my mom could find the words that were stuck in my throat. I see now that this strategy also positioned my mom in an emotional minefield. My response to a wrong guess was "I can't believe you think I want to talk about that!!" Sobbing ensued. My response to the right guess was similar: "Never mind, I don't want to talk about it!" More sobbing ensued.

Now that I am a parent, I am better able to put myself in my mom's shoes. I imagine that on one hand, she was grateful that I wanted to talk at all after stretches of silence. On the other hand, she was likely exasperated by the impossible position I put her in.

It's common for teens to turn their backs when they're desperate for conversation. I suggest that as parents, we all take a note from my mom's book and consistently find a perch at our kids' sides to assure them that we are willing to guess, apologize when we are wrong, and try again. We are willing to initiate awkward and cringey conversations about sex, bodies, relationships, and technology. We are willing to say, "I feel a little awkward about this too . . . but I love who you are and who you are becoming. It is my job to give you the information you need to make safe and healthy choices." Research says that whether adolescents are under a blanket, rolling their eyes, engaging in conversation, laughing at us, or turning their backs, they do hope we keep talking, asking, and listening. And when we do, they are far more likely to do the same.

■ ■ ■

PART 3

"Where Do I Belong?"

CHAPTER 8

Belonging with Friends

*"There is no house
like the house of belonging."*
—DAVID WHYTE, "THE HOUSE OF BELONGING"

"**M**y kid says that he doesn't mind school, but he never seems particularly excited to go," a parent shared with me. "I am worried he is lonelier this fall than he was online all last year." We were chatting at a back-to-school event after returning from more than a year of online school during the early COVID-19 pandemic.

"What do you think is going on?" I asked.

"Honestly, I don't know. He just has trouble fitting in sometimes. He has some pretty niche interests." She laughed lovingly and went on, "He has a few good friends he games with online but doesn't have a crew yet at school. I figured it would be easy now that we are back in person. Maybe it will just take time," she concluded hopefully.

"Everyone is still so wobbly. It's helpful you have your eye on it. I bet he will find his way," I responded.

I ran into this same parent later in the year and asked how things were going. She had good news to report: "Social stuff is still tricky for him. But things have settled down a bit, and he seems to have found a couple of his people through theater. They really get him. Plus, he still keeps up with his gaming friends. It makes all the difference."

It makes sense that this parent was concerned as she watched her son struggle to find his people at school. A sense of connectedness at school has been linked to better stress management, higher levels of motivation and achievement, and greater feelings of optimism.[1] Disconnectedness can be wrenching. Exclusion activates the same neural networks in the human brain as physical pain does.[2] Loneliness puts us at higher risk of mental illness, poor physical health, and feelings of hopelessness. The high costs of loneliness recently prompted the US Surgeon General to release an advisory outlining evidence of an "epidemic of loneliness" in the United States.[3] This is an issue that affects everyone. However, the negative effects of loneliness, social evaluation, and rejection are especially potent during adolescence.[4]

Changing Brains, Changing Social Sensitivity

"I'm ready for school!" my seven-year-old announced. I glanced over and marveled at how different his standards of preparedness were from his older sibling's. His long curls had become one massive snarl sticking out from the back of his head, he had a Band-Aid across his forehead, and his shirt was on backward.

"How about you give your hair a brush and check that your clothes are how you want them before you head out?" I prompted.

He went to find a brush but first informed me, "No one cares what my hair looks like, and I don't care what my shirt looks like." Fair enough.

Plenty of elementary-age kids have opinions about how they look. My kid's forehead Band-Aid was clearly a fashion-driven choice, because he hadn't sustained any recent flesh wounds. The hair and his shirt, not so much. Younger children tend to be unself-conscious around peers.

Most teens are far more sensitive to social evaluation than younger children are. This is partly because kids' external and internal social landscapes shift when they hit adolescence. Playdates scheduled by families become plans coordinated among friends. As their brains develop, teens are better able to consider and understand the perspectives of others. This change can strengthen empathy and social reasoning and accelerate self-consciousness. Psychologists call this developmental shift "imaginary audience ideation."[5] Adolescents are more likely than younger children to believe that the world is watching them, even when no one is around. This feeling is especially strong if they think they are being evaluated,[6] and it can make family communication more challenging. But this sensitivity serves an important function with friends. It helps adolescents prioritize the social awareness and skills that they will ultimately need to navigate adult friendships and relationships.

It makes sense that teens tune in to social feedback at the same time that they start forging beyond their families to find their people. If you were suddenly transported to a new community in a faraway place with a culture and traditions different from your own, what would you do? You would likely take your cues from the people around you. That is essentially what adolescents are doing. They are leaving childhood and entering puberty. They have to discover how they fit into this unfamiliar terrain. They don't know exactly how to act, so they look to their peers in this new territory.

Phones and Friendships

Kids don't need to be at the center of a vast social network to experience the benefits of belonging. While some studies indicate that having more friends helps young people cope with stress, the quality of friendships matters more than the quantity.[7] So are phones and technology improving relational quality and bringing young people closer? Or are teens, in the words of Sherry Turkle, "alone together?"[8] As usual, it depends.

Parents frequently lament that their kids would rather be on their phones than with each other. Research does indicate that technoference erodes the quality of adolescent friendships. A study of young adults showed lower relationship quality and increased loneliness when young people perceived themselves as distracted by their phones or when they perceived their friends' phone use as dismissive.[9] So, when teens are sitting side by side hunched over their phones, technoference might indeed be at play.

Yet the presence of phones doesn't inevitably lead to disconnection. The levels of "digital social multitasking" (multitasking on digital devices during social interactions) alone were not directly associated with lower relationship quality or loneliness.[10] As mentioned above, the association hinges on the *negative perception* of phone use. Dr. Chia-chen Yang, a researcher who has dedicated her career to the psychosocial development of young people in the digital age, invites us to consider scenarios like these:[11]

- **Scenario 1:** Two friends are hanging out. One is sharing a vulnerable experience about their day. The other is only half-listening, responding to unrelated texts from friends.

- **Scenario 2:** Two friends are hanging out. One is sharing a vulnerable experience about their day and asks for support. The other pulls out their phone to look for a helpful resource or a meme that might cheer up their friend.

Even without much detail, it's clear that the first scenario wouldn't feel very good for either friend. The second scenario, on the other hand, could strengthen both friends' feelings of engagement and connection.

Let's consider another common pair of scenarios:

- **Scenario 1:** Two friends are hanging out. Both have their phones out. They are enjoying showing each other videos that they both think are hilarious.

- **Scenario 2:** Two friends are hanging out. Both initially have their phones out and are enjoying showing each other entertaining videos. One friend tires of this and wants to talk about other things. They put their phone away and try to shift the dynamic. The phone-focused friend doesn't notice and continues to watch and share videos.

The difference in these two scenarios isn't just the presence or absence of phones, it's also about whether the friends are tuning into each other's needs. That said, phones are strategically designed to grab and hold our attention, making social interference more likely. Even when teens are on the same page, digital social multitasking can lead to increased "digital stress" (which is, in turn, associated with greater depressive symptoms) as teens try to balance face-to-face interactions with a constant stream of notifications, feelings of FOMO (fear of missing out), and pressure to be "always available" for friends online.[12] Remember, we human beings aren't great multitaskers.

Research shows that younger adolescents are more likely to perceive their levels of digital distraction as negative.[13] Skills like impulse control and other goal-directed behaviors are under construction in early adolescence, making it harder for kids to resist the allure of their phones. Remember, devices are distracting by design. Dr. Yang argues that relationship skills like self-awareness and communication are key to helping teens get on the same page about digital social multitasking.[14] Having plenty of device-free spaces for young people to hang out can help with this. Learning to read emotions and respond to them is hard work, and it requires face-to-face time. Adolescents are learning to navigate the tricky contours of relational communication. If they don't practice, they won't do it as well. The brain gets good at whatever it does a lot.

That said, lecturing teens that phones always ruin relationships or that hanging out with phones isn't real connection oversimplifies their digital lives. Instead, the next time you see your teen with friends and phones are part of the mix, try observing with these questions in mind: Do they seem in sync with each other? Are they engaged and tuned in, or are they more distracted and disconnected?

◀ REFLECT DIGITAL SOCIAL MULTITASKING

Kids need practice gaining awareness of how they and the people they interact with are using and communicating about technology during in-person social interactions. The first step in helping your kid gain these skills is to become aware of your own use. Here are some questions to help you do that. Think about them during an upcoming social interaction or take time now to think back to a recent social interaction.

Self-awareness:

- Why am I using my device right now?
- How is this use affecting my relationships?
- How and when does it benefit my relationships?
- How and when does it get in the way?

Communication:

- What does my family want and expect?
- What does this group of friends want and expect?

- What do I want and expect?
- How do we tell each other what we want and expect?
- What do we say when we aren't on the same page?

Awareness of tech design:

- If we could design devices to help strengthen and grow relationships, what features would they have? How would they be different from the features on this device?
- How distracted am I by this app or device? Why?
- Do I feel in control of when I use this device around my friends? If not, what strategies can I use to set myself up for success?

Reflecting on your own tech use grows your awareness and helps you model healthy habits. It also equips you to set boundaries and start important conversations with your teen that lay the groundwork for building essential relationship skills. For example, after driving your kid and their friends home, you might have a conversation like this:

Parent: "I noticed on the way home that your friends were on their phones for most of the drive. How did that feel to you?"

Teenager: "I don't know. Annoying."

Parent: "Say more."

Teenager: "I said I don't know, it's just annoying."

Parent: "Yeah, that makes sense. You kind of weren't talking to each other. Maybe they aren't aware of how it makes you feel. Or maybe they aren't sure what else to do. Have you ever thought about mentioning it to them?"

Teenager: "Why don't *you* tell them they can't be on their phones?"

Parent: "That's one idea. I'm curious, though: what would it feel like if you talked to them about how it feels?"

Teenager: "What would I say?"

Parent: "Maybe something like, 'When you are on your phone, it makes me feel like you don't care about me.'"

Teenager: "I would never ever say that."

Parent: "Got it. What would you say?"

Teenager: "I don't know. That it's annoying that they're on their phones."

Parent: "Yeah. You know, you can ask them to put away their phones. Do you think you could ask them that?"

Teenager: "I could just ask them to do something else."

Parent: "Want to try talking to them on the way home tomorrow?"

Teenager: "Maybe. Yeah."

Belonging Versus Fitting In

Hanging out with peers, with or without devices, doesn't guarantee that kids feel connected to those peers. Loneliness cannot be measured objectively by quantifying group participation or social interactions. Loneliness is a subjective internal state.[15] You can feel lonely when you are surrounded by people. You can also feel connected when you are far away from the people you love.

As parents, we want our kids to feel connected, not lonely. So it's easy to worry about whether our kids fit in at school, in their teams or casts or choirs, or in their clubs or activities. We may think that fitting in will make our kids' lives easier. But we might want to ask ourselves whether fitting in is a healthy goal. As researcher Brené Brown explains, "Fitting in is about assessing a situation and becoming who you need to be in order to be accepted. Belonging, on the other hand, doesn't require us to *change* who we are; it requires us to *be* who we are."[16] Belonging means sharing a connection with others while staying true to oneself. Fitting in can get in the way of belonging if it requires kids to change important parts of themselves to be accepted.

Adolescents often work hard to fit in by hiding, downplaying, or altering important parts of themselves. This can take a toll on their mental health and well-being. For example, neurodivergent kids who mask more often, or who suppress or hide neurodivergent traits to appear neurotypical, report higher levels of anxiety.[17]

Given the loneliness and strain caused by trying to fit in that many adolescents feel, some kids turn to the internet to find belonging. Online groups—from Scratch communities to anime clubs to #blackgirlmagic threads to queer subreddits—are spaces where some kids can show up more fully as themselves. And some kids may turn to AI. In a recent report on youth perspectives on AI, one young person shared, "We use AI because we are lonely and also because real people are mean and judging sometimes and AI isn't."[18]

We should take very seriously the possibilities and risks associated with seeking comfort in chatbots. Friendships with humans are training grounds for a host of important social skills, including navigating conflict and tension— and chatbots are an emotionally frictionless substitute at best. We should be wary of settling for a world in which some kids need to go online or talk to an AI companion to experience belonging and to be who they are. But rather than second-guessing the value of all online communities, let's do everything we can to cultivate belonging at home and in our schools.

IN ACTION: BELONGING VERSUS FITTING IN

Talk to your kid about the difference between belonging and fitting in. Explain how fitting in can get in the way of belonging. Ask, "When do you feel pressure to fit in? What do you do to fit in? What is the purpose of these strategies? What is the cost to you?"

Notice your reactions. Maybe you were raised to fit in, or maybe you faced significant challenges because you didn't fit in. If that's the case, you might find it stressful to watch your kid show up with their peers in ways that don't fit your perception of fitting in as the norm. Try saying, "When I was a kid, I was taught that I needed to fit in (to stay safe, to make friends, or whatever your reason was). I want to teach you a different way. Let's practice together."

Acknowledge that building or seeking belonging can be risky. Don't ignore the ways that online socializing meets your teen's need for belonging. At the same time, work to connect your teen to offline spaces where they can experience similar ease. If parts of your kid's identities, abilities, or experiences aren't centered or supported at school or in activities, acknowledge how painful this can be. Remind your kid that they deserve to experience belonging.

Flush out toxins to belonging. Many young people don't show up as their full selves because it isn't safe to do so. Asking teens to show up as they are without creating the conditions for belonging isn't fair. Find out where you can show up and take action related to antiracism and antibias work in your teen's school or community. For example, perhaps you advocate to add accessibility features to the community playground or write an email to the school board in support of culturally responsive curriculum. This is lifelong work that never truly ends, but it's our job to strive toward a world where every teenager can experience belonging.

The Dark Side of Belonging Online

I received an email from a parent immediately after a racially motivated mass shooting. Investigations showed that the shooter had spent a lot of time communicating with far-right extremist groups on Discord, a popular voice, video, and texting app. The parent wrote, "My son is on Discord. Should I be concerned?"

In the wake of mass violence, we often search for answers and prevention within our circles of influence. But the frustrating reality is: there are no simple answers. There is no single experience, site, app, or reason that leads a teenager toward extremist beliefs. Even the most popular mainstream apps can be exploited by extremists. This means that casual exposure to hateful content is common for young people online. Most teens encounter hate content and do not go on to adopt extremist beliefs. But extremist groups do often use a powerful force to draw in young people: the promise of belonging.

Extremist groups know how to exploit feelings of pain and insecurity. They are good at convincing adolescents that they can find solutions to their problems in extremism.[19] According to the Southern Poverty Law Center, the following factors make teens more vulnerable to online predation:

- **Loneliness and isolation:** Extremists often prey upon young people's desire for belonging and friendship by promising a connection to people who "understand" them.

- **Feelings of anger or betrayal:** Young people who are angry and resentful about perceived unfair treatment or social exclusion are more vulnerable to the us-versus-them extremist framework.

- **Stress, trauma, or mental health issues:** The vast majority of people suffering from mental health issues will not be drawn down an extremist path. But some may be more vulnerable to the simple black-and-white "solutions" that extremists offer to resolve their psychological pain.[20]

News headlines sometimes portray violent extremists as lone wolves, but they are often deeply embedded in online communities. Fortunately, parents can help counteract these communities' messages. Let your kids know that they might encounter extremist messages or hate content on any platform or in any medium. According to Common Sense Media, extremist groups have targeted adolescents (especially young White men) through "coordinated meme campaigns, invitations to chat rooms, and through influencers who gradually introduce extremist content."[21] Extremist messages aren't defined by challenging a system or even advocating for radical change from the status quo. Instead, they are rooted in a belief that violence or domination is the only answer to identity-based conflicts.[22] Don't look the other way if:

- Your kid's views seem to be getting more and more extreme.

- Your kid expresses hatred toward specific groups of people.

- Your kid grows secretive and combative about what they are doing online.

Many adolescents resist the idea that they could be lured in by extremists online. That's why starting conversations about online belonging and exclusion early and often is so important. You can also ask your kid questions about their favorite online spaces and groups:

- "What do people say in this space about others who don't share your identity?"

- "Are people in this space accepting of other people's views and identities?"

- "Who do you think feels like they belong here? Why?"

- "Who might not feel welcome here? Why?"

Online Bullying, Social Conflict, and Drama

The most common source of hurtful online interactions isn't extremist groups or strangers. It is peers.[23] While cruelty and bullying have long been unfortunate elements of adolescence, the internet can transform and magnify these social dynamics in painful ways. Dylan Marron, host of the award-winning podcast *Conversations with People Who Hate Me*, says, "When you combine the instinctive desire for internet points with a person who becomes a target on which we can score those points, the results can be disastrous."[24]

Bullying and online cruelty have gotten a lot of attention—for good reasons. A slew of research shows that bullying in any form has negative effects on young people's emotional health, learning, and relationships—for both the target and the perpetrator.[25] Cyberbullying is not a rite of passage or an inevitable part of growing up. Youth cyberbullying victims are more than twice as likely as their peers to engage in self-harm (although this is rare compared to the emotional and mental health consequences of cyberbullying).[26] One pair of researchers found that young people who experience both offline bullying *and* cyberbullying are more than eleven times as likely to have attempted suicide compared to those who have not been bullied.[27] If your teen exhibits any warning signs of suicidality, such as talking about being a burden to others, feeling hopeless or trapped, withdrawing from friends, eating or sleeping more or less, increasing alcohol or drug use, or talking about dying by suicide, remember that talking directly about suicide is an important part of prevention. When in doubt, call 988, the National Suicide and Crisis Lifeline, for support.

The worst outcomes are not inevitable. The vast majority of young people who are cyberbullied do not die by suicide.[28] News coverage of bullying is skewed toward the most alarming cases. These cases deserve attention because the stakes are so high—and for any family who has lost a loved one to suicide where cyberbullying was a contributing factor, no quantification of risk ameliorates their pain. However, research does not support drawing an *inevitable* path from cyberbullying to mental health crises and suicide-related behaviors, and it isn't helpful messaging for parents or teens either.

Cyberbullying alone is unlikely to directly lead a young person to suicide. But it can certainly exacerbate existing struggles in harmful ways. When online cruelty is added to a young person's struggles with depression or other mental health disorders, major life stressors, or other forms of trauma, the toll can feel unbearable to some teens.

How common is cyberbullying? Estimates vary depending on how it is defined and measured. Defining cyberbullying as the use of technology to support calculated, repetitive abuse aimed at a less powerful target, Sameer Hinduja and Justin W. Patchin at the Cyberbullying Research Center found that about 30 percent of students they surveyed between 2007 and 2023 had been cyberbullied.[29] Comparatively more Asian American young people said they experienced cyberbullying since the COVID-19 pandemic began.[30] Queer and trans youth have been disproportionately targeted for decades.[31] Research also shows that while the following actions don't meet the formal criteria for cyberbullying, things like name-calling, rumor spreading, public shaming, and other forms of cruelty online affect many more teens.[32]

Parents don't always know when their kid is involved in cyberbullying, as either the target or the perpetrator. The most obvious sign is an abrupt change in digital activities or device use. In their third edition of *Bullying Beyond the Schoolyard,* Hinduja and Patchin note a few warning signs that a young person might be the target of cyberbullying:[33]

- They unexpectedly stop using their device.

- They appear nervous or startle easily when using their device.

- They appear uneasy about going to school or to social gatherings.

- They show signs of anger or worry after using their device.

- They want to spend more time with parents than with peers.

- They experience persistent change in mood, appetite, or sleep patterns. (See chapter 3 for more information on signs of distress.)

Many of us parents are already on the lookout for signs that our teens are targets of online bullying. It's harder to wrap our minds around the possibility that our kids might be the perpetrators. Stereotypes might be getting in the way. According to Dr. Elizabeth Englander, the founder of the Massachusetts Aggression Reduction Center (MARC) at Bridgewater State University, the stereotype of a scrawny kid getting picked on physically by a bigger kid with "emotional problems" is long outdated. Most bullying today is psychological, and it tends to target young people who are perceived as socially vulnerable. Bravely acknowledging that our kids might be perpetrators makes it more likely that we will recognize red flags in our kids *and* that everyone involved will get the support and interventions they need. Following are a few signs that a young person might be engaged in cyberbullying:

- They quickly switch or close out of games and apps when an adult is nearby.

- They use their device at all hours of the night.

- They get unusually upset when they can't use their device.

- They seem to have multiple accounts.

- They experience increasing behavioral challenges at school or after school.

- They appear highly concerned about social status, social power, and popularity.

- They behave cruelly or callously toward peers.

- They avoid conversations with adults about online activities.

Keeping these signs and symptoms in the back of our minds is helpful. What isn't helpful is constantly trying to assess our kids' every move based on formal definitions or a rigid checklist. Addressing cruel or callous behavior and teaching relationship skills early and often are more effective approaches than memorizing specific red flags.

Same Cruelty, New Challenges

"I experienced all kinds of cruelty when I was in high school," a social worker named Ana shared during a professional development session on cyberbullying. She placed her hands over her heart and stomach at the same time, as if acknowledging old wounds. We had been asked by the presenter to talk in small groups about trends we were observing with clients or in our communities. She briefly shared personal context, noting that the transition from the South American nation of Colombia to a largely White Midwestern community in North America during adolescence had been socially difficult. She went on, "But what I experienced as a young person was nothing compared to the suffering of some of my clients."

"What do you mean?" another participant asked.

"For starters, when I had difficulties at school, at least I could go home and be in a loving and affirming space. I could get *away* from it. My adolescent clients have nowhere to go—because they experience it at school and then at home through their devices. It takes an enormous toll. There is no time or space for refuge or repair."

Ana's observations are a powerful reminder that technology doesn't just mirror offline cruelty, it can magnify and transform its impact. Digital design has transformed the social landscape in challenging ways.[34] Today's kids must navigate relationships within digital environments defined by the following:

- **Absence of physical cues:** Most digital platforms allow for fewer social cues like tone of voice, facial expression, and volume. The absence of reliable cues can quickly confuse social interactions and escalate drama. At worst, online environments are fertile ground for "online toxic disinhibition."[35] In other words, teens might say something cruel online that they would never say face-to-face. That said, online cruelty is usually not anonymous. Most teens say they know the identities of their cyberbullies.[36]

- **Constant connection:** Pre-internet, you could find refuge from cruelty, drama, and bullying when you had space and time away from the source of the conflict. Today, online cruelty and drama can follow teens wherever they go.

- **Scalability:** With a single tap, a kid can send a nasty message, share a rumor, or expose information about someone to an entire school. In one study, most teens reported that it would take fifteen minutes or less for a digital rumor to get around a school to one hundred kids.[37]

- **Public harassment:** Online cruelty often plays out in front of a large audience, making the sting of rejection or harassment that much more potent. Even initially private messages and photos are easily screenshotted and shared. Peers can amplify the pain if they pile on, share, or post additional cruel comments.

These digital design features can make the pain of exclusion, cruelty, and aggression more intense for many teens. Emerging AI features such as deepfake videos, "nudify" or "undressing" apps, catfishing (setting up fake profiles on social media), doxxing (publishing private information), and troll bots may amplify the pain even further. Online cruelty is usually deeply entangled with offline behaviors.[38] Conflict playing out online is likely showing up in school buildings as well. Getting rid of certain apps or taking digital breaks may reduce fuel for the fire, but it is unlikely to extinguish the flame altogether. Plus, confiscating devices entirely can increase loneliness just when teens need extra support. I talked with Dr. Englander about these dynamics. She noted that instead of taking phones away as a punishment or a "solution" to online cruelty, parents should teach kids to use digital breaks as a strategy for getting relief, managing distress, and lowering the temperature of online conflicts.[39]

By the time young people hit adolescence, they don't usually use the terms *cyberbullying* and *bullying*. They are more likely to refer to even very toxic dynamics as "drama." Follow-up questions can help adults discern whether this "drama" is part of an abusive pattern causing distress and harm or is part of a typical two-way social conflict. This is an important distinction. If we approach every disagreement or painful social slight as bullying, we may rob our teens of opportunities to practice skills like self-advocacy and conflict resolution. One study found that 62 percent of the teens who believed that they were bullied were actually using the word to describe different problems, such as fights with friends.[40] Kids rely on parents to be strong and steady through emotional storms. Overresponding to typical social conflicts can inadvertently send the signal that even typical conflict is an emergency. Social conflict is a normal part of adolescence. Bullying, online or offline, is not.

Try to distinguish between situations that call for hands-on support and those that call for lighter social problem-solving. There's no perfect roadmap here, but Dr. Englander has found that certain dynamics are likely to have a much bigger negative emotional impact. Ask yourself:

- Is this part of a pattern of cruelty, aggression, or exclusion?

- Did this happen in front of a wide and unsympathetic online audience?

- Is the cruelty being inflicted by someone that my kid thought they could trust, such as a friend, as opposed to a more distant and less emotionally significant peer?

- Is my child living with mental health challenges or dealing with other major stressors that might make handling online cruelty more challenging?

Responding in helpful ways requires slowing down, asking questions, and listening. Dr. Englander told me that she understands the impulse to rush in and heroically defend one's kid. But, based on her decades of experience in the field, she notes that this impulse isn't particularly helpful. Instead, here's her advice for parents:

> Keep your cool and ask your child what's going on. Gather information. It can be really hard to tell what is actually going on in these situations. If it is really serious, then your child is going to be reassured that you are in control. You are saying to them: "We're going to talk about this. We're going to figure out what's going on. We are going to work together to come up with a solution." And if it turns out that it's not a big deal, then your kid feels like, "Okay, I can talk to them without them flying off the handle every time."[41]

Keeping a cool head is easier said than done. The impulse to protect and defend our kids is strong. But the reality is that we don't always understand the full picture or have the best solution in mind. What we can offer is support at home and practice thinking through problems. We can also advocate for our kids, remove them from harmful situations, and reach out to schools as good-faith partners. These steps or any others are likely to be much more helpful after deliberation and thoughtful teamwork with our own kids.

REFLECT CYBERBULLYING AND ONLINE CRUELTY

Helping your teen navigate online conflict and cruelty is not easy. Use the statements below to reflect on how you currently approach these issues. For each statement, think about which response best represents where you currently stand: "I hadn't thought of this," "I try," or "I got this." Then ask yourself: What are you most proud of? What do you want to work on?

- My teen can name one trusted adult that they could go to if they experience or witness cruelty online.
- If my teen is being cyberbullied, I reassure them that it isn't their fault and encourage them to save all evidence.

- I know what my child's school policies are related to bullying and cyberbullying and can explain them to my teen so they know what to expect.
- I understand that my teen might be the one trying out cruelty, aggression, or bullying online.
- I know that just saying "shut your phone off" doesn't solve all online conflict or cyberbullying.
- I know that digital breaks can help young people cope with distress and lower the temperature of online conflicts.
- I understand that online conflict isn't entirely avoidable, and I avoid blaming my teen for getting into drama online.
- I acknowledge that most social slights online are distressing and painful, even if they don't rise to the level of cyberbullying.
- I have made my expectations for online kindness and respect clear *and* I remind my teen that I am here for them when they make mistakes.
- I understand that listening, empathizing, and problem-solving first can be more helpful than rushing to intervene.

Peer Influence and the Power of Bystanders

"I just assumed that my kid would stand up and do the right thing," a parent named Clara shared with me. She described how a group text had devolved into a toxic barrage of messages led by a popular girl and aimed at one of her daughter's friends. "When we asked Ava about it, she didn't have much to say at first, which felt even worse. It's surprising to me, because she has always seemed to have such a good compass about right and wrong when we talk about these things. Ugh. Clearly, we missed something."

"That is so hard," I responded. "Ideally someone would have spoken up to shift the dynamic. But I know these social situations are tough for kids to navigate. It takes some practice."

Clara went on to say that Ava eventually admitted to feeling awful about the whole thing. As Clara talked, I recalled Liam's experience, which I described in chapter 1. Liam had sat in silence as someone took and shared a video of a crying classmate. Like Ava, Liam had been a bystander to an act of cruelty. Also like Ava, he felt awful about it. It took time, reflection, and practice for him to make it right, and the same would be true for Ava.

Saying in the comfort and safety of your home that you would stand up for a friend is quite different from actually doing that in the stormy waters of peer relationships, when there is no script and the outcome is uncertain. The power of peer approval and influence is strong. Fear of peer rejection means that most teens are unlikely to go against the social grain. Public health campaigns often leverage this reality. For example, young people who learn that *most teens* don't engage in bullying are less likely to do so than teens who think bullying is common are.[42] When a group text gets toxic, a group norm of kindness might make it easier to stand up for a friend. Unfortunately, many online interactions don't have clear social norms, and popular peers can easily sway things in the wrong direction.[43]

Peer approval can fuel decisions teens might not make in other contexts. For example, young drivers are more likely to get into an accident when peers are in the car. The conventional thinking is that passengers in the car distract the driver or pressure them to drive recklessly. But it turns out that teens drive more recklessly even if their friends do nothing at all. Simply the presence of peers during a driving game can activate young people's reward systems and lead to riskier decisions.[45] On the positive side, peers can provide emotional fuel for social risk-taking on behalf of someone else.[46] Negative risk-taking behaviors and positive prosocial behaviors rely on overlapping neural circuitry.[47] The rewarding feeling of doing what is right feels better in the presence of approving friends.

The research is clear on one thing: Peers can transform the experience of peer cruelty.[48] Dramatic public service announcements often show bystanders disrupting cruelty by powerfully calling out the perpetrator in front of a large audience. That type of action might seem out of reach for young people like Liam or Ava, who are just getting their feet under them. And according to Dr. Englander, such examples aren't realistic or even helpful. She told me, "Adults' favorite fantasy is that kids are going to stand up in the face of a bully and confront them. What we find is that this is not a particularly effective method. It's something that is more often going to make the situation worse for the target or have no effect." What can young people do instead? Dr. Englander was clear: "Help the target. Look around for someone who needs help and help them."[49]

Rejection and loneliness tend to be the most painful parts of online cruelty. That's why showing up for the target is such a powerful and protective act. As codirectors of the Cyberbullying Research Center note, "The moment when somebody's being harassed, teased, threatened or humiliated is probably the moment when [they] feel most alone. That person needs a reminder that others really do care."[50]

There are other ways that kids can disrupt cruelty, deescalate drama, and contribute to a culture of belonging. Publicly calling out a peer might be off the table for some teens, but they can take some kind of action. It's helpful to review a variety of practical strategies, such as these:

- empathizing with the target

- responding directly to the bullying behavior

- refusing to react positively to cruelty

- refusing to share cruel or inappropriate content

- talking to a trusted adult

- anonymously reporting the incident

Digital citizenship advice like "Be kind online!" or "Just put down your phone!" is no match for the complicated social dynamics kids are navigating. As a young person interviewed in the book *Behind Their Screens* says, "You can't just always 'shut your phone off' and be done with it." Digital conflicts spill over into "the real world."[51] Our teens deserve more. We can ask thoughtful questions like "What are some ways you might support someone who has been hurt?" or "What might you do if someone shares a hurtful rumor with you? What are all the ways you might respond?" Generating specific strategies together goes a lot further than giving one-size-fits-all advice. Our kids need us to acknowledge that there aren't always simple answers. They also need to know that they don't have to navigate these dynamics alone.

Navigating conflict online is complicated. Young people need practice workshopping possible scenarios, perspectives, and actions. Keep the following framework in mind as you talk to your teen.

1. **Identify an expectation you have around online social behaviors.** For example: "We are positive bystanders, and we do something if we see cruelty, racism, or mean behavior online."

2. **Ground your expectations in real-life scenarios.** Ask:
   - "When might you need to stand up for someone or yourself?"
   - "How might you feel if this happened?"
   - "How might others involved feel?"

3. **Instead of assuming your teen knows what to do, work together to brainstorm specific actions or skills.** For example:
   - Take five deep breaths in the moment. Slow down.
   - Refuse to give cruelty an audience. Don't like, share, or otherwise amplify cruel interactions.
   - Empathize with the target in person or by sending a nice personal message online.

4. **Acknowledge that this is challenging.** "Sometimes it is easier to talk about doing the right thing than actually do it. I'm here for you when you do things you are proud of, when you wish you could get a do-over, and when things fall apart. I don't expect you to always get it right the first time. I just expect us to talk about it and learn from it."

▓ Belonging Matters

"You two look like twins!" a counselor commented.

My friend Gretchen and I were attending a YMCA camp that had swimming, hiking, and horseback riding. We looked at each other, pleased that someone had noticed our matching Indigo Girls t-shirts and soccer shorts. Convinced no one would know, we loved secretly coordinating outfits and then feigning surprise and delight when someone mentioned the similarities. Gretchen and I both grew up with brothers, so we had claimed each other as sisters in kindergarten and never looked back.

"I have just the horses for you two," the counselor went on.

Gretchen and I were even more pleased. While we had no experience with horses, we imagined ourselves cantering through the woods—twin sisters on twin horses. Gretchen and I didn't actually look much alike. And we each had our self-conscious ideas about the differences. From my perspective, Gretchen was tall, tan, and gorgeous. I was . . . the opposite.

Meanwhile, our counselor was leading our horses out of the barn toward us. It was easy to see why she had chosen these animals for us. They were both white and speckled all over with light brown. They were both horses. That was where their similarities ended. The counselor brought the first horse toward Gretchen. It was a stunning specimen: tall, strong, impressive, and sweet. After handing the reins to Gretchen, our counselor turned toward me. "Meet Tweety," she said. Tweety was short, squat, and appeared to be in a terrible mood. Her disposition was confirmed the minute I tried to ride her and she laid down on the trail, refusing to move. Gretchen and her horse were prepared to canter off into the countryside.

Gretchen and I are still close friends. We have kids the same age and live blocks from each other in South Minneapolis. We have been friends for nearly four decades and have been through a lot together. But that experience at camp is among my most vivid preteen memories. It isn't because I love horses. Instead, that memory sticks out because those horses made a powerful internal comparison visible in the most ridiculous way. This unflattering opportunity for public comparison could have been mortifying. My real and imaginary audiences could have been cruel. Instead, this memory is salient precisely because it *wasn't* mortifying. I didn't have a superpower that made me immune to the judgment of imaginary audiences. Rather, it wasn't mortifying because I had Gretchen. We belonged to each other. And that grumpy horse made us laugh so hard we almost peed in our matching soccer shorts. Having each other made all the difference in the world.

During adolescence, our kids move out into the world to find their people. Sometimes the road is smooth. Often it is rocky and painful. Gretchen and I are both parenting middle schoolers now. It is abundantly clear that the presence of social media and phones has changed their social landscape. These digital tools mirror, magnify, and transform dynamics in ways that are hard for anyone who grew up without phones to understand. What hasn't changed is young people's fundamental need to experience belonging with their friends. This isn't something we can measure by the presence or absence of phones. We can't measure it by how many online friends they have, how many interactions they have at school, or whether they seem to fit in. We measure it by whether our kids can form a meaningful connection with those around them while staying true to themselves. This takes time. It takes practice. And kids can't do it on their own.

■ ■ ■

CHAPTER 9

Self-Worth

"If you could be anyone, would you choose to be yourself?"
—NAOMI SHIHAB NYE, *HABIBI*

"It was fun—until it really, really wasn't," eighteen-year-old Anjali shared. She was a guest speaker for a group of eighth graders gathered in a small classroom as part of a mental health advocacy club. Perched on a tall stool in front of the group, Anjali explained that she had posted a dance video of herself on social media, and it caught the attention of a much wider audience than usual. At first, Anjali said, she loved the attention and interaction. "I've been a dancer forever and have taken Indian dance since I was little." She tapped one foot on the lowest bar of her stool.

I sat in the audience with the students, moved by Anjali's willingness to share a personal story. It was clear that the students were moved too. She went on, "Sometimes dancing is the only thing that can get me out of my head. It's a huge part of my connection to my community. But to get such positive feedback from people I didn't even know? I loved it."

"So, what happened?" a student asked bluntly, clearly sensing an impending turn for the worse.

"Well, it turns out that people had *lots* of opinions about my dancing—and not all positive. I tried not to look at the critical comments, but it was hard to ignore them. People commented on my body and my clothing. The comments about my dancing were the hardest to ignore. Although I said I didn't care,

I did. I was consumed by what people thought about me." All the eighth graders nodded knowingly.

"The worst part wasn't the stuff people said, though. The worst part was that it took dancing from me for my whole junior year. I mean, I still danced. But before that, I used to feel like I could be playful and push myself and experiment. I loved that. But that social media experience completely shook my confidence. I wasn't dancing for myself anymore. I was chasing approval from strangers online. I really lost myself."

The group went on to talk about how to take care of themselves in an online world of constant appraisal. While few in the room had firsthand experience with internet fame, they all knew what it felt like to lose themselves to the opinions of others.

The Fragility of Self-Esteem

Self-esteem is a household term today, but the concept dates back to 1890, when psychologist William James first wrote about self-esteem. He defined it as a "set of opinions I have about myself."[1] According to James, an opinion has two parts: facts and emotional responses to those facts. The same facts can elicit very different emotional responses. For example, the facts might be that a teen made multiple missteps in a dance performance. The emotional response might be one of several things:

- satisfaction that they improved their abilities from a previous performance
- frustration that they didn't do better because they didn't practice enough
- devastation because they feel that anything but a perfect performance proves that they are a bad dancer

When missteps lead to devastation, parents often try to help by reminding kids that they *are* talented and amazing. We want to fill the breach in our kids' confidence with our positive appraisals. We might even blame others for our kids' mistakes. After all, we want to protect our kids from experiences that might hurt their self-esteem.

These responses don't come out of thin air. Many of us grew up with programs and curricula promising to boost self-esteem that focused solely on boosting children's positive emotional responses regardless of life's real ups and downs. In other words, they focused on trying to help kids *feel better* about themselves.

There is nothing wrong with feeling good. But too often this kind of self-esteem relies on the opinions of others or on feedback from a constant treadmill of accomplishments. This works when kids are doing well and generating praise. It tends to fall apart in the face of challenges, social comparison, mistakes, and difficult feelings.

Online Approval and the Quest for Likes

"I know that so much of it is fake. But when I'm scrolling or looking for likes, I still don't *know* that," a teenager shared with me. We agreed that there is a big gap between logic and emotions when it comes to social feedback and comparison online. On one hand, most people realize that images are curated, edited, and produced. We also know that our value as human beings isn't determined by how many likes we get on the internet. Yet we still experience the emotional thrill of social praise and the sting of social judgment as we scroll. This is especially true for adolescents.

I met Marlin a few years ago. His eighth-grade daughter Sanya had her own phone, and she did okay with it when her social interactions were limited to group chats. "Once she got onto social media, it quickly became clear that she was in over her head," Marlin shared.

"How so?" I asked.

"It's all she thinks about. We were unprepared for this, because her older sister did just fine at Sanya's age. Although she spent time on social media, her entire sense of self-worth didn't rise and fall with what people said about her online," Marlin shared. He continued, "Every time we have a conversation about social media, Sanya rolls her eyes and assures us that she knows that there is more to life than her phone. But she is hooked emotionally."

Marlin's observation about his daughters is a good reminder that every kid is unique. Some kids, like Sanya's sister, are indeed just fine with social media. As explored in previous chapters, many teens express their emerging identities and find their people online. Comments and messages can be a positive part of building friendships and community.[2] But Sanya's experience is common. In a 2023 Common Sense Media study, most of the teen girls reported that they had struggled with "focusing too much" on metrics, including views, followers, shares, and likes.[3] This experience was especially common among girls who were already struggling.

Developmental psychologists have been theorizing about imagined audiences for decades. But for young people today, their audiences aren't only imagined. They are also online. And audience opinions are clear and quantifiable in the form of likes, shares, streaks, tags, and views. No one is indifferent to social feedback received online. If I post something online, I am pleased to see positive feedback. Young people are no different. In an experiment at UCLA's Ahmanson-Lovelace Brain Mapping Center, reward circuits were activated within teens' brains when they saw large numbers of likes on their pictures or the pictures of friends.[5] The sensation of these rewards is likely to be more pleasurable for teens than for adults. The teenage brain is more sensitive to rewards, more driven to seek them out, and more sensitive to the pleasure associated with them. The opposite—online judgment, criticism, or indifference—can feel devastating. Adolescents navigate the emotional highs and lows of peer opinion offline too. But the public and portable nature of online social platforms, the absence of interpersonal cues, and the quantification of peer feedback can make the thrill of approval and the sting of rejection more intense and sustained.

Excessive investment in social status online can take its toll. Dr. Jacqueline Nesi and her colleague Mitchell Prinstein set out to learn more about young

> **INSIDE INSIGHTS**
> Remember, the emergence of "imaginary audiences" during adolescence means that adolescents are more likely than younger children are to feel that others are watching and evaluating them.[4] Teens may feel that they are on stage in front of their peers. This can make it difficult for adolescents to distinguish between their own preoccupations and those of their imagined audiences. In other words, if a young person is worried about how their new haircut looks, they assume others are evaluating it with similar intensity. The reality, of course, is that other young people are likely focused on their own worries and challenges—each managing their own perceived exposure on their own stage.

people who engage in "digital status seeking." These teens tend to use social media more often, believe that online metrics are important, and use various strategies to get more likes, comments, followers, and interactions on their posts. Nesi and Prinstein found that more digital status seeking predicted higher levels of health risk behaviors, such as substance abuse and risky sexual behaviors.[6] This is just one study, but it illustrates how young people's heightened focus on status combined with the design features of social media platforms is a tricky mix for some teens.

Young people like Sanya aren't just scanning their own social metrics. They are likely *comparing their metrics to others'*. Since the teen brain is especially sensitive to status and respect, receiving fewer likes than expected or fewer than peers receive can deliver an intense emotional blow. In a national survey of US adolescents, more than half of the respondents said it was a negative experience to post content on social media and not receive enough likes.[7] Insufficient online validation is a new form of social threat. A group of researchers set out to try to understand how these dynamics affect adolescent well-being. They found that young people who received fewer likes than their peers reported more distress, felt stronger rejection, and had more negative thoughts about themselves. This was especially true for teens who had been victimized by peers in the past. Young people who showed stronger negative reactions to low metrics were more likely to develop depressive symptoms over time.[8]

It's normal for kids to have feelings about peer opinions. On its own, this isn't a reason for adults to swoop in like mental health first responders. But we shouldn't ignore signs that our kids are becoming preoccupied with online feedback or that their entire sense of self-worth rises and falls with social metrics or social feedback online.

Adolescents are, of course, capable of accurately evaluating online feedback, but the features of digital platforms create the perfect conditions for cognitive distortions. Technology can intensify anxious thoughts and self-doubt. These thoughts may sound like this:

- "They didn't comment on my post; they *must be* mad at me."

- "Not enough people liked my post; I am *worthless*."

- "I *should* have a skin-care routine like everyone on social media."

The Center for Digital Thriving at the Harvard School of Education is tackling this issue head-on. Dr. Emily Weinstein, cofounder of the Center, told me, "In the spirit of 'name it to tame it,' I really believe that giving teens the language to name these thinking traps is powerful."[9] Dr. Weinstein notes that learning about these common traps can also shift thinking patterns. For example, a young person who's aware of cognitive distortions might move from the automatic thought of "She must be mad at me" toward healthier self-talk, such as "There's the personalizing trap again. There are plenty of reasons for this that have nothing to do with me." You can find a rich set of resources on thinking traps co-created by the Center for Digital Thriving and adolescents in the Recommended Resources at the end of this book.[10]

My Body, My Worth?

"A little part of me died inside when my daughter told me *at age seven* that she didn't like her belly," a friend told me. "I felt like we had worked so hard to inoculate her from all that toxic messaging. I guess it just comes at her from everywhere. Now that she's thirteen, it's the same thing on overdrive. I get that she is going to focus more on her looks at this age. I just worry that it's driven by feeling bad about her body."

"Yeah, it doesn't help that most teens are bombarded with content related to their appearance all the time," I replied. "It's just so hard."

Many parents can recall, with a bit of heartbreak, the first negative comments their children made about their bodies. These comments might relate to bellies, skin tone, hair texture and style, height, eye shape, and on and on. No body part is immune to self-scrutiny. These are the moments when we wish we had a magic spell we could cast around our kids to repel the effects of digitally altered advertisements or social media reels spewing narrow and unattainable Western standards of beauty that center Whiteness as well as thinness *and* muscularity.[11] Though no such magic spells exist, there are things we can do to promote positive body image. For example, one study showed that building a strong ethnic-racial identity may protect against negative outcomes associated with appearance dissatisfaction and self-objectification among Black youth.[12] Yet fostering positive body image can feel like trying to swim upstream. According to a 2022 poll, nearly two-thirds of parents of eight- to eighteen-year-olds in the United States report that their child is self-conscious about some element of their appearance. Of those parents, nearly one-third say that their kids make overtly negative comments about it.[13]

Negative self-talk tends to escalate in adolescence, especially among teen girls. When kids hit adolescence, their bodies start changing exactly when they are exploring who they are in front of the perceived scrutiny of imaginary audiences. It's no surprise, then, that adolescents tend to operate in a stronger "appearance culture" than younger children do.[14] Teens are more likely than younger children are to start talking about physical attractiveness, work to align their looks with dominant beauty standards, and compare their appearance to that of others. The societal focus on female physical appearance helps explain why girls are more likely than boys to believe that their self-worth is contingent on their appearance.[15] Add social media to that volatile mix of ingredients, and things can get toxic very quickly for some teens.

Dr. Sophia Choukas-Bradley, director of the Teen and Young Adult Lab at the University of Pittsburgh, is a clinical psychologist who studies how specific social media experiences shape mental health, body image, and identity development. She notes that for some teens, social media creates the "perfect storm" for body image concerns.[16] Overall time on social media is not consistently connected to body image issues. But in highly visual media, upward social comparison, or comparing yourself to people you think have higher social status than you, *is* connected to body image issues.[17] Highly visual and quantifiable apps, such as Instagram and Snapchat, tend to be flooded with edited images of peers, celebrities, and online influencers. For some teens, this can feel inspiring. For many, though, it adds hot air to the storm, since appearance-focused content dominates the algorithms. Influencers document their weight loss, share daily workout routines, encourage multistep skin-care regimens, and dole out advice alongside hashtags like #fitspiration and #thinspiration. A team of researchers at the University of Vermont analyzed one thousand TikTok videos from ten popular nutrition, food, and weight-related hashtags. Altogether, the videos were viewed more than one billion times. Only 3 percent of the posts were "weight inclusive," and most of the posts were created by "white female adolescents and young adults."[18] The average scroll through social media is far from an accurate reflection of the lives, identities, and bodies of real kids.

Young people have long been bombarded with unrealistic messages and images. But this doesn't mean that body image concerns are a teenage phase that kids grow out of. Sidelining body image from broader conversations about social media and adolescent mental health is a mistake. Body image concerns are risk factors for depressive symptoms and disordered eating—and an extraordinary number of adolescents are struggling with these issues. A 2023 study estimated that one in five teens may struggle with disordered eating globally.[19] From 2018 to 2022, health visits related to eating disorders more than doubled among young people under the age of seventeen in the United States.[20] This might turn out to be another pandemic-related high-water mark in the data, but it is concerning nonetheless.[21] Body image concerns are a pathway linking social media use to poor mental health for some teenagers.

We need more research on the body image struggles of LGBTQ+ young people, but a 2020 review of studies indicates that these teens experience a greater incidence of eating disorders and disordered eating behaviors than their straight and cisgender peers.[22] A 2023 national survey on LGBTQ+ youth mental health found that nearly nine in ten queer youth reported being dissatisfied with their bodies.[23] These findings align with other signs of the great toll transphobia and homophobia take on the health and well-being of LGBTQ+ adolescents. Trans youth in particular must navigate a complex set of body image concerns as they negotiate the tensions between their own experience of identity, gender, and appearance and the expectations of peers, family, and society.

Cisgender boys aren't immune to appearance-related content either. The toxic waters they swim in just look a little different. For starters, research indicates that boys tend to be socialized to be self-reliant and strong and to minimize and manage problems on their own.[24] As a result, boys may be less likely to reach out for help when they do face body image challenges, which the data indicate they will. I connected with Dr. Jason Nagata, an adolescent and young adult medicine specialist and an expert in eating disorders in boys and men. He noted that "there's still a stereotype that eating disorders only affect girls. And because of that, a lot of the research and even guidance is focused on thinness and weight loss, reflecting the female body ideal."[25] Yet according to one of Dr. Nagata's own studies, 61 percent of teen boys want to change their weight, and a rapidly growing percentage of eating disorder patients identify as male.[26] He reminded me that "eating disorders don't affect one type of individual. They can affect people of all genders, sexual orientations, races, ethnicities, sizes, and socioeconomic backgrounds."

The images of male social media influencers are mostly unrealistic and unattainable. A team of researchers analyzed one thousand appearance-related posts from men and boys on Instagram. They found that the majority showed high levels of leanness and muscular bodies.[27] Boys are more likely to get positive feedback for posting muscular content on their profiles and stories. This trend has an impact on kids. Dr. Nagata shared with me the finding from his study that one-third of teen boys report trying to gain weight and bulk up.[28] Focusing on physical fitness and building strength isn't inherently problematic. But for many young men, an unhealthy preoccupation with food, exercise, muscularity, or biohacking (making lifestyle changes to "hack" your body's biology and optimize physical or mental performance) can have devastating impacts.[29]

This was certainly the case for Justin. Justin had two older siblings, one female and the other nonbinary. Understandably, his parents were quite vigilant around body image issues with their first two kids. His dad told me, "It's not that we didn't care about Justin's body image, it's just that some unconscious part of us figured that our first two were at risk and that Justin wasn't. It all seems painfully obvious now that no teenager is immune, but at the time we just didn't see it."

Justin's parents noted that he started getting more serious about sports in eighth grade. "Honestly, we were relieved!" his mom said. "It's not easy getting kids to move, so having the structure and motivation was great. It made sense to me that he started following a lot of fitness people online, because he was really into becoming more of an athlete, and he's always been a perfectionist. His For You page on TikTok was *all* about fitness and nutrition." His dad added, "Eating healthy and getting strong just seemed like part of how he was committing himself to sports. I used to praise him for it! I didn't realize it was a disorder until he was in so deep."

Justin's parents described how he started following the rigid diets of his favorite influencers, counting calories, and compensating for extra food he ate with harder and more frequent workouts. "It was his coach who ended up reaching out to us. I am so grateful, because we were already starting to notice that things were off. The coach confirmed our concerns and helped us break through to Justin that what he was doing wasn't healthy. By the time we got him evaluated, he was to the point of needing medical monitoring. It was awful."

Justin's parents were wise to reach out to their doctor for an evaluation and to plan next steps. Dr. Nagata says that eating disorder treatment is best supported by an interdisciplinary team that includes mental health, medical, and nutrition specialists. If you are concerned about the possibility that your child has an eating disorder, reach out to your primary care provider and get referrals from there.[30] Holistic, individualized care is key to recovery.

Justin and other young people like him aren't led into disordered eating behaviors by online influencers alone. And eating disorders aren't an inevitable outcome for all young people using social media. Beauty ideals are culturally specific, and many young people find plenty of affirming representations of their identities online. Even problematic content doesn't always lead to disordered eating and depression. Additional risk factors, such as genetics, stress and trauma, other mental health issues, and food insecurity, play a role. That said, for all ages and genders, going down an appearance-focused rabbit hole is usually a recipe for feeling worse. Algorithms and ad targeting can quickly create a personalized ecosystem of unrealistic and unhealthy images and messages.

The Costs of Being Camera Ready

"I used to just constantly think about what everything, including myself, would look like online. I saw everything through filters and potential posts," a young woman shared with me after presenting a project to help young people be more thoughtful about their online activities.

I met her as part of a program in which I, along with others in my field, served as a mentor for young thought leaders striving to improve the digital landscape. These young leaders were thoughtful, innovative, and committed to a future in which their self-worth wasn't tied to corporate earnings. They created projects ranging from journaling exercises to mindfulness apps to phone-free in-person events.

The same young woman said, "I don't want to have to log off to feel good about myself. But I also know that I can easily lose my sense of self online. I want to change that."

Being camera ready takes a psychological toll. The "perfect storm" of body image concerns that Dr. Choukas-Bradley describes in her research can intensify when teens become preoccupied with producing, editing, and curating images of themselves. Dr. Choukas-Bradley and her collaborators have developed and validated a scale to measure the extent to which young women's "thoughts and behaviors reflect ongoing awareness of whether they might look attractive to an online audience."[31] They call it the appearance-related social media consciousness (ASMC) scale. The scale measures things like imagining how photos might look to online audiences, zooming in on specific body parts to see what they look like in online photos, looking at photos of oneself on social media again and again, and carefully editing and curating photos before posting them to social platforms. If you've ever been at a gathering and found yourself thinking about what it might look like on social media rather than enjoying the event itself, you have experienced a little taste of this. Higher-than-typical ASMC is associated with worse mental health outcomes. In one study, Dr. Choukas-Bradley and her colleagues found that higher baseline ASMC predicts higher body dissatisfaction and depressive symptoms over time.[32] ASMC seems to be higher in teens who identify as girls, but ASMC is associated with depressive symptoms across all genders, even when controlling for time spent on social media.

I heard Dr. Choukas-Bradley and one of her graduate students share some of their research findings on body image and social media use at the Digital Media and Developing Minds International Scientific Congress. As I sat in the audience, I couldn't help thinking about possible solutions. In addition to holding social media companies responsible for harmful algorithms, I thought, what if we were to fill our feeds with more affirming imagery? I resisted the urge to pull out my phone and start curating images to better reflect the stunning diversity of bodies in the world. During the question-and-answer session, another audience member asked the same question I was wondering about. The presenters' answer made me grateful that I hadn't invested hours in photo curation quite yet. They said that research does indicate that consuming photos depicting more realistic and diverse bodies can help,[33] and it is undoubtedly better than scrolling nonstop through dieting and fitness posts. But the most protective images are those that don't portray bodies at all.[34] Taking breaks from body photos altogether is an important antidote to the stress of consuming appearance-related content. If teens want some relief, they might consider following body-neutral feeds (those that focus less on appearance and emphasize body acceptance and function) and training their algorithms to include more baby animal videos.

Unfortunately, algorithms are not built to boost soothing panda and cat content. Social media companies use a kind of artificial intelligence called recommendation algorithms to push similar and often more extreme content to hold our attention. So, for example, once you've clicked on a workout video, you get more workout videos—and maybe more extreme ones. Understanding how these algorithms serve up content is an essential skill for anyone who uses social media. Thanks to recommendation algorithms, different people see different content. The differences in individual For You feeds on TikTok illustrate this point. I might be enjoying cross-country skiing videos and middle-age parenting memes while my kid is being inundated with #fitspiration posts and videos urging him to bulk up. It's easy to forget that my feed isn't just "how things are," because recommendation algorithms are relentless. Most young people understand intellectually that social media doesn't reflect real life. But it takes ongoing conversations, algorithm literacy, and maybe some cat videos to shift their emotional responses to social media.

IN ACTION: RECOMMENDATION ALGORITHMS

Explore these questions with your kid to remind them that what they see online isn't just the way things are:

- "Do you know why certain content shows up in your feed?"
- "What do you know about recommendation algorithms? Why do companies use them? What do you think of them?"
- "What's working for you in your feed? What's not working for you?"
- "What do you already do or want to start doing to take control of the content in your feed?"

SELF-WORTH AND SOCIAL MEDIA

This is not a diagnostic tool, nor is it an official scale of any kind. This is a starting place for reflection on the role that social comparison might be playing in your teen's sense of self-worth. For each statement below, think about which response best represents your teen: "I'm not sure," "Not really," "Sometimes," or "Often." If your reflections make you feel concerned, reach out to your child's primary care physician, the school mental health professional, or another trusted advisor.

- My teen's sense of self-worth rises and falls based on online feedback.

- My teen doesn't bounce back easily from perceived negative feedback online.

- My teen tends to read even ambiguous social feedback as negative.

- My teen spends a lot of time editing and curating photos of themselves to post on social media.

- My teen always uses filters to alter their appearance before posting on social media.

- My teen deletes images that don't receive enough positive feedback online.

- My teen follows a lot of appearance-focused influencers or celebrities.

- My teen feels bad about themself when they compare themself to others online.

The Antidote Is Self-Compassion

As parents, it's painful to watch our kids compare themselves to others online and conclude that they are inferior to their peers. It is heartbreaking to watch them lose their sense of self in the opinions of others or compensate for their insecurities by casting judgment or seeking status online.

In these moments, it is tempting to offer strong positive appraisals to counteract the distortions of social media. We want to yell, "Your belly is just right! Your skin is beautiful! Your dancing isn't the sum of who you are! Your appearance is not your worth!" For every self-disparaging comment saying, "I'm bad," we want to respond with a louder, "No, you're good!"

Our desire to reassure is understandable. After all, who among us doesn't want to bolster our kids' self-worth? There is nothing wrong with reminding kids that they are stunning, precious, whole humans—even if we get an eye roll in response.

We should remember, though, that trying to bolster self-worth by showering our kids with praise and reassurance is unlikely to work even if our kids are receptive. This leaves our kids still looking for external cues of their worth. If we want to equip our teens to resist comparison and judgment, they need to learn how to be good friends to themselves. They need to learn self-compassion.

Dr. Kristin Neff is an associate professor at the University of Texas at Austin. She is also one of the world's leading experts on self-compassion research. Self-compassion is treating yourself the way you would treat a friend. Neff and her collaborator Dr. Christopher Germer note that learning self-compassion is learning "to become an inner ally rather than an inner enemy."[35] Self-compassion is a much more stable resource for adolescents than self-esteem, because it doesn't depend upon getting things "right," generating positive appraisals, or comparing yourself to others. Instead, practicing self-compassion gives you emotional resources to be kind to yourself even when you are imperfect or suffering. According to Drs. Neff and Germer, self-compassionate people focus on love, connection, and presence:[36]

- **Love:** Instead of blaming themselves and engaging in self-criticism when they make mistakes, self-compassionate teens practice putting "a supportive arm around [their] own shoulder,"[37] just like they would for a best friend.

- **Connection:** Comparison is isolating and can make teens feel like they are the only ones struggling. Self-compassionate teens recognize that everyone makes mistakes and everyone experiences pain. No one has found a way to avoid failure and challenges.

- **Presence:** Scrolling through social media certainly sparks a lot of emotions. It can also be a way to numb them. Self-compassionate teens are open to the reality of what is happening in the present. They welcome feelings as information about their experiences rather than permanent features of their personalities.

A growing body of research demonstrates the benefits of self-compassion to physical and mental health.[38] People who are more self-compassionate experience less depression, anxiety, stress, and shame. There is no way to immunize adolescents against social comparison. But we can help our teens handle it by encouraging them to practice compassion for themselves.

Dr. Neff and her collaborators have developed entire courses focused on teaching the skills of mindful self-compassion to parents and teens.[39] One exercise that you can try right away is to model talking to yourself the way that you would talk to a good friend. Modeling healthy self-talk requires important inner work. Start by tracking how you talk about yourself, and if you find that you're a self-critic, try adjusting to a more compassionate stance.

You can model self-compassion by saying things like "I have been managing a lot this week. It's hard to remember everything! Everyone drops a ball sometimes. I'm sorry I forgot about your appointment. We will reschedule it for next week." Or "I was feeling so down on myself this morning because I was embarrassed by how envious I felt looking at my friend's vacation pictures. Then I realized that everyone feels envy sometimes. It's just part of being human. So I told myself, 'It's okay to feel this way. Nobody is perfect.' I took a little break from social media, and that helped."

You can also prompt your teen to practice self-compassion during times of struggle. For example, you might say, "It sounds like you are feeling bad about how some people responded to your video. It makes sense that it didn't feel good. We all take things personally sometimes. What would you say to a friend in the same position? Do you think you can give yourself that same comfort?" Or you could say, "There are so many negative messages coming at us about our bodies on social media. I heard you say something negative about your belly earlier. Can you offer yourself a little more kindness? You could say to yourself, 'Ugh, this hurts. It's awful to feel bad about my body and to see so many unrealistic images online. I know I'm not the only one who feels like this. I am enough just as I am.'"

IN ACTION: MODELING AND INVITING SELF-COMPASSION

If your inner critic is strong, it can be challenging to model self-compassion. You aren't alone. Most people are more compassionate to others than they are to themselves. Practice relating to yourself with compassion by reflecting on the following questions.

- Write down a mistake you made or a challenge you recently faced.
- How did your inner critic respond to this mistake or challenge?
- How do you think a caring friend would respond?
- Offer yourself those same caring words. (Give yourself bonus points for saying them out loud in front of your teen.)

It's You I Like

Two essential developmental questions of adolescence discussed in previous chapters are "Who am I?" and "Where do I belong?" Let's add "Am I enough?" to that list. Mister Rogers, the beloved and legendary master of child development, was crystal clear about the protective power of self-worth for healthy development. In every song, skit, and story he produced, he found ways to communicate to children, "It's you I like. Every part of you."[40] The wisdom of Mister Rogers holds throughout the lifespan and across contexts. Educator and author Alex Shevrin Venet argues that experiencing "unconditional positive regard" is essential to young people's learning and mental health.[41] She says the stance of unconditional positive regard is: "I care about you. You have value. You don't have to do anything to prove it to me, and nothing will change my mind."[42]

For parents, unconditional positive regard means accepting kids for who they are, not what they do. I had the opportunity to produce a podcast episode with Shevrin Venet about what this looks like in practice. She admitted, "Most people hear [about unconditional positive regard] and think, 'Oh yeah—that's so nice,' but it can actually be very difficult."[43] I appreciated her honesty. Parenting teenagers is a wild ride. It's common for adolescents to push parents away, test limits, and externalize negative feelings. These rocky moments are exactly when young people need unconditional positive regard the most. This doesn't mean setting no boundaries or not holding teens accountable for poor choices. It means that when we do hold kids accountable, we communicate that "what you have done isn't okay" instead of "who you are is unacceptable."

Unconditional positive regard tells your kid that their value isn't contingent on their performance, their choices, their appearance, their identity, or social media metrics. It provides a sturdy sense of self-worth that's essential in a world that constantly tells teens what they could or should be instead of themselves.

Few of us parents would admit to communicating anything other than unconditional love for our kids. Yet young people are quick to point out the gap between our words and their experiences. Jennifer Breheny Wallace, author of the book *Never Enough,* found that 50 percent of the young adults she surveyed thought that their parents loved them more when they were more successful.[44]

REFLECT UNCONDITIONAL POSITIVE REGARD

Read each statement and think about which response best describes where you are right now: "I hadn't thought of this," "I try," or "I got this." Then ask yourself: What are you most proud of? What do you want to work on?

- I avoid comparing my teen to their siblings or friends.
- I avoid criticizing my teen's appearance, identity, or interests.
- I express my belief that mistakes and imperfections are part of being human.
- I don't withhold affection when my teen falls short of my expectations.
- I separate my teen's worth from their actions and choices.
- I don't judge my self-worth by my teen's achievements.
- I provide warm and accurate praise to my teen when they meet their goals.
- I try to be curious instead of critical when things aren't going well.
- I communicate the purpose behind my expectations and boundaries.
- I make sure my teen knows that nothing they could ever do would make me love them any less.
- I make sure my teen knows that there is nothing they need to do to make me love them more.

Self-Worth Starts at Home

Just as belonging with friends can't be measured by the number of social interactions our kids have, their worth can't be measured by social feedback. Yet social feedback is part of the digital landscape that they are navigating. Try as we might, we can't force our kids to be kinder and more compassionate with themselves as they travel through their world. There is no magic spell we can cast to skip them over all the hard parts.

But we can step bravely toward self-compassion ourselves. We can notice when our digital activities evoke painful feelings of inferiority. And when we inevitably feel painful emotions, make mistakes, or experience the sting of social comparison, we can offer ourselves kindness. We can model a different relationship with ourselves than what is served up by social media algorithms.

We can also give our kids a very powerful taproot for self-worth: absolute certainty that they are loved for all that they are. We invite them to belong to themselves when we communicate, "I love you just the way you are—your strengths, your struggles, your identities, your spark, and your dark. All of you."

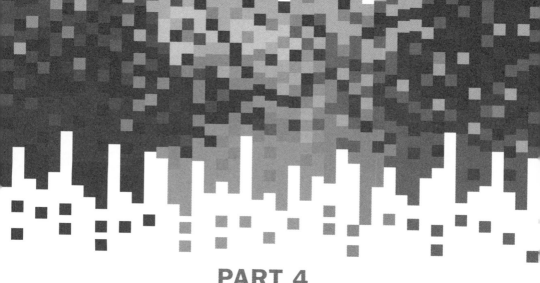

PART 4

"How Can I Contribute?"

CHAPTER 10

The Power of Purpose

*"Tell me, what is it you plan to do
with your one wild and precious life?"*
—MARY OLIVER, "THE SUMMER DAY"

"Why is that squirrel eating a nut? Where do you think it lives? Why are there nuts on that tree? Where are the other squirrels?"

I can still remember my kids' incessant questions when they were preschoolers. Every step down our neighborhood sidewalk brought intense investigations. Simple walks were constantly punctuated with "Why? Where? How come?"

These endless Q and A sessions weren't always delightful. Sometimes after a long day of inquiry, the only response I could muster was "Because!" When I wasn't rushed or exhausted, though, I could appreciate that curiosity is a childhood superpower. Exploring a squirrel's complex relationship with trees can be exasperating, but inquisitiveness helps kids gain more than just squirrel facts. It motivates learning, helps them take the perspectives of others, and boosts their mood.[1]

My middle schooler is less likely to verbalize the kinds of curious questions he asked when he was a toddler. Indeed, most young people are more likely to *inform* their parents how the world works instead of asking for explanations. But despite the appearance of assurance, adolescents are every bit as curious as toddlers are. As their understanding of the world and their place in it expands, the scale and scope of their questions grow as well. Adolescents are built to ask questions like "Where am I headed?" and "What is the point?" These aren't just philosophizing exercises. Exploring these questions is key to their development.

What Is the Point?

"I can see my teen's motivation really shifting this year," a parent shared.

"What do you mean?" I asked.

"Carter's always been a pretty diligent student," the parent responded. "He's one of those rare kids who loves to check things off his to-do list. Lately, though, lists aren't doing much for him. He seems almost existential about his priorities."

"What do you think is going on?" I asked.

"Part of it is probably just getting older. He's pretty engaged with politics and global issues—and honestly totally overwhelmed by it. The other day he said, 'Is this math assignment really that important given what's going on in the world? I just don't see the point right now.' My observation is that he just scrolls and scrolls through headlines that would make anybody question whether homework assignments matter. My attempts to reassure him seem to fall flat."

Carter isn't unique. Most young people today aren't just following the latest dance challenges or checking out their friends' activities online. They are also scrolling through coverage of current events, making broad observations about their communities, and sharing stories online about everything from climate change to racism to politics.

It's tempting to write this off as doomscrolling and try to shut it down in hopes of restoring a more positive outlook (and to get kids back to their to-do lists). Doomscrolling is spending an excessive amount of time reading large quantities of negative news online. Unsurprisingly, research indicates that this isn't good for mental health.[2] But not all online activity puts teens on an inevitable road toward existential crisis and poor mental health. Growing awareness of the bigger picture happens during adolescence regardless of digital habits. The sheer amount of online information about that picture can certainly overwhelm kids, just as it can overwhelm adults. It can also serve as an on-ramp for something teens desperately need: purposeful participation in something bigger than themselves.

The Search for Purpose in Adolescence

I was going through a box of old belongings after my parents politely reminded me that their home was not my storage unit. I was quick to recycle some items, wondering why I thought I would want to look at term papers twenty years later. But like most old memory boxes, mine contained a few gems from my adolescent years. One was a journal I kept as a fifteen-year-old while attending a wilderness canoe camp in northern Minnesota. As I turned the pages, I found myself laughing out loud. There in my daily updates was a written record illustrating the shift to meaning-making that happens during adolescence. I'll spare you from the entire contents of the journal, but here is a sample of the shift:

> Day 1. We had oatmeal for breakfast. It was good. I hope we see a moose today. It's nice to be away from my brothers and I bet I will be stronger than them when I get home. We had four portages today. We had GORP for lunch which was good except for the raisins. I hope we have pizza for dinner.

> Day 2. [More of the same]

> Day 3. [More of the same]

> Day 4. [More of the same]

> Day 5. We had pancakes for breakfast. I am so grateful for this fuel that helps me do things I didn't know I was capable of doing. Being out here for this long, I am starting to notice so many things that nobody pauses long enough to see at home—the taste of good food that we've really worked for, the way we make deeper friendships out here, and the endless night sky. A day on trail is so simple and yet the world feels way bigger . . .

How far I had come in five short days. I went from listing menu preferences to describing a soul-expanding journey of a lifetime! I even tried my hand at poetry and watercolor drawings on later pages. I made it clear in no uncertain terms that I was forever changed by this experience. As I reread these entries, I could see my capacity to reflect on my emotions and my place in the world maturing. The context, a wilderness trip with a small group of peers led by an influential young adult, certainly helped facilitate this. But no matter how young people spend their summers, they experience a growing capacity for self-exploration and reflection. This is developmentally right on schedule. Changes in the teenage brain allow young people to look up from a meal menu and toward the sky.

The combination of personal reflection and collective awareness is what distinguishes the broader search for purpose from task completion. Researcher William Damon, director of the Stanford Center on Adolescence, has studied the power of purpose in adolescent development for more than twenty years. Drawing on research in psychology and philosophy, he and his colleagues share three key criteria that define purpose:[5]

INSIDE INSIGHTS

Chapter 5 explores the benefits of both "looking out" and "looking in." As their brains mature, adolescents are capable both of reacting to concrete things in their environments *and* of thinking abstractly and making meaning of what they are experiencing. Intense emotions help drive this deep thinking and reflection.[3] When teens explore the question "Who am I?" they often ask big questions about how they will show up in the broader world. Researchers Mary Helen Immordino-Yang and Douglas R. Knecht note that abstract thinking during adolescence is a "brain builder."[4] More abstract thinking explains why purpose takes center stage in adolescence.

- Purpose is about committing to a longer-term goal. It isn't just a quick or momentary impulse to do something.

- Purpose is personally meaningful. It isn't something that others say you should care about.

- Purpose is relevant to the broader community or world. It is an "externally oriented quest."

In other words, purpose isn't something that teens can check off a list. It's something they discover over time as they connect their strengths and interests to the needs of the world. Young people won't identify one purpose early on and stick with it. Instead, they may have varying purposes depending on context and age. These range from smaller purposeful actions aligned with shorter-term goals, such as leading a sports team or a school club, to purposeful actions aligned with longer-term goals, such as a career or passion project.

The Benefits of Purpose

Exploring purpose doesn't just make young people feel good. Adolescents who cultivate purpose experience all kinds of positive outcomes. For starters, exploring purpose can help them answer that nagging question "What's the point?" as they weigh finishing their math homework against video games or hanging out with friends. While tedious tasks or deadlines may be stressful or boring, young people with purpose tend to see them as more worthwhile.[6] But the benefits don't stop there. Studies have also linked adolescent sense of purpose with other benefits, including fewer risk-taking behaviors and healthier physical and mental health outcomes.[7] The benefits reach into the digital world as well. Young people who have a greater sense of purpose tend to rely less on social media likes for validation and self-esteem.[8] No matter which way you cut the data, it appears that teens thrive when they start trying to answer the questions "What's the point?" and "What gives my life meaning?"

Given all these benefits, it would be nice if we could assign our adolescents a sense of purpose when they hit high school or when their motivation starts to lag. Unfortunately, purpose doesn't work this way. My wife, who has twenty years of experience working with adolescents in schools, consistently reminds me that the "sit down and let me tell you what you should care about" approach tends to backfire. We can do things to help our kids manage daily tasks. But we can't give them purpose. Purpose isn't a prepackaged thing that can be given, or that they can just go out and grab. According to the authors of a report from the National Scientific Council on Adolescence, "For adolescents, developing a *sense* of purpose . . . matters more than the particular purpose that is being cultivated."[9] So how do teens start exploring purpose? A team of researchers set out to answer that question. They found three common pathways to purpose:[10]

- **Proactive exploration:** Some teens actively seek out experiences and information related to their potential purpose. Think of a young person who is interested in making films and applies for an internship at an independent theater.

- **Reactive exploration:** Some teens stumble upon their purpose after having a powerful experience. Picture the teen who decides they want to pursue coding after participating in a Lego robotics tournament at school.

- **Social learning:** Some young people align their actions with those of a purposeful person they admire. Imagine a teen who wants to mimic their favorite YouTuber, who creates content about the environment and climate solutions.

Kids are more likely to find purpose when they seek it out or when they have access to transformative experiences and purposeful adults. Most young people experience a growing sense of purpose *following* transformative experiences and relationships. This means that purpose, like so many things in young people's lives, results from explorative trial and error. It's normal for teens to shift passions and interests across contexts and over time. A young person might feel that their purpose is to lead the school newspaper during the academic year and then shift to career aspirations in the summer. All teens deserve access to experiences that inspire purpose in and out of school.

Adolescents Need Opportunities to Cultivate Purpose

"I have plenty of things that I like doing," a seventeen-year-old told me. "I like school okay, helping with my siblings, and I like playing soccer. But most of the time I'm just head-down getting through the day."

This young person is certainly not alone. Some teens struggle to enjoy school, work, or extracurricular activities because of difficult things happening in their lives. But even teens who don't have major complaints may not have time and space to learn more about what makes them come alive. Dr. Kendall Cotton Bronk, an educational psychologist who has spent her career studying the moral development of adolescents, says that living a life of purpose is a "beneficial but rare experience" for young people. Only about one-fifth of high schoolers and one-third of college-age young adults report leading a life of purpose.[11] Research indicates that not all teens have opportunities to cultivate their purpose.[12] This inequity is concerning because purpose is especially beneficial for adolescents who face barriers to healthy development. For example, purpose can protect against the worst effects of daily experiences of racism.[13]

Young people today are acutely aware of the structural barriers that unjustly block their paths, such as racism, transphobia, xenophobia, and poverty. Indeed, many young people find purpose in organizing to make the world a more equitable and accessible place. Adults should follow their lead.

Doomscrolling Versus Participation

Let's return to Carter, the young man I introduced at the beginning of this chapter. He was weighing the significance of his math homework against the pressing world challenges that dominated his social feeds. Carter's parent was quick to note that scrolling through the world's problems didn't seem to be helping him, but is this an inevitable outcome of online activities?

Many adults lament that young people today are obsessed with entertainment over substance or that they scroll past life instead of engaging with it. Yet the data paint a different picture when it comes to civic engagement. In the early 2000s, young people were criticized for engaging in "slacktivism" online (slacker activism). More than two decades later, young people still charge each other with "performative activism" if a peer doesn't back up their public posts with meaningful actions.

Despite these charges, studies show that most teens who are politically active online are not slackers.[14] Young people who seek political information and who produce and share content about it online are more likely than their peers are to participate in public life. All those clicks, likes, and shares can be an important part of building a civic identity. Even nonpolitical participation in online social communities, like interest-based chat rooms or fandoms, allows young people to learn more about the things they care about.[15] Many of these digital spaces also help connect personal interests to opportunities for purposeful action. Whether it is remixing videos to share commentary about a school issue or sharing stories with movement hashtags, young people are participating in broader conversations than they would have access to without digital tools.

Posting political opinions or sharing about issues online can be fraught, though. Each post, share, or hashtag comes with its own complications. Teens must consider the reactions of their intended and unintended audiences before acting. They must think critically about what, where, and when to post. This analysis has high stakes in a polarized and often toxic political climate. As Emily Weinstein and Carrie James report in their book *Behind Their Screens,* middle and high school kids alike want to share their opinions about social issues. At the same time, they are acutely aware of the complicated digital afterlife of their contributions. In interviews with hundreds of young people across the country, Weinstein and James note that young people confront two truths: "Posting is a must and there are countless ways to get it wrong."[16] So, how can we help ensure that digital tools enrich young people's quest for purpose instead of undermining it?

It's tempting to just hand our kids devices and hope they gravitate toward online activities that inspire purposeful action. But popular platforms and the algorithms that drive content aren't designed with purpose in mind. That's why reflection and skill building around doomscrolling, online activism, and misinformation are so important.

That said, online activities *can* be a portal to purpose. Dr. Ellen Middaugh, who studies youth civic engagement online, has documented the ways in which online participation can help young people find their voices, their passions, and their communities. What distinguishes these purposeful teens from young people who are scrolling the day away? It isn't about motivation, caring, or skill. Dr. Middaugh argues that it often comes down to opportunity. Young people are more likely to link their personal interests to community concerns when they are invited to do so.[17]

Bridging Digital Interests and Purposeful Action

"I'm already totally over the summer, and it's only June," a parent named Jared shared with me. We were standing on the sidelines in our neighborhood park watching our middle schoolers bomb around the field.

"Oh no," I said. "Is it that bad?"

"I thought more downtime would be fine for Aiden now that they are in eighth grade and old enough to do their own thing. But now I feel like they have settled into a summer of YouTube, and all we do is battle. I just wish they had any interests at all!"

"Yeah, competing with YouTube is not easy," I sympathized. "I am wondering about something though."

"What's that?" he asked.

"Because of the amount of time Aiden spends on YouTube, I'm curious if they have any interests related to that. Those interests might have something to do with the creators they are following. Or maybe they are interested in video production itself?"

"Yeah, I guess so. They actually just got an app that helps them create cool jump cuts and stuff. But I don't want to encourage any more time on screens."

"Totally. Sitting alone in front of a screen all summer probably isn't healthy. But I wonder if learning video skills with others might spark something in Aiden?" We went on to brainstorm free opportunities for youth media production in Minneapolis.

I ran into Jared a year later at a school event. I reminded him that the last time we connected, he had been in a battle with Aiden about YouTube and asked how things were going.

"You know what? Last summer didn't ended up being so horrible," Jared responded. "After we talked, Aiden got into a youth media production class at the community center. It wasn't all unicorns and rainbows, but they made cool videos and ended up staying involved off and on during the past school year. They are going back this summer as a peer facilitator in the same program."

Like Aiden, most young people spend an extraordinary amount of time online. And there are some benefits to just hanging out and socializing online. Dr. Mizuko (Mimi) Ito, a professor at the University of California, Irvine, and director of the Connected Learning Alliance, has spent her career studying young people's learning experiences with new media. Dr. Ito and her collaborators have identified a group of practices they call HOMAGO, which stands for Hanging Out (including social practices such as spending time on TikTok or texting a friend), Messing Around (such as trying a new app or editing a home movie), and Geeking Out (deep, interest-driven engagement with technology).[18] Ito and her team have found that young people benefit from HOMAGO when adults help them shift from simply hanging out to messing around and geeking out. Too many teens don't have the opportunities, support, guidance, and resources they need to make this shift.

Kids like Aiden benefit when a caring adult notices a digital interest and offers an opportunity to pursue that interest with peers and purposeful adults. Building on HOMAGO principles, Dr. Ito and her colleagues have worked with libraries and other organizations across the country to design "connected learning" experiences for young people.[19] Connected learning is designed to connect youth interests, supportive relationships, and academic, civic, and career opportunities.[20] It doesn't necessarily involve digital media, but it often does. When done well, connected learning is associated with positive outcomes such as increased academic engagement, persistence, career aspirations, and sense of connectedness.[21] That said, it's not enough to just invite teens into a space and hand them cameras or give them access to coding programs. Instead, four major components predict positive outcomes:

- **Sponsorship of youth interests:** Sponsorship doesn't mean writing a check and walking away. It's about adults and institutions recognizing and investing in young people's digital interests and activities. In Nashville, for example, Studio NPL connects students to mentors to do everything from producing music to building robots.[22] At YOUmedia Hartford in Connecticut, young people connect with visiting artists and get project support from community mentors.[23]

- **Shared practices:** Connected learning is, first and foremost, about doing stuff together. Concrete and purposeful activities like designing new video games, creating digital art, producing films, or writing fanfiction help youth practice interest-driven skills together. The adolescent brain is built for this kind of hands-on, experiential learning with friends.

- **Shared purpose:** Connected learning isn't just fun; it also gives young people an opportunity to contribute meaningfully to their communities. Shared purpose might include showcasing work to larger audiences, creating resources for family or community, or advocating for solutions to real-world problems. For example, at YOUmedia Chicago, music makers have their own record label, and gamers produce a weekly podcast.[24]

- **Connections across settings:** Connected learning allows young people to build connections across home, school, community, and digital spaces. For example, libraries and museums might sponsor programming and also connect adolescents to a wider network of supports and opportunities online and offline.

Let's Prioritize Purpose

Jared was right that a summer of YouTube scrolling wasn't a promising recipe for a thriving Aiden. To complete the recipe, Aiden needed opportunities to make connections between their online interests and purposeful real-world exploration. Teens benefit when they are invited to explore, try new things, and meet purposeful peers and adults through formal or informal connected learning experiences. Adolescents are built to explore their identities and discover how their personal interests intersect with humankind's collective concerns. The changes that occur between childhood and the mid-twenties create the conditions for important questions like "Why?" and "What's the point?" The constant barrage of information online and the sheer amount of time adolescents spend there can overwhelm their capacity to pause, reflect, and make meaning. This is precisely why so many young people are organizing around digital well-being and mental health. Other young people are *using* their digital skills in podcasting, video production, social media strategy, and media arts to explore interests and take purposeful action. They aren't doing this because adults told them to. They are doing it because their brains are built to care, connect, explore, and learn. We all benefit when young people have opportunities to tinker with the tools in front of them and then look inside themselves to consider questions like "What does this mean?" and "Where do I want to go with this?"

REFLECT CULTIVATING PURPOSE

You can't assign your teen a sense of purpose. But you can give them opportunities to explore and discover things that they find meaningful. Read each statement and think about which response best describes where you are right now: "I hadn't thought of this," "I try," or "I got this." Then ask yourself: What are you most proud of? What do you want to work on?

- I understand that my teen's digital activities are valid interests.
- I show that I care about my teen's interests, skills, and values by asking questions and listening.
- I can identify one or two of my teen's friends who share interests with them.
- I connect my teen to purposeful adults who have similar interests.
- I introduce my teen to spaces, places, or programs that provide opportunities to explore purpose—in and out of school.
- I work to ensure that all young people have access to opportunities to explore their purpose.
- I provide emotional support when my teen experiences setbacks as they experiment with purpose.
- I encourage my teen to volunteer and engage in community work.
- I create opportunities for my teen to reflect on their purpose and share their purpose with others.

IN ACTION: PATHWAYS TO PURPOSE

Building bridges between your teen's digital interests and purposeful exploration starts with noticing what your teen is interested in or passionate about online:

- **What are your teen's digital interests?** If you are having a hard time coming up with a list of things your kid loves to do, watch for when they get most engaged, passionate, or curious. If their stated passion is video games, that is great! Pay attention to other gaming-related interests as well. Does your kid love creating worlds? Characters? Coding? Sound production? Collaboration?

- **What programs, clubs, jobs, or community roles might help your adolescent bridge their digital interests to experiences that have the following?**
  - » purposeful adults and peers
  - » exploration, tinkering, and skill building
  - » opportunities to share work with broader audiences or help solve a community problem

You can't tell your kid to be passionate about a specific activity or program. But you can be on the lookout for meaningful pathways to explore purpose in your community.

CHAPTER 11

The Power of Voice

"If you are going to invite us to speak, you need to be ready to listen."
—JUSTIN, AGE SIXTEEN

"I love hearing about these opportunities," a fellow parent turned toward me and said. "We missed the boat on this kind of stuff the first time around." We had met an hour earlier, when we found ourselves at the same table during a parent night at our kids' school. We already felt like old friends. The room was buzzing with beginning-of-the-school-year excitement and energy. Educators had just finished sharing opportunities for students to get involved in school decision-making and community partnership programs. Our school is in a large urban district that often struggles with funding, so I was amazed by all the genuine invitations for middle schoolers to participate in their new school community.

"What do you mean you missed the boat?" I asked.

"My older kid, Jin, is in high school. He struggled last year in eighth grade to stay motivated. He had so much on his plate between work and school. I was like, 'You don't have time for distractions!' I just wanted him to stay focused, so I kept trying to take responsibilities off his plate. But now I think replacing some of his commitments with stuff like this might have been better."

We went on to talk about how challenging it is to watch motivation drain from our kids without a clear sense of how to help. "It was Jin's school counselor who helped us identify what might be going on. He was really busy, but he didn't have much opportunity to contribute to anything. He was on autopilot everywhere he went."

"But things are a little better now? What shifted?" I asked, eager to hear the end of the story before we got up from our table. I wasn't sure I would find her again in the sea of caregivers.

"Jin's counselor connected him with an advisory board for an organization working on artificial intelligence ethics—something that fascinates him."

She went on to describe little changes in her son's motivation and energy. When she asked him to describe what had changed, he said simply, "I don't know, it just feels good to actually *do* something. They really care about what I have to say."

By this point, we were the last two people at our table. "Thanks for that little window into the future," I said.

She laughed and replied, "We are all just figuring it out as we go, aren't we?"

Wired to Contribute

As my sixth grader embarked on middle school, Jin's experience was instructive. Adolescents lead busy lives. Increased responsibilities and packed schedules make it easy to slip into checklist mode. This isn't young people's fault. Many school and work settings prioritize compliance and completion over engagement. But Jin's thoughtful observation that "it just feels good to actually *do* something" is a good reminder that adolescents aren't built for autopilot. They are built to contribute.

While human beings are capable of inflicting extraordinary harm on others, a long line of scholarship has helped us understand that we are actually wired to help. Multiple studies show that people voluntarily give time, resources, and skills to support others and solve collective problems. Even very young children spontaneously offer help to those around them.[1] I remember being so grateful when my toddlers started doing things like opening doors for me and picking up things I had dropped on the floor. Of course, the ratio of things toddlers drop to what they pick up from the floor is wildly lopsided. But their desire to be of service is nonetheless delightful.

This innate desire to help doesn't disappear during adolescence. It's common for teens to temporarily feign disinterest around their parents. But remember, they are deeply attuned to the feelings and needs of those around them. This is the stage when many of our kids respond well to prompts to "broaden their circles of concern" to include people beyond their family and closest friends.[2] One look at how young people are leading the way on issues such as climate change, disability rights, and mental health awareness tells us that teens are quite capable of contributing solutions to our collective concerns.

Dr. Andrew Fuligni is a developmental scientist at the University of California, Los Angeles. After reviewing dozens of studies on the topic, he concluded that the importance of contribution shouldn't be an afterthought in adolescent development.[3] He writes, "I believe it's time to move away from outdated stereotypes of adolescents as only selfish and dangerous risk-takers and to consider how they are ripe for learning about contributing to others and their communities."[4]

INSIDE INSIGHTS
As their social brain networks mature, adolescents become better able to consider the perspectives and needs of others and find creative ways to show up for them. Increased reward sensitivity can fuel prosocial risk-taking (not just the negative risk-taking that dominates headlines about adolescents). These risks pay off. Teens who are deemed prosocial by their friends through caring and contribution enjoy higher status than those who attempt to gain status through bullying behaviors.[5] Given that the teen brain is especially sensitive to respect and status, contributing can be a compelling pathway to building community.

Contributing isn't just something that teens *can* do because their brains are capable of it. It is something that young people *need* to experience for healthy development. Working with others to influence something that they care about helps build a sense of autonomy, competence, and relatedness.[6] Contributing also tends to strengthen young people's sense of belonging. Finally, physical and psychological benefits flow from helping others.[7] If we want adolescents to be able to participate meaningfully in their communities as adults, they need to practice doing that now. The brain gets good at what it does a lot.

Youth Voice Matters

It's easy for parents to make a quick list of ways they would *like* their kids to contribute. My list might start with putting away the dishes. And indeed, one study found that daily helping improved young people's moods. The effect was particularly strong among those who suffered higher levels of depressive symptoms. Another study found that teens were significantly happier on days when they helped their families.[8]

But the kind of contributing that really benefits adolescents isn't just doing things that adults tell them to do. Instead, teens gain a lot from participating in family rule-making, engaging in school or community decision-making, or leading social change. Meghan Lynch Forder of the Center for the Developing Adolescent calls these "contributions of consequence—actions that have substantial benefits to others that help to reach a shared goal. This type of contributing involves not simply taking a single action but playing an important role within a group—whether it's a family, school, or community."[9]

Contribution is closely related to the kind of purposeful exploration we explored in chapter 10. Another important path to contribution is youth voice. The United Nations Convention on the Rights of the Child asserts that kids and teens have the right to access information and influence matters that affect them.[10] Youth voice ranges from simply asking young people for input to creating true adult-youth partnerships in which teens help make consequential decisions.

Let's imagine that a nonprofit mental health organization wants to create an app that addresses adolescent health and well-being. Centering youth voice might include things like this:

- surveying young people about their experiences online

- seeking youth opinions and ideas about what they want or need from their digital experiences

- creating accessible structure and support for adolescents to co-create digital experiences alongside designers and other adults

Each of these strategies has potential value, but the last one is the gold standard. Young people can quickly sniff out tokenism. Asking young people to serve on an advisory board without being clear about how and why tends to backfire. It also allows adults to tout their commitment to youth voice without investing in it.

This is exactly the dynamic that Josefina faced at her school. I met her a few years ago at a youth development conference. She offered a scathing summary of her experience on a school cell phone policy committee. She shared, "They said they wanted student voice at my school, but it felt like they just wanted student attendance at their meetings."

When I asked her what that meant, she said, "They invited me to participate, and then they didn't want to hear what I had to say. One of the things that I felt strongly about was that our school's cell phone policy wasn't being enforced evenly across the student body. My White friends often just got told to put their phones away, while my Black friends had their phones confiscated or were disciplined in other ways. I like my teachers and I'm sure it's not intentional, but it still feels messed up."

"Sounds like you didn't get the response from adults at your school you deserved or expected," I said.

"Not at all. They did not want to hear it. I didn't expect them to act immediately on my input, but I did expect to be respected. If they didn't want to hear our thoughts, they should've just said so from the beginning," she concluded.

Giving young people a voice requires more than just inviting teens to attend meetings. It means centering their experiences and perspectives in decision-making—even when those perspectives challenge "the way we do things." When it comes to technology and adolescent mental health, there are a lot of adults talking about the issues, but not nearly enough opportunities for kids to have a voice in the policies, products, and solutions created for them. A survey by Dosomething.org found that "71 percent of young people look to their peers for tips and tricks to navigate the digital landscape, yet young people rarely have a seat at the table when designing new solutions."[11]

Community leaders and researchers are taking these lessons to heart. For example, the Chicago-based foundation Susan Crown Exchange launched the Youth Voice in the Digital Age Challenge to bring together organizations that support youth leadership. Supported by these organizations, young people have created a range of projects, from antibullying PSAs to digital media arts programming to text messaging challenges designed to inspire better conversations about tech between parents and their kids.[12] Harvard School of Education's Center for Digital Thriving explicitly takes inspiration from the disability rights movement, which declared, "Nothing about us without us."[13] The Center partners with young people to codesign accessible resources for teens on digital thriving. Using research and existing evidence as a starting place, it engages young people in prototyping solutions, tinkering with versions, creating a product, and gathering input on the product from stakeholders such as educators, parents, and psychologists. Youth-centric organizations such as #HalftheStory are not only creating space for authentic storytelling and programming related to mental health and digital well-being but also advocating for policy that prioritizes a safer and healthier internet.[14] The result of these efforts and others like them is a set of resources that young people are far more likely to use and benefit from than products made by tech companies for the average adult user or by well-meaning adults who haven't engaged a diverse group of young people in the process.

IN ACTION: YOUTH VOICE

Consider asking your teen if they have opportunities to contribute at school, after school, in online communities, at work, or in volunteer or activism settings. Find your own language to ask these questions:

- "Do you feel that your thoughts, opinions, and skills are valued there? What does that look like?"

- "Do you feel that other kids' thoughts, opinions, and skills are valued there? What does that look like?"

- "Do you ever get to play a role in decision-making or in creating or upholding community guidelines?"

- "If you have an idea for how to improve things or feedback about your experience, what do you do?"

- "Do you feel welcome there? Do you think others feel welcome there?"

- "If you have a goal or project, are there opportunities to work with others to make it happen?"

Contributing at Home: Co-creating Media Agreements

Not every teen is going to serve on a youth advisory panel for the Harvard School of Education. But opportunities exist in every space that includes adolescents—online communities, sports teams, arts programming, at school, after school, at job sites—for kids to have a voice in the decisions that affect them. And contributing isn't something that happens only outside the home. Family decision-making is an important place for contribution too. Family interactions are the first places where kids start to answer the questions "How can I contribute?" and "Does anyone care about what I have to say?"

Chapter 1 of this book explores the benefits of shifting from control-based screen time strategies to connection-based strategies. Connection-based strategies give kids opportunities to share their experiences, voice dissent, and contribute to media rule-making. The more often we parents can create a sense of teamwork related to digital challenges, the more likely it is that our kids will get into the driver's seat of their digital lives. Family decision-making doesn't put teens entirely in charge of the rules. Teens rely on us to set clear and consistent boundaries. But it does mean that we center kids' ideas, feelings, and perspectives in the process. We can communicate, "It's my job as your parent to help you take care of your safety. That's why we have these boundaries. It's also my job as your parent to learn from you, listen to you, and figure things out together."

IN ACTION: CO-CREATING FAMILY MEDIA AGREEMENTS

Chapter 5 helps you identify the media boundaries that matter most to you right now. These might be your nonnegotiables. Co-creating a family media agreement allows you to brainstorm additional ideas together related to everyone's media habits (including those of adults). This does not have to be a formal process. Visit the American Academy of Pediatrics website for an extensive Family Media Plan template. Otherwise, consider creating a flexible document that includes the following information:

- We use [device/game/platform] because: [positive reasons for tech use].
- We will stay safer by: [expectations related to monitoring, downloading apps, photos, and texts].
- This is what we care about most in how we treat other people online: [priorities and values regarding interactions with others].
- We will stay balanced by: [limits on spaces or times of day when tech use is okay].
- When we hit challenges or conflict, we will: [plan for working through challenges and resolving conflicts].

IN ACTION: ADDRESS DIGITAL CHALLENGES TOGETHER

A family media agreement will not prevent all arguments or tech-related challenges. Instead of responding to conflicts or challenges with new rules or escalating consequences, try addressing challenges together as they arise by inviting, listening, problem-solving, and checking in:

Invite: When things are calm and you aren't in active conflict, start a conversation by saying, "I've noticed that . . . " For example: "I've noticed that you are grabbing the tablet more often to look things up and then staying on longer than you probably mean to."

Listen: Share your perspective. Invite your kid to share theirs. For example: "This means I end up nagging you to get off the tablet more often. It doesn't feel good to me, and I'm guessing it doesn't feel good to you. Have you noticed this? How is it for you?"

Problem-solve: Work together to find a solution by asking, "How can we try this differently? What can we each agree to?" For example: "Okay, I'll agree to be a little more flexible before dinner. You will agree to try to keep your searches more focused. Then after dinner we will just put the tablet away, so it isn't tempting."

Check in: Make a plan to check in and talk about how things are going. For example: "Let's try this for a few days and check in over the weekend."

Creating space for youth voice in family decision-making is not always going to be pretty. Adolescents are unlikely to say, "Thank you so much for this collaborative process!" Instead, they might just grumble, say nothing, or protest, "Do we really have to talk about this?" Don't let this stop you from collaborating with your kid. In the long run, engaging your kid in the process will likely have a longer and more powerful impact on their life than any specific part of a family agreement. Remember: the brain gets good at what it does a lot.

The Art of Listening

"Wait," my older kid interrupted me. "Aren't you supposed to be lending me your ears?"

"What?" I responded, annoyed at being interrupted—but also momentarily distracted by the mental image of lending him a set of giant costume ears. By the time I erased this picture, I was ready to dive right back into my list-of-very-important-things-my-kids-must-understand-and-that-I-must-tell-them-right-now. Then I remembered what he was referring to.

The week before, I had presented at a children's mental health conference. The keynote speaker, Dr. Anne Gearity, had said something that I shared with my kids when I got home. Her wise advice went something like this: "Young children often need your words. Older children often need your ears." In other words, young children sometimes need parents to help make sense of their experiences by giving words to describe them. As kids get older, they need parents to listen as they make sense of their experiences themselves.

My irritation at having been interrupted by my kid dissipated when I realized he was right. My impulse to inform, opine, or lecture is strong. After all, I have so much experience and wisdom to impart! I've lived so long! I know so many things! I especially know a lot about all the things that could go wrong.

For us parents, lending teens our ears sometimes requires significant impulse control. This is especially true when kids and teens don't have much to say. That's why we need to practice the art of listening.

IN ACTION: LISTENING TAKES PRACTICE

Listening is more important than talking. Listening shows your kid that you respect them and care about what they have to say.

Instead of: cutting off your teens in the middle of their sentences . . .
Try: using short words or phrases, such as "Ah," to let your teen know you're listening.

Instead of: assuming you know what your kid will say or is trying to say . . .
Try: asking clarifying questions, such as "Can you explain that again? I want to be sure I get what you are saying."

Instead of: thinking about how you're going to respond to your teen while they're talking . . .
Try: listening to understand their perspective and ideas.

Instead of: trying to have the last word or ending the conversation with your thoughts . . .
Try: sitting with what your kid has shared. For example: "Thanks for sharing that. I want to think about it for a little bit, if that's okay with you."

Instead of: assuming you know what is best in every situation . . .
Try: being open to the idea that your kid has important insights, ideas, and contributions to share.

IN ACTION: QUESTIONS THAT HELP YOU LISTEN

It can be helpful to have questions that put you in a listener's frame of mind ready to go:

- "Is there anything else you want or need me to know?"
- "Is there anything you wish I understood better about this?"
- "Is there anything I can do to not make this worse?"
- "Would it help to write it down or send it in a text?"
- "Do you want me to help you think about solutions or just listen?"

IT'S THEIR WORLD

It's Their World—Are We Ready to Partner with Them to Make It Better?

My elementary-age child informed me that "adults don't understand kids' worlds as well as you think you do."

"I think you are probably right," I responded, trying not to laugh at his casual, matter-of-fact manner. "It was a while ago when I was your age. And the world looks a little different now."

"Yes," he replied, pleased that I agreed. "What do you think I am thinking about right now?" he asked, clearly confident that I was about to fail miserably at mind-reading.

"Hmm," I responded. "Are you thinking about what's for lunch today at school?"

"Not at all!" he replied triumphantly. "I am wondering why every week the days are the same and in the same order. I wish every week had different days in a different order. I am also thinking about recess and why we don't have it twice a day."

He went on from there to inform me that he was also thinking about snakes. As the list went on, I was increasingly eager to replace my own mental to-do list with his expansive thoughts about how we measure time, how we spend our days, and which animals we hope to encounter that day.

I have thought about this conversation quite a bit since then. I wasn't entirely convinced that all adults are completely out of touch with the world of kids and teens. But I think there was a lot of wisdom in the second half of my kid's statement: "as well as you think you do."

We adults know a lot about a lot of things. But when we decide that *we already know everything* about teens and tech, we close the door to young people's contributions to our understanding of the situation. Similarly, when we decide that *we know nothing,* we miss out on opportunities to step meaningfully into our kids' lives when they need us most.

Our teenagers' brains are transforming at the same time that their digital worlds are expanding. Parenting adolescents can be scary, isolating, and overwhelming. Growing up can be too. There is no shortage of things to worry about. We are facing daunting and disorienting collective challenges. Trending topics, headlines, clips, and snippets continuously hijack our nervous systems and pull our attention outward.

When I started in this field, I coped by shoving more research into my presentations. When I was wobbly as a young parent, I searched for more rigorous studies. I scoured journals for guidance. I still do. That's a big part of why I wrote this book. Science at its best provides supportive handholds when we've only got a couple of fingers on the wall.

But since I started out in this field and as a parent, I've had the opportunity to be with young people and the teams of adults who care about them in cafeterias, theaters, auditoriums, and media centers across the country. When I have settled my body enough to listen, young people have shifted my understanding, challenged my assumptions, and sparked insights I never would have had on my own. My kids have done the same. They've helped me see that some parts of growing up in a digital world are way harder than I thought—and other parts are way better than I could have imagined.

The complicated research about teens and tech tells the same story that's been true about adolescence since scientists started studying adolescence. It is a story about connection above all else. The adolescent brain and the adult brain have a lot in common. We are all wired for connection, contribution, purpose, and discovery. We just need to open ourselves up to practicing those things together.

When it comes to parenting in the digital age, the summative wisdom is not that different from the advice of the nurse who helped my wife and me out the door with our first newborn. "You have everything you need," she said. "Remember, you are a team." I don't think it is young people's responsibility to solve all the challenges we face related to technology. I just don't think we can do it without them.

D o parents still matter? I used to teach a course on digital media, storytelling, and social change to undergraduate students in Minneapolis. One of our first field experiences every semester was to visit the studio of Minneapolis-based visual artist Ricardo Levins Morales. My students tended to be emerging filmmakers and media makers, so many were surprised that we weren't starting the semester with camera operation or editing techniques. Instead, we always started with story.

Ricardo often greeted my students in his studio by saying, "Welcome to my medicine shop." Every surface of his studio was covered with visual art—vibrant prints of community leaders and connected communities. Ricardo explained that each print he creates is a source of nutrients or antibodies for people who are suffering. Each print reframes or transforms a story that has been inaccurate, incomplete, or harmful.

Stories have always been the primary way that humans pass down culture, values, and identity. Sharing stories is how we communicate who we are and who we want to be. When my kids were young, I loved curling up to read them a good book or sharing well-worn family stories. But narratives are everywhere, and they don't always start with "once upon a time."

We add to the story of humanity when we pick up a camera or post to social media. We absorb stories from news coverage, articles, conversations, policies, video game plots, graphics, memes, advertisements, and on and on. They shape our understanding of the world and each other. They focus our attention and help us make meaning out of our experiences.

Whoever Tells the Stories Defines the Culture

Stories about teens and screens are running at a fever pitch. Woven through them are narratives about risk, adolescence, and parenting. These stories shape the framing of problems and solutions. Kids absorb stories about adolescence that drive whether they see themselves as broken or built for discovery. Parents absorb stories about digital media use that shape whether they see technology as a toxic substance or a powerful tool.

I'm tempted to try to resolve these narrative conflicts and bring this story to a descending or ascending close. For example, I could close with a warning that AI will undoubtedly undermine any sense of digital well-being teens have left. Alternatively, I could close with an optimistic prescription that promises digital success in five simple steps.

But of course, the plot is more complicated than that. Technology will keep changing at a dizzying pace, and there is no single true story about raising thriving kids. Raising healthy and whole humans requires sitting in the tension of an "oscillating narrative"—one that goes up, down, and all around.[1] The oscillating narrative of teens and screens is about both strengths *and* vulnerabilities. It is about both personal experiences *and* policies, systems, and culture. It is about both harm and possibility. *Both. And.*

Embracing this complexity has helped me identify the narratives that sustain families and disrupt those that are inaccurate, incomplete, or harmful. Rather than offer one tidy narrative in this book, I invite you to consider letting go of the narratives of inevitability, shame, one size fits all, and personal solutions to collective problems.

Inevitability

The narrative of inevitability says that teens plus screens equals harm, full stop. But as I've noted throughout this book, the data tell a more complicated and nuanced story. For any individual teen, outcomes are shaped by who they are and what they are doing.

I'm not saying, "See? It's not all bad for all teens!" Nor am I ignoring the real and insidious ways technology contributes to young people's suffering. But the narrative of inevitability can inadvertently make young people more vulnerable to the very harms adults are trying to protect them from.

Some researchers have suggested that it is more helpful to think about digital media use as driving a car rather than as exposure to a harmful toxin.[2] We can and should address road conditions, assess readiness, invest in driver's education, attend to safety standards, and hold poor corporate actors accountable. And just as with driving a car, there are things to learn and be watchful of; parents and teens are not passengers in an inevitable digital car wreck. Young people do better when they step into the driver's seat of their digital lives. They also do better when they know they aren't alone on the road.

Shame

Parents often tell me that they have "lost the battle" with their kids over technology, offering embarrassed explanations for their choices. I am always quick to reassure them that there is no need to be embarrassed. Yet the feeling of constant failure hangs over many conversations about screen time.

I recently talked with Dr. Linda Charmaraman, a scientist and contributing author of the American Psychological Association's Health Advisory on Social Media Use in Adolescence and director of the Youth, Media & Wellbeing Research Lab at Wellesley College. I asked her to share her top concerns related to teens and tech, expecting to hear about issues like sexting, cyberbullying, or rising levels of anxiety. She *is* concerned about those things, but the issue she mentioned first was the corrosive nature of parental shame related to digital media use. She said that parents often "feel that they are failing their kid by not adhering to some kind of unwritten rule that the goal [for screen time] is zero."[3]

Dr. Charmaraman is not alone in her conviction that screen time shame is not helpful for parents or their kids. Drs. Megan Moreno and Jenny Radesky, medical directors of the American Academy of Pediatrics' Center of Excellence on Social Media and Mental Health, published a commentary in which they note that "good decisions that work for diverse families are not made from a place of shame or oversimplification."[4] Shame tends to shut down curiosity, learning, reflection, and growth. These are the exact tools needed for parenting adolescents. We aren't engaged in a battle with our teens that we can win or lose. Rather, we are turning toward our teens to say, "This is hard, isn't it? My job is to hold the boundaries that matter most. We will figure the rest out together."

One Size Fits All

Just like apps designed for the average user, screen time advice that is designed to be universal is likely to fall short in meeting everyone's needs. Adolescence includes common developmental tasks. Understanding these tasks can help us parents meet our kids' needs and help us feel less alone.

A developmental perspective also recognizes that variation is the norm. There are many paths to healthy development. What works for one teen may not work as well for another. Every kid has a unique brain and body. Each family has a unique set of values, identities, cultures, priorities, and access to resources and support. While parenting advice and news headlines often make it feel like we are walking along a tightrope over a crevasse, developmental science reminds us that there are lots of ways to get it right as parents. Letting go of the one-size-fits-all narrative allows us to parent the kids that we have, rather than the kids we think we should have.

Personal Solutions to Collective Problems

You're not alone if you feel overwhelmed by the sheer number of parental controls, platforms, and settings that exist. Unfortunately, the current corporate and policy landscapes place nearly all the burden on caregivers and teens to find or create spaces of connection, purpose, and belonging *despite* platform design. This is unfair, and it amplifies risk inequities. Research evidence shows clearly that manipulative design features are at odds with kids' developmental needs. The data that companies collect on adolescents drive algorithms that put kids directly in harm's way.

When we focus solely on parental controls and personal habits, we miss the opportunity to center young people's voices and ideas in conversations about the policies, laws, and investments that shape their digital lives. Let's let go of the idea that teens and parents just need to do better on their own to navigate digital spaces that weren't designed with their needs in mind. Instead, let's tell a story that prioritizes collective solutions and good policy, youth-centered digital design, and broad supports for adolescent mental health. Tech companies can no longer ignore the specific needs and vulnerabilities of their young users or outsource all responsibility to parents.

It's Their World

I vividly remember standing at my kitchen counter in the early months of pandemic lockdowns, trying to get some work done on my computer. My phone buzzed constantly with notifications from school, work, and friends. Next to me, my younger child diligently swiped his little fingers across the screen of his school-issued iPad, even though he couldn't yet read the text on it. Behind me, my niece and older child were hunched over their Chromebooks, hoodies up and headphones on. Everywhere I looked, there was a screen.

This memory helps explain my daydreams at the time about what the "end" of the pandemic might look like. I imagined taking a measured approach: walking around my home, unplugging all the devices one by one. I would change my Zoom name to "Be Back Never" and conveniently forget the kids' passwords to Google Classroom. Then I would take my kids deep into the forest to start a new tech-free life.

These fantasies were probably a reaction to the intense digital overload we were all experiencing. Eventually, though, my family had to make real preparations to return to school and life in person. Having thought a great deal about what *I* wanted out of the transition, I was curious about my kids' perspectives. So, I asked them: "What do you hope we keep doing? What do you want to change?"

I expected that they would prefer to continue scrolling through videos uninterrupted but also be excited to see friends in person again. But my younger kid had something else to say. He responded immediately and without hesitation: "Don't stop coming to my worlds."

This might sound like an odd choice of words, but I knew exactly what he meant. He was referring to the adventures we had enjoyed together in Minecraft, an online sandbox game that allows users to create, build, and explore worlds together. He wasn't asking me to play because I was good at it. My skills were comical at best. But during those months at home, I'd had a front row seat to my kid's digital life. It came with immense challenges. But I was also more likely to join both of my kids *where they were*. My younger child was old enough to put words to these shared experiences and young enough to admit that they mattered.

Now that my kids are older, I don't get direct invitations into their digital worlds as often. But I know that doesn't mean that they want me to stay out of the spaces that matter to them—online and offline. I still dream of retreating into the forest with my family, and I take this impulse seriously. It reminds me to prioritize ample time and space where our devices don't claw for our attention. *And* my son's request—"Don't stop coming to my worlds"—serves as a powerful, evidence-based guide for parenting teens in the digital age.

Your teen doesn't need you to take this invitation too literally. It's not about jumping into every platform or becoming their online best friend. Instead, your teen needs you to embrace the spirit of the invitation—to stay engaged with their worlds, to remain curious, and to keep showing up as they grow, grow, grow.

We Are Growing Too

"Whoa! Back to back!" my mother-in-law said to my middle schooler after a few months between visits. In a well-worn routine, they both kicked off their shoes and stood back to back.

"It's not even close," I reported, breaking the news that my kid was now almost an inch taller than her. "It's the end of an era," I said, knowing that within a few short years, both of my kids would be towering over her.

Put a sixth grader and a twelfth grader side-by-side, and you can see the obvious transformations that happen during adolescence. We've spent this entire book exploring the developmental questions that take center stage as adolescents grow:

- "What am I capable of?"

- "Who am I?"

- "Where do I belong?"

- "How can I contribute?"

Our task as parents is to give our kids the space, skills, and support to explore these questions in healthy ways—online and offline.

It's tempting to see ourselves as spectators to our kids' metamorphoses. After all, our height remains the same. The reality, however, is that parenthood transforms us as well. During our kids' adolescence, we ask our own developmental questions, such as "How do I share power?" and "How do I handle rejection?" Our adult brains may have made it through the major construction zones of childhood and adolescence, but we are still learning and changing. We grow new neurons throughout our lifetime.

This process can be painful, isolating, and overwhelming—especially when our kids are pulling away or turning toward their friends and phones. One of the more vulnerable questions I hear from parents during this stage is "Do

I still matter?" During adolescence, many of us feel like our influence shrinks compared to that of friends, videos, chatbots, creators, influencers, and tech companies. There are times when we don't just *imagine* that our opinions don't matter. Our kids tell us as much.

But once again, research offers some helpful beams of light in the dark. It shows that parents, families, and other caring adults still matter a lot to young people.[5] Whether in risk-taking or decision-making, the data are clear that adult influence remains strong[6]—if we are willing to grow alongside our kids.

Adolescents need us to loosen without letting go. They need us to give them space to explore new terrain and discover who they are and what they can contribute to the world. They need us to move from control to connection.

We can't expect our teens to tell us, "Keep coming to my worlds" and "Yes, you matter." Parenting teenagers can be a delayed-gratification activity. We experience the reward when our kids-turned-adults look back on their adolescence and say, "I couldn't articulate it at the time, but it really mattered to me that you . . .

> . . . played video games with me."
>
> . . . held purposeful boundaries."
>
> . . . encouraged me to create and code."
>
> . . . didn't ignore or try to fix my big feelings."
>
> . . . expressed unconditional positive regard."
>
> . . . encouraged me to explore and roam."
>
> . . . helped me learn from trial and error."
>
> . . . supported me through mistakes."
>
> . . . talked to me about digital dilemmas."
>
> . . . apologized for mistakes and repaired harm."
>
> . . . maintained rituals and traditions."
>
> . . . watched my favorite videos."
>
> . . . advocated for a safer and healthier internet."
>
> . . . asked questions and listened to me."
>
> . . . grew alongside me."
>
> . . . were on my team."

It mattered. All of it.

◼ ◼ ◼

Acknowledgments

This book has been living for more than a decade in my head, on the stage, in short-form writing, and in my conversations with preteens, teens, and their adults. My first thank-you goes to the many young people, educators, school administrators, mental health professionals, and caregivers who have trusted me with personal stories, questions, worries, and reflections: I have learned more from you than any other source.

I am indebted to the many researchers who bring their giant brains and hearts to this field. Your scientific integrity, connection to youth, and commitment to equity and impact have changed so many lives. Including my own.

Thank you to the web of supporters who made this project possible. Thank you to Diver Van Avery, my friend, early reader, and creative collaborator, for pushing me to believe that the book I was writing in my head belonged on the page. To my writing advocates Craig Martin, Juliet Patterson, Miré Regulus, and Sally Zimney and the LAB crew. To my acquisitions editor, Tom Rademacher, who invited a proposal and championed this project every step of the way. Thank you to my brilliant editor, Christine Zuchora-Walske, for the care, collaboration, and expertise you brought to every single page. I feel so lucky to have worked with you. I am immensely grateful to the entire team at Free Spirit Publishing for enhancing this book at every stage. Special thanks to Colleen Pidel for bringing the inviting and vibrant cover design to life.

Huge gratitude to my parents, Monica and David Walsh, for walking alongside me with unconditional love throughout my own adolescence. I am aware of how special it is that we keep choosing to walk with each other in adulthood. Your legacy, generosity, and curiosity are at the heart of this work. You are at the heart of me.

We thrive rooted in relationships. My life is buoyed by the support of beloved grandparents, Jean and Dan Fritz, Cathy Seward, and Tom Peichel, along with my siblings, Dan, Annie, Brian, Rocío, Amy, and Nate. Thank you to the super cousins—Ellis, Luci, Miles, Fiona, Emmett, Graham, and Lupita—whose energy and love for each other are the best fuel for life. To Gretchen Hansen: thank you for being a source of belonging at every stage of our development since show-and-tell in kindergarten. Let's grow old together. To my village of beloved friends and chosen family: I am beyond grateful we are raising community, our kids, and each other. We are better together.

To Miles and Emmett: thank you for holding up mirrors, being my taproots, cheering me on, and being my favorite humans to hang out with. It's your world—and I love you to the end of the earth and back again.

This book would not exist without the love and support of my wife, Katie Fritz. Katie, you are a steady presence in the storm, a prairie woman who juggles our life and home when I am in the writing cave, and someone who models what it looks like to grow alongside kids. Your professional expertise, insights, and deep respect for adolescents are on every single page of this book.

Recommended Resources

BOOKS

Teens and Tech

Behind Their Screens: What Teens Are Facing (and Adults Are Missing) by Emily Weinstein and Carrie James
    This book provides a nuanced exploration of digital age challenges by combining the latest research with rich and instructive insights from teens themselves.

Bullying and Cyberbullying: What Every Educator and Parent Needs to Know by Elizabeth Kandel Englander
    This extensive guide examines the complex issue of bullying in both traditional and digital contexts and delivers strategies and tools to help create safer environments for kids.

Growing Up in Public: Coming of Age in a Digital World by Devorah Heitner
    In an age where teens' lives are often shared and compared, this book helps parents navigate the complexities of digital issues such as boundaries, identity, privacy, and reputation.

Hanging Out, Messing Around, and Geeking Out: Kids Living and Learning with New Media (Tenth Anniversary Edition) by Mizuko Ito, Sonja Baumer, Matteo Bittanti, danah boyd, Rachel Cody, Becky Herr-Stephenson, Heather A. Horst, Patricia G. Lange, Dilan Mahendran, Katynka Z. Martinez, C. J. Pascoe, Dan Perkel, Laura Robinson, Christo Sims, and Lisa Tripp
    This research-driven book offers compelling case studies that showcase young people's everyday uses of entertainment media and challenges the notion that screen time is inherently harmful.

Kids Across the Spectrums: Growing Up Autistic in the Digital Age by Meryl Alper
    This book explores the media experiences of children on the autism spectrum and offers practical suggestions for parents and educators to better support neurodivergent kids online.

The Mediatrician's Guide: A Joyful Approach to Raising Healthy, Smart, Kind Kids in a Screen-Saturated World by Dr. Michael Rich
    With a blend of research, clinical expertise, and compassionate advice, this book helps families create a balanced media plan from early childhood through adolescence.

Parenting for a Digital Future: How Hopes and Fears about Technology Shape Children's Lives by Sonia Livingstone and Alicia Blum-Ross
    This book challenges the idea that there are one-size-fits-all solutions to screen time and situates parenting decisions about technology in context, personal trade-offs, and values.

Technology's Child: Digital Media's Role in the Ages and Stages of Growing Up by Katie Davis
    This book reminds parents that "good enough" digital parenting is just what kids need. It describes how digital media affects children's development at various stages of growth, from infancy to adolescence.

Adolescence

10 to 25: The Science of Motivating Young People by David Yeager
    This book explores the science behind why traditional approaches often fail to inspire young people and provides actionable strategies for tapping into the power of the adolescent brain to ignite motivation and engagement.

The Addiction Inoculation: Raising Healthy Kids in a Culture of Dependence by Jessica Lahey
    Parents and educators who want to identify the root causes of substance abuse and learn practical strategies for prevention from early childhood through adolescence will find a compassionate roadmap in this book.

The Breakthrough Years: A New Scientific Framework for Raising Thriving Teens by Ellen Galinsky
    This comprehensive exploration of adolescent development presents the latest scientific research, challenges outdated models and stereotypes, and points to strategies for parents and caring adults.

The Emotional Lives of Teenagers: Raising Connected, Capable, and Compassionate Adolescents by Lisa Damour
    Drawing on scientific research and clinical experience, this book offers insights into the powerful emotions of adolescence and offers parenting strategies for supporting healthy emotional development and mental health.

Fourteen Talks by Age Fourteen: The Essential Conversations You Need to Have with Your Kids Before They Start High School by Michelle Icard
    A guide for parents that outlines crucial conversations to have with kids in early adolescence, covering topics such as technology use, friendship dynamics, and decision-making skills.

How to Raise an Adult: Break Free of the Overparenting Trap and Prepare Your Kid for Success by Julie Lythcott-Haims
    This book encourages parents to step back and allow their children to learn from mistakes, emphasizing the importance of teaching life skills and resilience.

The Mindful Self-Compassion Workbook: A Proven Way to Accept Yourself, Build Inner Strength, and Thrive by Kristin Neff and Christopher Germer
    This rich resource provides practices, exercises, guided meditations, and prompts to help you cultivate self-compassion in your daily life.

Social Justice Parenting: How to Raise Compassionate, Anti-Racist, Justice-Minded Kids by Tracy Baxley
    This thoughtful and practical guide offers advice for raising compassionate and socially conscious children who have healthy self-image and care for others.

This Is So Awkward: Modern Puberty Explained by Cara Natterson and Vanessa Kroll Bennett
    This relatable guide addresses the uncomfortable yet essential topic of puberty for preteens and their parents.

ORGANIZATIONS AND WEBSITES

Adolescence

Center for Parent and Teen Communication
parentandteen.com
    Find articles, tips, and strategies focused on fostering healthy communication and relationships between parents and adolescents.

Healthy Native Youth
healthynativeyouth.org
    This site hosts culturally relevant resources and tools to promote healthy relationships, emotional well-being, and positive decision-making among Native youth.

Inside Out 2
movies.disney.com/inside-out-2
    This sequel to the popular film *Inside Out* tackles the science of teenage emotions as the main character, Riley, enters puberty.

RESilience: Uplifting Youth Through Healthy Communication About Race
apa.org/res
    This initiative by the American Psychological Association focuses on helping children develop healthy racial identities and build skills for coping with and navigating racism.

Spark & Stitch Institute
sparkandstitchinstitute.com
    Cofounded by Erin Walsh and Dr. David Walsh, Spark & Stitch uses science to spark understanding and stitches science to practical strategies for raising connected and courageous kids in the digital age.

This Teenage Life
thisteenagelife.org
    This podcast and online platform offers a place where teens share their experiences and perspectives on sensitive topics, including stories about tech and digital well-being.

UCLA Center for the Developing Adolescent
developingadolescent.semel.ucla.edu
    The Center conducts research on adolescent development and offers resources aimed at improving the well-being of young people through evidence-based practices.

Teens and Tech

#HalftheStory
halfthestoryproject.com
>This global movement and nonprofit empowers young people to share their real experiences with social media and promotes digital well-being and positive mental health.

Center for Digital Thriving
digitalthriving.gse.harvard.edu
>This research and innovation center at Harvard Graduate School of Education creates content and research-based resources to help young people thrive in a tech-filled world.

Center for Humane Technology
humanetech.com
>This advocacy and education nonprofit aims to change the digital landscape in ways that prioritize people's well-being and strengthen democracy.

Center of Excellence on Social Media and Youth Mental Health
aap.org/socialmedia
>The Center of Excellence of the American Academy of Pediatrics provides evidence-based resources and guidance to support the mental health of children and teens as they navigate social media.

Children and Screens: Institute of Digital Media and Child Development
childrenandscreens.org
>This organization provides scientific information and expert advice on the impact of digital media on children's development and well-being.

The Connected Wellbeing Initiative
connectedwellbeing.org
>This initiative focuses on fostering digital well-being in ways that are youth centered, socially connected, and strength based.

Design It For Us
designitforus.org
>This youth-led national coalition advocates for safer online platforms and social media.

Digital Parenthood
aura.com/digital-parenthood
>This is a virtual parenting support group where parents can ask questions about tech-related challenges, get access to expert insights, and connect with other caregivers.

Digital Wellness Lab
digitalwellnesslab.org
>Based in Boston Children's Hospital and Harvard Medical School, this nonprofit center shares science and promotes positive digital media experiences for infants, children, and teens.

LiveMore ScreenLess
livemorescreenless.org
>This organization is dedicated to promoting digital well-being through meaningful partnerships with youth and educators.

Spark & Stitch Institute
sparkandstitchinstitute.com
>Cofounded by Erin Walsh and Dr. David Walsh, Spark & Stitch uses science to spark understanding and stitches science to practical strategies for raising connected and courageous kids in the digital age.

Techno Sapiens
technosapiens.substack.com
>Leading researcher on tech and teens Dr. Jacqueline Nesi shares the latest research on pscychology, technology, and parenting in easy-to-understand language.

Youth, Media, & Wellbeing Research Lab
wcwonline.org/Youth-Media-Wellbeing-Research-Lab/youth-media-wellbeing-research-lab
>This research lab at Wellesley Centers for Women studies issues related to youth, media, and well-being and facilitates digital well-being summer workshops open to teens across the country.

Mental Health

988 Suicide & Crisis Lifeline
988lifeline.org
>This crisis line provides free, confidential support and crisis intervention services for individuals experiencing emotional distress or thoughts of suicide, via call, text, or chat.

The AAKOMA Project
aakomaproject.org
>Dedicated to positively impacting the mental health of youth and young adults of color, the AAKOMA Project provides

resources to young people themselves, engaging families and communities, and changing systems.

Child Mind Institute
childmind.org
This institute offers clinical care, research, and resources to support children and families struggling with mental health and learning disorders.

Cyberbullying Research Center
cyberbullying.org
This center offers research, resources, and strategies for understanding and preventing cyberbullying and online harassment.

Effective Child Therapy
effectivechildtherapy.org
A resource by the Society of Clinical Child and Adolescent Psychology, this site provides evidence-based information on mental health treatments for kids and teens.

The Jed Foundation
jedfoundation.org
JED is committed to protecting emotional health and preventing suicide for teens and young adults by providing resources to individuals, schools, and communities.

National Alliance on Mental Illness
nami.org
NAMI is dedicated to improving the lives of people affected by mental illness through advocacy, education, support, and public awareness.

The Trevor Project
thetrevorproject.org
This nonprofit provides crisis intervention and suicide prevention services to LGBTQ+ youth, offering support through a 24/7 helpline, online chat, and educational resources.

Cyberbullying and Online Cruelty

Cyberbullying Research Center
cyberbullying.org
This center provides research, resources, and strategies to understand, prevent, and address cyberbullying among young people.

Family Online Safety Institute
fosi.org
The institute offers tools, resources, and advocacy to promote safe and responsible

technology use by families, emphasizing digital citizenship and online well-being.

Project Zero: Digital Dilemmas
pz.harvard.edu/projects/digital-dilemmas
An effort by Harvard's Project Zero, Digital Dilemmas explores ethical issues in digital life and offers resources for educators and students to reflect on and navigate the complexities of online interactions.

Project Zero: The Good Play Project
pz.harvard.edu/projects/
the-good-play-project
A program of Harvard's Project Zero, the Good Play Project focuses on understanding how young people engage with digital media and fostering ethical online behavior and citizenship.

Raising Good Gamers
raisinggoodgamers.com
Dedicated to fostering positive and inclusive gaming communities for young people, this organization promotes respectful communication, digital literacy, and ethical gameplay.

ReThink Citizens
rethinkcitizens.org
This group empowers young people to recognize and prevent online hate and cyberbullying through innovative digital tools and educational programs that promote positive online behavior.

StopBullying.gov
Various government agencies offer information on bullying prevention and response for kids, parents, and schools.

Sexual Health

Amaze
amaze.org
Amaze provides age-appropriate animated videos and resources to help young people understand sexual health, relationships, and puberty in a direct, inclusive, and engaging way. The site includes resources for parents on how to talk to kids about online porn.

Sex, Etc.
sexetc.org
This sexual health education website is created by teens for teens, offering reliable information on sex, relationships, and reproductive health.

Love Is Respect
loveisrespect.org
> A project of the National Domestic
> Violence Hotline, Love Is Respect focuses
> specifically on teen dating violence. It
> offers resources on digital abuse and
> how tech can be used in unhealthy
> relationships.

Teen Health Hub
doh.wa.gov/teenhealthhub
> This website from the Washington State
> Department of Health offers comprehen-
> sive health resources and information
> for teens on topics such as mental health,
> sexual health, and substance use.

Take It Down
takeitdown.ncmec.org
> This service helps remove online nude,
> partially nude, or sexually explicit photos
> and videos taken before people are eigh-
> teen years old.

Ratings, Reviews, and Monitoring

Common Sense Latino
commonsensemedia.org/es/
celebra-cultura-latina
> This site provides culturally relevant media
> reviews, advice, and resources in Spanish.

Common Sense Media
commonsensemedia.org
> Common Sense Media offers expert
> reviews, ratings, and resources to help
> families and educators navigate media,
> technology, and entertainment, ensuring
> safe and healthy digital experiences for
> children.

Family Media Plan
healthychildren.org/English/fmp/Pages/
MediaPlan.aspx
> This interactive tool from
> the American Academy of Pediatrics helps
> families create personalized plans for
> balanced, healthy media use.

Notes

Introduction

1. Lisa Damour, *Under Pressure: Confronting the Epidemic of Stress and Anxiety in Girls* (Ballantine Books, 2019), 7.

2. David Yeager, *10 to 25: The Science of Motivating Young People: A Groundbreaking Approach to Leading the Next Generation—And Making Your Own Life Easier* (Avid Reader Press, 2024).

3. Victoria Rideout, Alanna Peebles, Subreet Mann, and Michael B. Robb, "The Common Sense Census: Media Use by Tweens and Teens" (Common Sense, 2022), commonsensemedia.org/sites/default/files/research/report/8-18-census-integrated-report-final-web_0.pdf.

4. Jacqueline Nesi, Eva H. Telzer, and Mitchell J. Prinstein, eds., *Handbook of Adolescent Digital Media Use and Mental Health* (Cambridge University Press, 2022), doi.org/10.1017/9781108976237.

5. Linda Charmaraman, J. Maya Hernandez, and Rachel Hodes, "Marginalized and Understudied Populations Using Digital Media," in *Handbook of Adolescent Digital Media Use and Mental Health*, ed. Eva H. Telzer, Jacqueline Nesi, and Mitchell J. Prinstein (Cambridge University Press, 2022), 188–214, doi.org/10.1017/9781108976237.011.

Chapter 1: Built for Discovery

1. Ellen Galinsky, *The Breakthrough Years: A New Scientific Framework for Raising Thriving Teens* (Flatiron Books, 2024).

2. Lisa Damour, *The Emotional Lives of Teenagers: Raising Connected, Capable, and Compassionate Adolescents* (Ballantine Books, 2023), 77.

3. Angela Prencipe, Amanda Kesek, Julia Cohen, Connie Lamm, Marc D. Lewis, and Philip David Zelazo, "Development of Hot and Cool Executive Function during the Transition to Adolescence," *Journal of Experimental Child Psychology* 108, no. 3 (March 2011): 621–637, doi.org/10.1016/j.jecp.2010.09.008.

4. Galinsky, *The Breakthrough Years*, 24.

5. Victoria Rideout, Alanna Peebles, Subreet Mann, and Michael B. Robb, "Common Sense Census: Media Use by Tweens and Teens" (Common Sense, 2022), commonsensemedia.org/sites/default/files/research/report/8-18-census-integrated-report-final-web_0.pdf.

6. Mary Madden, Amanda Lenhart, Sandra Cortesi, Urs Gasser, Maeve Duggan, Aaron Smith, and Meredith Beaton, "Teens, Social Media, and Privacy," *Pew Research Center: Internet, Science & Tech* (blog), 2013, pewresearch.org/internet/2013/05/21/teens-social-media-and-privacy.

7. UCLA Center for the Developing Adolescent, "The Science Behind Adolescent Risk Taking and Exploration," Accessed on November 4, 2024, developingadolescent.semel.ucla.edu/topics/item/science-of-risk-taking.

8. Agnieszka Tymula et al., "Adolescents' Risk-Taking Behavior Is Driven by Tolerance to Ambiguity," *Proceedings of the National Academy of Sciences* 109, no. 42 (October 16, 2012): 17135–17140, doi.org/10.1073/pnas.1207144109.

9. Laurence Steinberg, *Age of Opportunity: Lessons from the New Science of Adolescence*, Reprint edition (Harper Paperbacks, 2015).

10. The American Academy of Pediatrics, "Where We Stand: Screen Time," HealthyChildren.org, December 13, 2024, healthychildren.org/English/family-life/Media/Pages/Where-We-Stand-TV-Viewing-Time.aspx.

11. Sonia Livingstone and Ellen J. Helsper, "Parental Mediation of Children's Internet Use," *Journal of Broadcasting & Electronic Media* 52, no. 4 (November 7, 2008): 581–599, doi.org/10.1080/08838150802437396, 581.

12. David Hill et al., "Media and Young Minds," *Pediatrics* 138, no. 5 (November 1, 2016): e20162591, doi.org/10.1542/peds.2016-2591.

13. Patti M. Valkenburg, Adrian Meier, and Ine Beyens, "Social Media Use and Its Impact on Adolescent Mental Health: An Umbrella Review of the Evidence," *Current Opinion in Psychology* 44 (April 1, 2022): 58–68, doi.org/10.1016/j.copsyc.2021.08.017.

14. Common Sense Media, "A Double-Edged Sword: How Diverse Communities of Young People Think About the Multifaceted Relationship Between Social Media and Mental Health" (Common Sense Media and Hope Lab, 2024), commonsensemedia.org/sites/default/files/research/report/2024-double-edged-sword-hopelab-report_final-release-for-web-v2.pdf.

15. Liang Chen and Jingyuan Shi, "Reducing Harm From Media: A Meta-Analysis of Parental Mediation," *Journalism & Mass Communication Quarterly* 96, no. 1 (March 1, 2019): 173–193, doi.org/10.1177/1077699018754908.

16. Noah T. Kreski et al., "Experiences of Online Bullying and Offline Violence-Related Behaviors Among a Nationally Representative Sample of US Adolescents, 2011 to 2019," *Journal of School Health* 92, no. 4 (2022): 376–386, doi.org/10.1111/josh.13144.

17. Megan A. Moreno, Kole Binger, Qianqian Zhao, Jens Eickhoff, Matt Minich, and Yalda Tehranian Uhls, "Digital Technology and Media Use by Adolescents: Latent Class Analysis," *JMIR Pediatrics and Parenting* 5, no. 2 (May 4, 2022): e35540, doi.org/10.2196/35540.

18. Jason M. Nagata et al., "Associations between Media Parenting Practices and Early Adolescent Screen Use," *Pediatric Research*, June 5, 2024: 1–8, doi.org/10.1038/s41390-024-03243-y.

19. Chen and Shi, "Reducing Harm From Media."

Chapter 2: Primed for Rewards

1. Adriana Galván, "Adolescent Development of the Reward System," *Frontiers in Human Neuroscience* 4 (February 12, 2010): 6, doi.org/10.3389/neuro.09.006.2010.

2. Adriana Galván, *The Neuroscience of Adolescence* (Cambridge University Press, 2017).

3. Agnieszka Tymula et al., "Adolescents' Risk-Taking Behavior Is Driven by Tolerance to Ambiguity," *Proceedings of the National Academy of Sciences* 109, no. 42 (October 16, 2012): 17135–17140, https://doi.org/10.1073/pnas.1207144109.

4. Anna Vannucci, Lior A. Rosenberg Belmaker, Amy K. Roy, Lital Ruderman, Kirk Manson, Paul W. Glimcher, and Ifat Levy, "Social Media Use and Risky Behaviors in Adolescents: A Meta-Analysis," *Journal of Adolescence* 79, no. 1 (2020): 258–274, doi.org/10.1016/j.adolescence.2020.01.014.

5. American Psychological Association, "Potential Risks of Content, Features, and Functions: The Science of How Social Media Affects Youth," accessed November 4, 2024, (American Psychological Association, 2024), apa.org/topics/social-media-internet/youth-social-media-2024.

6. Mimi Ito and Katie Salen, "Supporting Youth Wellbeing Through Equitable and Relatable Online Connection," *Connected Learning Lab* (blog), March 1, 2021, connectedlearning.uci.edu/blog/supporting-youth-wellbeing-through-equitable-and-relatable-online-connection.

7. Mizuko Ito, Candice Odgers, and Stephen Schueller, *Social Media and Youth Wellbeing: What We Know and Where We Could Go* (Connected Learning Alliance, June 2020), clalliance.org/publications/social-media-and-youth-wellbeing-what-we-know-and-where-we-could-go.

8. Amanda Lenhart and Kellie Owens, *The Unseen Teen* (Data & Society, May 5, 2021), datasociety.net/library/the-unseen-teen.

9. Jenny Radesky, Heidi M. Weeks, Alexandria Schaller, Michael B. Robb, Supreet Mann, and Amanda Lendart, "Constant Companion: A Week in the Life of a Young Person's Smartphone Use | Common Sense Media" (Common Sense, 2023), commonsensemedia.org/sites/default/files/research/report/2023-cs-smartphone-research-report_final-for-web.pdf.

10. Radesky et al., "Constant Companion."

11. Monica Anderson, Michelle Faverio, and Jeffrey Gottfried, "Teens, Social Media and Technology 2023" (Pew Research Center, 2023), pewresearch.org/internet/2023/12/11/teens-social-media-and-technology-2023.

12. Jacqueline Nesi, Supreet Mann, and Michael B. Robb, "Teens and Mental Health: How Girls Really Feel About Social Media" (Common Sense Media, 2023), commonsensemedia.org/sites/default/files/research/report/how-girls-really-feel-about-social-media-researchreport_web_final_2.pdf.

13. Katie Davis, interview by Erin Walsh, Riverside, March 21, 2024.

14. Katie Davis, *Technology's Child: Digital Media's Role in the Ages and Stages of Growing Up* (The MIT Press, 2023).

15. David Friedman, Robin Goldman, Yaakov Stern, and Truman R. Brown, "The Brain's Orienting Response: An Event-Related Functional Magnetic Resonance Imaging Investigation," *Human Brain Mapping* 30, no. 4 (May 8, 2008): 1144–1154, doi.org/10.1002/hbm.20587.

16. Mary K. Rothbart and Michael I. Posner, "The Developing Brain in a Multitasking World," *Developmental Review* 35 (March 1, 2015): 42–63, doi.org/10.1016/j.dr.2014.12.006.

17. Colin M. Gray, Yubo Kou, Bryan Battles, Joseph Hoggatt, and Austin L. Toombs, "The Dark (Patterns) Side of UX Design," in *Proceedings of the 2018 CHI Conference on Human Factors in Computing Systems* (CHI '18: CHI Conference on Human Factors in Computing Systems, Montreal QC Canada: ACM, 2018), 1–14, doi.org/10.1145/3173574.3174108.

18. Jenny Radesky et al., "Prevalence and Characteristics of Manipulative Design in Mobile Applications Used by Children," *JAMA Network Open* 5, no. 6 (June 17, 2022): e2217641, doi.org/10.1001/jamanetworkopen.2022.17641.

19. Radesky et al., "Constant Companion."

20. National Scientific Council on the Developing Child, "Understanding Motivation: Building the Brain Architecture That Supports Learning, Health, and Community Participation: Working Paper No. 14" (Center on the Developing Child at Harvard University, 2018), developingchild.harvard.edu/resources/understanding-motivation-building-the-brain-architecture-that-supports-learning-health-and-community-participation.

21. Henry H. Wilmer, Lauren E. Sherman, and Jason M. Chein, "Smartphones and Cognition: A Review of Research Exploring the Links between Mobile Technology Habits and Cognitive Functioning," *Frontiers in Psychology* 8 (April 25, 2017): 605, doi.org/10.3389/fpsyg.2017.00605.

22. Bill Thornton, Alyson Faires, Maija Robbins, and Eric Rollins, "The Mere Presence of a Cell Phone May Be Distracting," *Social Psychology* 45, no. 6 (November 2014): 479–488, doi.org/10.1027/1864-9335/a000216.

23. Adam Alter, *Irresistible: The Rise of Addictive Technology and the Business of Keeping Us Hooked* (Penguin Press, 2017).

24. Amanda Raffoul, Zachary J. Ward, Monique Santoso, Jill R. Kavanaugh, and S. Bryn Austin, "Social Media Platforms Generate Billions of Dollars in Revenue from U.S. Youth: Findings from a Simulated Revenue Model," *PLOS ONE* 18, no. 12 (December 27, 2023): e0295337, doi.org/10.1371/journal.pone.0295337.

25. Brian M. Galla, Sophia Choukas-Bradley, Hannah M. Fiore, and Michael V. Esposito, "Values-Alignment Messaging Boosts Adolescents' Motivation to Control Social Media Use," *Child Development* 92, no. 5 (September 2021): 1717–1734, doi.org/10.1111/cdev.13553.

26. Rothbart and Posner, "The Developing Brain in a Multitasking World."

27. Despina Stavrinos, Benjamin McManus, Andrea T. Underhill, and Maria T. Lechtreck, "Impact of Adolescent Media Multitasking on Cognition and Driving Safety," *Human Behavior and Emerging*

Technologies 1, no. 2 (April 2019): 161–168, doi.org/10.1002/hbe2.143.

28. Rothbart and Posner, "The Developing Brain in a Multitasking World."

29. Melina R. Uncapher and Anthony D. Wagner, "Minds and Brains of Media Multitaskers: Current Findings and Future Directions," *Proceedings of the National Academy of Sciences* 115, no. 40 (October 2, 2018): 9889–9896, doi. org/10.1073/pnas.1611612115.

30. Anna Mattson, "Sludge Videos Are Taking Over TikTok—And People's Mind," *Scientific American*, January 10, 2024, scientificamerican.com/article/ sludge-videos-are-taking-over-tiktok-and-peoples-mind1.

31. Victoria Rideout and Michael B. Robb, "Common Sense Census: Media Use by Tweens and Teens, 2019" (Common Sense Media, 2019), commonsensemedia. org/sites/default/files/research/ report/2019-census-8-to-18-full-report-updated.pdf.

32. Richard B. Lopez, Julia M. Salinger, Todd F. Heatherton, and Dylan D. Wagner, "Media Multitasking Is Associated with Altered Processing of Incidental, Irrelevant Cues During Person Perception," *BMC Psychology* 6, no. 1 (October 11, 2018): 44, doi.org/10.1186/ s40359-018-0256-x.

33. Wilmer, Sherman, and Chein, "Smartphones and Cognition."

34. Amishi P. Jha, *Peak Mind: Find Your Focus, Own Your Attention, Invest 12 Minutes a Day* (HarperOne, 2021).

35. Douglas A. Gentile et al., "Internet Gaming Disorder in Children and Adolescents," *Pediatrics* 140, no. Supplement_2 (November 1, 2017): S81–85, doi.org/10.1542/peds.2016-1758H.

36. World Health Organization, "Addictive Behaviours: Gaming Disorder," October 22, 2020, who.int/news-room/questions-and-answers/item/addictive-behaviours-gaming-disorder.

37. Digital Wellness Lab, "Family Guide to Problematic Interactive Media Use (PIMU)," Boston Children's Digital Wellness Lab, May 5, 2022, digitalwellnesslab.org/family-guides/ family-guide-to-problematic-interactive-media-use-pimu.

38. Gentile et al., "Internet Gaming Disorder in Children and Adolescents."

39. Candice Odgers et al., "Engaging, Safe, and Evidence-Based: What Science Tells Us about How to Promote Positive Development and Decrease Risk in Online Spaces," (PsyArXiv, November 30, 2022), doi.org/10.31234/osf.io/rvn8q.

Chapter 3: Sensitive to Stress

1. Common Sense Media, "A Double-Edged Sword: How Diverse Communities of Young People Think About the Multifaceted Relationship Between Social Media and Mental Health" (Common Sense Media and Hope Lab, 2024), commonsensemedia.org/sites/default/ files/research/report/2024-double-edged-sword-hopelab-report_final-release-for-web-v2.pdf.

2. Office of the Surgeon General, "Protecting Youth Mental Health: The U.S. Surgeon General's Advisory" (US Department of Health and Human Services, 2021), pubmed.ncbi.nlm.nih. gov/34982518; American Academy of Pediatrics, "AAP-AACAP-CHA Declaration of a National Emergency in Child and Adolescent Mental Health," 2021, aap.org/en/advocacy/child-and-adolescent-healthy-mental-development/ aap-aacap-cha-declaration-of-a-national-emergency-in-child-and-adolescent-mental-health.

3. Centers for Disease Control and Prevention, "Youth Risk Behavior Survey Data Summary & Trends Report: 2009–2019," 2020, cdc. gov/healthyyouth/data/yrbs/pdf/ YRBSDataSummaryTrendsReport2019-508.pdf.

4. Centers for Disease Control and Prevention, "Youth Risk Behavior Survey Data Summary & Trends Report: 2011–2021," 2023, cdc.gov/healthyyouth/ data/yrbs/pdf/YRBS_Data-Summary-Trends_Report2023_508.pdf.

5. Alfiee Breland Noble and The AAKOMA Project, "State of Mental Health for Youth and Young Adults of Color 2022" (The AAKOMA Project, 2023), aakomaproject.org/somhyoc2022.

6. Richard Weissbourd et al., "Caring for the Caregivers: The Critical Link Between Parent and Teen Mental Health," Making Caring Common Project, Harvard Graduate School of Education, July 11, 2023, mcc.gse.harvard.edu/reports/caring-for-the-caregivers.

7. Sophia Solano, "Parents Are Suffering from Depression and Anxiety as Much as Their Teens," *Washington Post*, July 11, 2023, washingtonpost.com/parenting/2023/07/11/parents-teens-anxiety-depression.

8. Vivek H. Murthy, "Surgeon General: Parents Are at Their Wits' End. We Can Do Better," *The New York Times*, August 28, 2024, nytimes.com/2024/08/28/opinion/surgeon-general-stress-parents.html.

9. Office of the Surgeon General, "Parents Under Pressure: The U.S. Surgeon General's Advisory on the Mental Health & Well-Being of Parents" (US Department of Health and Human Services, 2024), hhs.gov/sites/default/files/parents-under-pressure.pdf.

10. Weissbourd et al., "Caring for the Caregivers."

11. Weissbourd et al., "Caring for the Caregivers."

12. Bruce D. Perry and Maia Szalavitz, *Born for Love: Why Empathy Is Essential—and Endangered* (William Morrow Paperbacks, 2011).

13. National Scientific Council on the Developing Child, "Excessive Stress Disrupts The Architecture of the Growing Brain: Working Paper 3" (Center on the Developing Child at Harvard University, 2014), developingchild.harvard.edu/resources/wp3/.

14. Zhuang Miao, Yan Wang, and Zhongsheng Sun, "The Relationships Between Stress, Mental Disorders, and Epigenetic Regulation of BDNF," *International Journal of Molecular Sciences* 21, no. 4 (February 18, 2020): 1375, doi.org/10.3390/ijms21041375.

15. Devika Bhushan et al., "The Roadmap for Resilience: The California Surgeon General's Report on Adverse Childhood Experiences, Toxic Stress, and Health" (Office of the California Surgeon General, December 9, 2020), osg.ca.gov/2021/09/27/roadmap-for-resilience-california-surgeon-generals-report.

16. Brendesha M. Tynes, Henry A. Willis, Ashley M. Stewart, Matthew W. Hamilton, "Race-Related Traumatic Events Online and Mental Health Among Adolescents of Color," *Journal of Adolescent Health* 65, no. 3 (September 1, 2019): 371–377, doi.org/10.1016/j.jadohealth.2019.03.006.

17. Perry and Szalavitz, *Born for Love*.

18 David S. Yeager et al., "A Synergistic Mindsets Intervention Protects Adolescents from Stress," *Nature* 607, no. 7919 (July 2022): 512–520, doi.org/10.1038/s41586-022-04907-7.

19. Child Mind Institute, "2017 Children's Mental Health Report, Anxiety and Depression in Adolescence," Child Mind Institute, 2017, childmind.org/awareness-campaigns/childrens-mental-health-report/2017-childrens-mental-health-report/anxiety-depression-in-adolescence.

20. Lisa Damour, *The Emotional Lives of Teenagers: Raising Connected, Capable, and Compassionate Adolescents* (Ballantine Books, 2023), 27.

21. Nicole L. Rosen and Stacey Nofziger, "Boys, Bullying, and Gender Roles: How Hegemonic Masculinity Shapes Bullying Behavior," *Gender Issues* 36, no. 3 (September 1, 2019): 295–318, doi.org/10.1007/s12147-018-9226-0.

22. Catharine Evers, Agneta H. Fischer, P. M. Rodriguez Mosquera, Antony S. R. Manstead, "Anger and Social Appraisal: A 'Spicy' Sex Difference?," *Emotion* 5, no. 3 (September 2005): 258–66, doi.org/10.1037/1528-3542.5.3.258.

23. Rebecca Epstein, Jamilia Blake, and Thalia González, "Girlhood Interrupted: The Erasure of Black Girls' Childhood," *SSRN* Scholarly Paper (June 27, 2017), papers.ssrn.com/abstract=3000695.

24. Elizabeth Englander, Interview by Erin Walsh, Riverside, April 10, 2024.

25. Jonathan Haidt, *The Anxious Generation: How the Great Rewiring of Childhood Is Causing an Epidemic of Mental Illness* (Penguin Press, 2024).

26. Patti M. Valkenburg, Adrian Meier, and Ine Beyens, "Social Media Use and Its Impact on Adolescent Mental Health: An Umbrella Review of the Evidence," *Current Opinion in Psychology* 44 (April 1, 2022): 58–68, doi.org/10.1016/j.copsyc.2021.08.017.

27. Valkenburg, Meier, and Beyens, "Social Media Use."

28. Office of the Surgeon General, "Social Media and Youth Mental Health" (US Department of Health and Human Services, 2023); American Psychological Association, "Health Advisory on Social Media Use in Adolescence" (American Psychological Association, 2023), apa.org/topics/social-media-internet/health-advisory-adolescent-social-media-use; National Academies of Sciences, Engineering, and Medicine, *Social Media and Adolescent Health* (The National Academies Press, 2024), doi.org/10.17226/27396.

29. American Psychological Association, "Health Advisory on Social Media Use in Adolescence"; Office of the Surgeon General, "Social Media and Youth Mental Health."

30. Amy Orben, Adrian Meier, Tim Dalgleish, and Sarah-Jayne Blakemore, "Mechanisms Linking Social Media Use to Adolescent Mental Health Vulnerability," *Nature Reviews Psychology*, May 7, 2024, 1–17, doi.org/10.1038/s44159-024-00307-y.

31. Andrew K. Przybylski and Netta Weinstein, "A Large-Scale Test of the Goldilocks Hypothesis: Quantifying the Relations Between Digital-Screen

Use and the Mental Well-Being of Adolescents," *Psychological Science* 28, no. 2 (2017): 204–215, doi.org/10.1177/0956797616678438.

32. Mizuko Ito, Candice Odgers, and Stephen Schueller, "Social Media and Youth Wellbeing: What We Know and Where We Could Go" (Connected Learning Alliance, 2020), clalliance.org/publications/social-media-and-youth-wellbeing-what-we-know-and-where-we-could-go.

33. Jacqueline Nesi, "From the Headlines: Social Media and Kids" (Aura Digital Parenthood Summit, The Times Center, June 4, 2024), digitalparenthood.com/kb/social-media/from-the-headlines-social-media--kids-/59.

34. Ahmed A. Alsunni and Rabia Latif, "Higher Emotional Investment in Social Media Is Related to Anxiety and Depression in University Students," *Journal of Taibah University Medical Sciences* 16, no. 2 (December 19, 2020): 247–252, doi.org/10.1016/j.jtumed.2020.11.004.

35. Amy Orben, Andrew K. Przybylski, Sarah-Jayne Blakemore, and Rogier A. Kievit, "Windows of Developmental Sensitivity to Social Media," *Nature Communications* 13, no. 1 (March 28, 2022): 1649, doi.org/10.1038/s41467-022-29296-3.

36. Linda Charmaraman, J. Maya Hernandez, and Rachel Hodes, "Marginalized and Understudied Populations Using Digital Media," in *Handbook of Adolescent Digital Media Use and Mental Health*, ed. Eva H. Telzer, Jacqueline Nesi, and Mitchell J. Prinstein (Cambridge University Press, 2022), 188–214, doi.org/10.1017/9781108976237.011.

37. Common Sense Media, "A Double-Edged Sword."

38. Steven A. Sumner et al., "Association of Online Risk Factors With Subsequent Youth Suicide-Related Behaviors in the US," *JAMA Network Open* 4, no. 9 (September 20, 2021): e2125860, doi.org/10.1001/jamanetworkopen.2021.25860.

39. Brendesha M. Tynes, Michael T. Giang, David R. Williams, and Geneene N. Thompson, "Online Racial Discrimination and Psychological Adjustment Among Adolescents," *Journal of Adolescent Health* 43, no. 6 (December 1, 2008): 565–569, doi.org/10.1016/j.jadohealth.2008.08.021.

40. Sophia Choukas-Bradley, Savannah R. Roberts, Anne J. Maheux, and Jacqueline Nesi, "The Perfect Storm: A Developmental-Sociocultural Framework for the Role of Social Media in Adolescent Girls' Body Image Concerns and Mental Health," *Clinical Child and Family Psychology Review* 25, no. 4 (December 2022): 681–701, doi.org/10.1007/s10567-022-00404-5.

41. National Alliance on Mental Illness, "Warning Signs and Symptoms," accessed November 5, 2024, nami.org/About-Mental-Illness/Warning-Signs-and-Symptoms.

42. Jennifer M. Whitehill, Libby N. Brockman, and Megan A. Moreno, "'Just Talk to Me': Communicating with College Students about Depression Disclosures on Facebook," *The Journal of Adolescent Health: Official Publication of the Society for Adolescent Medicine* 52, no. 1 (January 2013): 122–127, doi.org/10.1016/j.jadohealth.2012.09.015.

43. T. Dazzi, R. Gribble, S. Wessely, and N. T. Fear, "Does Asking about Suicide and Related Behaviours Induce Suicide Ideation? What Is the Evidence?," *Psychological Medicine* 44 (July 7, 2014): 1–3, doi.org/10.1017/S0033291714001299.

44. Corey H. Basch, Lorie Donelle, Joseph Fera, and Christie Jaime, "Deconstructing TikTok Videos on Mental Health: Cross-Sectional, Descriptive Content Analysis," *JMIR Formative Research* 6, no. 5 (May 19, 2022): e38340, doi.org/10.2196/38340.

45. Common Sense Media and Hopelab, "Getting Help Online: How Young People Find, Evaluate, and Use Mental Health Apps, Online Therapy, and Behavioral Health Information" (Common Sense Media, 2024), commonsensemedia.

org/research/getting-help-online-how-young-people-find-evaluate-and-use-mental-health-apps-online-therapy-and-behavioral.

46. Cody Mello-Klein, "Is TikTok Helping Autistic People Self-Diagnose? New Research Shows Role App Plays in Diagnosis," *Northeastern Global News* (blog), September 1, 2023, news.northeastern.edu/2023/09/01/self-diagnosing-autism-tiktok.

47. Jack Brewster, Lorenzo Arvanitis, Valerie Pavilonis, and Macrina Wang, "Misinformation Monitor: September 2022: Beware the 'New Google:' TikTok's Search Engine Pumps Toxic Misinformation to Its Young Users," *NewsGuard* (blog), September 14, 2022, newsguardtech.com/misinformation-monitor/september-2022.

48. Jacqueline Nesi, "Can TikTok Diagnose Your Anxiety?," *Techno Sapiens*, October 11, 2022, technosapiens.substack.com/p/mentalhealthtiktok.

49. Kristen Harrison, Lia Vallina, Amelia Couture, Halie Wenhold, and Jessica D. Moorman, "Sensory Curation: Theorizing Media Use for Sensory Regulation and Implications for Family Media Conflict," *Media Psychology* 22, no. 4 (July 4, 2019): 653, doi.org/10.1080/15213269.2018.1496024.

50. Emily Weinstein, "Teens, Screens & Wellbeing: Youth in the Digital Age," Panel Discussion, SXSW, Austin, Texas, March 8, 2024, https://schedule.sxsw.com/2024/events/PP145989.

Chapter 4: Separation and Connection

1. Peter Blos, "The Second Individuation Process of Adolescence," *The Psychoanalytic Study of the Child* 22, no. 1 (January 1, 1967): 162–186, tandfonline.com/doi/abs/10.1080/00797308.1967.11822595.

2. Bruce D. Perry and Maia Szalavitz, *Born for Love: Why Empathy Is Essential—and Endangered* (William Morrow Paperbacks, 2011), 16.

3. Julianne Holt-Lunstad, Theodore Robles, and David A. Sbarra, "Advancing Social Connection as a Public Health Priority in the United States," *The American Psychologist* 72, no. 6 (September 2017): 517–530, doi.org/10.1037/amp0000103.

4. Harvard Center on the Developing Child, "Building Adult Capabilities," Center on the Developing Child at Harvard University, March 9, 2016, developingchild.harvard.edu/innovation-application/key-concepts/adult-capabilities.

5. Yang Qu, Andrew J. Fuligni, Adriana Galvan, and Eva H. Telzer, "Buffering Effect of Positive Parent-Child Relationships on Adolescent Risk Taking: A Longitudinal Neuroimaging Investigation," *Developmental Cognitive Neuroscience* 15 (October 2015): 26–34, doi.org/10.1016/j.dcn.2015.08.005.

6. Lisa Delpit, *"Multiplication Is for White People": Raising Expectations for Other People's Children* (The New Press, 2013), 77.

7. Lisa Damour, "Family Relationships," Lisa Damour, PhD, 2024, drlisadamour.com/resources/topic/family-relationships.

8. Lee Rainie and Kathryn Zickuhr, "Americans' Views on Mobile Etiquette," Pew Research Center, August 26, 2015, pewresearch.org/internet/2015/08/26/americans-views-on-mobile-etiquette.

9. Jelena Komanchuk et al., "Impacts of Parental Technoference on Parent-Child Relationships and Child Health and Developmental Outcomes: A Scoping Review," *Cyberpsychology, Behavior and Social Networking* 26, no. 8 (August 2023): 579–603, doi.org/10.1089/cyber.2022.0278.

10. Brandon T. McDaniel and Jenny S. Radesky, "Technoference: Longitudinal Associations between Parent Technology Use, Parenting Stress, and Child Behavior Problems," *Pediatric Research* 84, no. 2 (August 2018): 210–218, doi.org/10.1038/s41390-018-0052-6.

11. Chioma Torres, Jenny Radesky, Kimberley J. Levitt, and Brandon T. McDaniel, "Is It Fair to Simply Tell Parents to Use Their Phones Less? A Qualitative Analysis of Parent Phone Use," *Acta Paediatrica* 110, no. 9 (September 2021): 2594–2596, doi.org/10.1111/apa.15893.

12. Search Institute, "The Rooted in Relationships Model," *Search Institute* (blog), accessed November 5, 2024, searchinstitute.org/resources-hub/the-rooted-in-relationships-model.

13. Search Institute, "Developmental Relationships Framework," *Search Institute* (blog), accessed November 5, 2024, search-institute.org/developmental-relationships/developmental-relationships-framework.

Chapter 5: Independence and Exploration

1. Devorah Heitner, *Growing Up in Public: Coming of Age in a Digital World* (TarcherPerigee, 2023).

2. Brooke Auxier, Monica Anderson, Andrew Perring, and Erica Turner, "Parenting Children in the Age of Screens" Pew Research Center, July 28, 2020, pewresearch.org/internet/2020/07/28/parenting-children-in-the-age-of-screens.

3. Ellen Cantarow, "No Kids," *Village Voice*, January 15, 1985, 10.

4. Peter Gray, David F. Lancy, and David F. Bjorklund, "Decline in Independent Activity as a Cause of Decline in Children's Mental Wellbeing: Summary of the Evidence," *The Journal of Pediatrics* 260 (February 1, 2023): 113352, doi.org/10.1016/j.jpeds.2023.02.004.

5. Julie Lythcott-Haims, *How to Raise an Adult* (St. Martin's Griffin, 2016), 7.

6. Kenneth R. Ginsburg, the Committee on Communications, and the Committee on Psychosocial Aspects of Child and Family Health, "The Importance of Play in Promoting Healthy Child Development and Maintaining Strong Parent-Child Bonds," *Pediatrics* 119, no. 1 (January 1, 2007): 182–191, doi.org/10.1542/peds.2006-2697.

7. Joseph L. Mahoney, Angel L. Harris, and Jacquelynne S. Eccles, "Organized Activity Participation, Positive Youth Development, and the Over-Scheduling Hypothesis," *SRCD Social Policy Report* 20 (December 1, 2006): 1–31, doi.org/10.1002/j.2379-3988.2006.tb00049.x.

8. Richard M. Ryan and Edward L. Deci, "Self-Determination Theory and the Facilitation of Intrinsic Motivation, Social Development, and Well-Being," *The American Psychologist* 55 (January 1, 2000): 68–78, doi.org/10.1037/0003-066X.55.1.68.

9. Natalie M. Saragosa-Harris, Alexandra O. Cohen, Travis R. Reneau, William J. Villano, Aaron S. Heller, and Catherine A. Hartley, "Real-World Exploration Increases Across Adolescence and Relates to Affect, Risk Taking, and Social Connectivity," *Psychological Science* 33, no. 10 (October 2022): 1664–1679, doi.org/10.1177/09567976221102070.

10. Francesco Recchia, "Physical Activity Interventions to Alleviate Depressive Symptoms in Children and Adolescents: A Systematic Review and Meta-Analysis," *JAMA Pediatrics* 177, no. 2 (February 1, 2023): 132–140, doi.org/10.1001/jamapediatrics.2022.5090.

11. Gray, Lancy, and Bjorklund, "Decline in Independent Activity," 6.

12. Suniya S. Luthar, Nina L. Kumar, and Nicole Zillmer, "High-Achieving Schools Connote Risks for Adolescents: Problems Documented, Processes Implicated, and Directions for Interventions," *American Psychologist* 75, no. 7 (2020): 983–995, doi.org/10.1037/amp0000556.

13. Catherine L. Ramstetter, Robert Murray, and Andrew S. Garner, "The Crucial Role of Recess in Schools," *Journal of School Health* 80, no. 11 (October 7, 2010): 517–526, doi.org/10.1111/j.1746-1561.2010.00537.x.

14. Phillip Atiba Goff, Matthew Christian Jackson, Brooke Allison Lewis Di Leone, Carmen Marie Culotta, and Natalie Ann DiTomasso, "The Essence of Innocence: Consequences of Dehumanizing Black Children," *Journal of Personality and Social Psychology* 106, no. 4 (2014): 526–545, doi.org/10.1037/a0035663.

15. Jenny S. Radesky, Heidi M. Weeks, Alexandria Schaller, Michael B. Robb, Supreet Mann, and Amanda Lenhart, "Constant Companion: A Week in the Life of a Young Person's Smartphone Use" (Common Sense Media, 2023), commonsensemedia.org/sites/default/files/research/report/2023-cs-smartphone-research-report_final-for-web.pdf, 44.

16. Baroness Beeban Kidron, "Putting Children at the Centre of the Digital World," Digital Media and Developing Minds International Scientific Congress, Washington, DC, September 20, 2023, beeban.com/media/putting-children-at-the-centre-of-the-digital-world.

17. Victoria Rideout, Alanna Peebles, Supreet Mann, and Michael B. Robb, "Common Sense Census: Media Use by Tweens and Teens" (Common Sense Media, 2022), commonsensemedia.org/sites/default/files/research/report/8-18-census-integrated-report-final-web_0.pdf.

18. Jonathan Haidt, *The Anxious Generation: How the Great Rewiring of Childhood Is Causing an Epidemic of Mental Illness* (Penguin Press, 2024).

19. Sapien Labs, "Age of First Smartphone/Tablet and Mental Wellbeing Outcomes," Sapien Labs, May 15, 2023, sapienlabs.org/wp-content/uploads/2023/05/Sapien-Labs-Age-of-First-Smartphone-and-Mental-Wellbeing-Outcomes.pdf.

20. D. S. Bickham, E. Hunt, J. R. Kavanaugh, and M. Rich, "Children's First Cell Phones: Parents' Perspectives on Risks and Benefits" (Digital Wellness Lab, 2021), digitalwellnesslab.org/wp-content/uploads/Pulse-Survey-Childrens-First-Cell-Phones-1.pdf.

21. American Psychological Association, "Potential Risks of Content, Features, and Functions: The Science of How Social Media Affects Youth," American Psychological Association, April, 2024, apa.org/topics/social-media-internet/youth-social-media-2024.

22. Linda Charmaraman, Alicia Doyle Lynch, Amanda M. Richer, and Jennifer M. Grossman, "Associations of Early Social Media Initiation on Digital Behaviors and the Moderating Role of Limiting Use," *Computers in Human Behavior* 127 (February 1, 2022): 107053, doi.org/10.1016/j.chb.2021.107053.

23. Amy Orben, Andrew K. Przybylski, Sarah-Jayne Blakemore, and Rogier A. Kievit, "Windows of Developmental Sensitivity to Social Media," *Nature Communications* 13, no. 1 (March 28, 2022): 1649, doi.org/10.1038/s41467-022-29296-3, 1.

24. Orben et al. "Windows of Developmental Sensitivity to Social Media."

25. Andrew K. Przybylski and Netta Weinstein, "A Large-Scale Test of the Goldilocks Hypothesis: Quantifying the Relations between Digital-Screen Use and the Mental Well-Being of Adolescents," *Psychological Science* 28, no. 2 (2017): 204–215, doi.org/10.1177/0956797616678438, 204.

26. Mariya Stoilova, Monica Bulger, and Sonia Livingstone, "Do Parental Control Tools Fulfil Family Expectations for Child Protection? A Rapid Evidence Review of the Contexts and Outcomes of Use," *Journal of Children and Media* 18, no. 1 (2024): 1–21, doi.org/10.1080/17482798.2023.2265512, 1.

27. Liang Chen and Jingyuan Shi, "Reducing Harm From Media: A Meta-Analysis of Parental Mediation," *Journalism & Mass Communication Quarterly* 96, no. 1 (March 1, 2019): 173–193, doi.org/10.1177/1077699018754908.

28. danah boyd, "FACETED ID/ENTITY: Managing Representation in a Digital World," Dissertation, Boston, MA, 2001.

29. Heitner, *Growing Up in Public*, 26.

30. David S. Yeager, Ronald E. Dahl, and Carol S. Dweck, "Why Interventions to Influence Adolescent Behavior Often Fail but Could Succeed," *Perspectives on Psychological Science* 13, no. 1 (January 2018): 101–122, doi.org/10.1177/1745691617722620.

31. Yeager, Dahl, and Dweck, "Why Interventions to Influence Adolescent Behavior Often Fail."

32. Wendy S. Grolnick and Rachel E. Lerner, "How Parental Autonomy Support, Structure, and Involvement Help Children Flourish: Considering Interactions, Context, and Diversity," in *The Oxford Handbook of Self-Determination Theory*, edited by Richard M. Ryan (Oxford University Press, 2023), doi.org/10.1093/oxfordhb/9780197600047.013.26.

33. Marta Benito-Gomez, Kenneshia N. Williams, Amy McCurdy, and Anne C. Fletcher, "Autonomy-Supportive Parenting in Adolescence: Cultural Variability in the Contemporary United States," *Journal of Family Theory & Review* 12, no. 1 (February 26, 2020): 7–26, doi.org/10.1111/jftr.12362.

34. Benito-Gomez, Williams, McCurdy, and Fletcher, "Autonomy-Supportive Parenting," 17.

35. American Psychological Association, "How Social Media Affects Teens' Mental Health, with Jacqueline Nesi, PhD," *Speaking of Psychology* (podcast), episode 238, 32:15, apa.org/news/podcasts/speaking-of-psychology/teen-social-media-use.

36. Maria Pagano, Valeria Bacaro, and Elisabetta Crocetti, "'Using Digital Media or Sleeping… That Is the Question'. A Meta-Analysis on Digital Media Use and Unhealthy Sleep in Adolescence," *Computers in Human Behavior* 146 (September 1, 2023): 107813, doi.org/10.1016/j.chb.2023.107813.

37. Michael B. Robb, "The New Normal: Parents, Teens, Screens, and Sleep in the United States" (Common Sense Media, 2019), commonsensemedia.org/sites/default/files/research/report/2019-new-normal-parents-teens-screens-and-sleep-united-states-report.pdf.

38. Radesky, Weeks, Schaller, Robb, Mann, and Lenhart, "Constant Companion."

39. Serena Bauducco, Meg Pillion, Kate Bartel, Chelsea Reynolds, Michal Kahn,

and Michael Gradisar, "A Bidirectional Model of Sleep and Technology Use: A Theoretical Review of How Much, for Whom, and Which Mechanisms," *Sleep Medicine Reviews* 76 (August 1, 2024): 101933, doi.org/10.1016/j.smrv.2024.101933.

40. Rea Alonzo, Junayd Hussain, Saverio Stranges, and Kelly K. Anderson, "Interplay between Social Media Use, Sleep Quality, and Mental Health in Youth: A Systematic Review," *Sleep Medicine Reviews* 56 (April 2021): 101414, doi.org/10.1016/j.smrv.2020.101414.

41. Jason M. Nagata et al., "Bedtime Screen Use Behaviors and Sleep Outcomes: Findings from the Adolescent Brain Cognitive Development (ABCD) Study," *Sleep Health* 9, no. 4 (August 2023): 497–502, doi.org/10.1016/j.sleh.2023.02.005.

42. John J. Ratey, *Spark: The Revolutionary New Science of Exercise and the Brain* (Little, Brown, and Co, 2008).

43. Tassia K. Oswald, Alice R. Rumbold, Sophie G. E. Kedzior, and Vivienne M. Moore, "Psychological Impacts of 'Screen Time' and 'Green Time' for Children and Adolescents: A Systematic Scoping Review," *PloS One* 15, no. 9 (2020): e0237725, doi.org/10.1371/journal.pone.0237725.

44. Ian Alcock, Matthew P. White, Benedict W. Wheeler, Lora E. Fleming, and Michael H. Depledge, "Longitudinal Effects on Mental Health of Moving to Greener and Less Green Urban Areas," *Environmental Science & Technology* 48, no. 2 (January 21, 2014): 1247–1255, doi.org/10.1021/es403688w.

45. Mary Helen Immordino-Yang, Joanna A. Christodoulou, and Vanessa Singh, "Rest Is Not Idleness: Implications of the Brain's Default Mode for Human Development and Education," *Perspectives on Psychological Science* 7, no. 4 (July 1, 2012): 352–364, doi.org/10.1177/1745691612447308.

46. Immordino-Yang, Christodoulou, and Singh, "Rest Is Not Idleness."

Chapter 6: Online Self-Expression

1. E. H. Erikson, *Identity: Youth and Crisis* (Norton & Co., 1968).

2. Erikson, *Identity*.

3. Carl Rogers, *On Becoming a Person: A Therapist's View of Psychotherapy* (Houghton Mifflin, 1961).

4. Katie Davis and Emily Weinstein, "Identity Development in the Digital Age: An Eriksonian Perspective," in *Identity, Sexuality, and Relationships Among Emerging Adults in the Digital Age*, edited by M. F. Wright (Information Science Reference/IGI Global, 2017), papers.ssrn.com/abstract=2982613, 5.

5. Emily Weinstein and Carrie James, *Behind Their Screens: What Teens Are Facing (And Adults Are Missing)* (The MIT Press, 2022).

6. Devorah Heitner, *Growing Up in Public: Coming of Age in a Digital World* (TarcherPerigee, 2023).

7. Lurie Children's Hospital, "Parenting Teens in the Age of Social Media," *Parenting Teens in the Age of Social Media* (blog), September 1, 2020, luriechildrens.org/en/blog/social-media-parenting-statistics.

8. Sonia Livingstone, "Taking Risky Opportunities in Youthful Content Creation: Teenagers' Use of Social Networking Sites for Intimacy, Privacy and Self-Expression," *New Media & Society* 10, no. 3 (June 1, 2008): 393–411, doi.org/10.1177/1461444808089415.

9. Heitner, *Growing Up in Public,* 167.

10. Mizuko Ito, Crystle Martin, Rachel Cody Pfister, Matt Rafalow, Katie Salen, and Amanda Wortman, *Affinity Online: How Connection and Shared Interest Fuel Learning* (NYU Press, 2018).

11. Meryl Alper, *Kids Across the Spectrums: Growing Up Autistic in the Digital Age* (The MIT Press, 2023).

12. Common Sense Media, "A Double-Edged Sword: How Diverse Communities of Young People Think About the Multifaceted Relationship Between Social

Media and Mental Health" (Common Sense Media and Hope Lab, 2024), commonsensemedia.org/sites/default/files/research/report/2024-double-edged-sword-hopelab-report_final-release-for-web-v2.pdf.

13. Crystal Abidin and Jing Zeng, "Feeling Asian Together: Coping With #COVIDRacism on Subtle Asian Traits," *Social Media + Society* 6, no. 3 (July 1, 2020): 2056305120948223, doi.org/10.1177/2056305120948223.

14. Linda Charmaraman, J. Maya Hernandez, and Rachel Hodes, "Marginalized and Understudied Populations Using Digital Media," in *Handbook of Adolescent Digital Media Use and Mental Health*, edited by Eva H. Telzer, Jacqueline Nesi, and Mitchell J. Prinstein (Cambridge University Press, 2022), https://doi.org/10.1017/9781108976237.011.

15. Nicole D. Reed, Roger Peterson, Thomas Ghost Dog, Carol E. Kaufman, Allyson Kelley, and Stephaie Craig Rushing, "Centering Native Youths' Needs and Priorities: Findings from the 2020 Native Youth Health Tech Survey," *American Indian and Alaska Native Mental Health Research* 29, no. 3 (September 2022): 1–17, doi.org/10.5820/aian.2903.2022.1.

16. Jacqueline Nesi, Supreet Mann, and Michael B. Robb, "Teens and Mental Health: How Girls Really Feel About Social Media (Common Sense Media, 2023), commonsensemedia.org/sites/default/files/research/report/how-girls-really-feel-about-social-media-researchreport_web_final_2.pdf.

17. UCLA Center on the Developing Adolescent, "This Is Me: Race and Identity in Adolescence," *Adaptivity* (podcast), transcript, October 2, 2021, developingadolescent.semel.ucla.edu/podcasts/item/this-is-me-race-and-identity-in-adolescence.

18. Brendesha M. Tynes, Devin English, Juan Del Toro, Naila A. Smith, Fantasy T. Lozada, and David R. Williams, "Trajectories of Online Racial Discrimination and Psychological Functioning among African American and Latino Adolescents," *Child Development* 91, no. 5 (September 2020): 1577–1593, doi.org/10.1111/cdev.13350.

19. Brendesha M. Tynes, Adriana J. Umaña-Taylor, Chad A. Rose, Johnny Lin, and Carolyn J. Anderson, "Online Racial Discrimination and the Protective Function of Ethnic Identity and Self-Esteem for African American Adolescents," *Developmental Psychology* 48, no. 2 (2012): 343–355, doi.org/10.1037/a0027032.

20. Henry Willis, Interview by Erin Walsh, Riverside, May 22, 2024.

21. Weinstein and James, *Behind Their Screens,* 125.

22. Emily C. Weinstein, Margaret Rundle, and Carrie James, "A Hush Falls Over the Crowd?: Diminished Online Civic Expression Among Young Civic Actors," *International Journal of Communication* 9 (January 5, 2015): 84–105, ijoc.org/index.php/ijoc/article/view/2901.

23. Linda Charmaraman, Huiying Bernice Chan, Stephen H. Chen, and Amanda Richer, "Asian American Social Media Use: From Cyber Dependence and Cyber Harassment to Saving Face," *Asian American Journal of Psychology* 9, no. 1 (2018): 72–86, doi.org/10.1037/aap0000109.

24. Valeriya Safronova, "On Fake Instagram, a Chance to Be Real," *The New York Times,* November 18, 2015. nytimes.com/2015/11/19/fashion/instagram-finstagram-fake-account.html.

25. Alicia Blum-Ross and Sonia Livingstone, "'Sharenting,' Parent Blogging, and the Boundaries of the Digital Self," *Popular Communication* 15, no. 2 (April 3, 2017): 110–125, doi.org/10.1080/15405702.2016.1223300.

26. Jennifer Valentino-DeVries and Michael H. Keller, "A Marketplace of Girl Influencers Managed by Moms and Stalked by Men," *The New York Times,* February 23, 2024, nytimes.com/2024/02/22/us/instagram-child-influencers.html.

27. Karen Verswijvel, Michel Walrave, Kris Hardies, and Wannes Heirman, "Sharenting, Is It a Good or a Bad Thing? Understanding How Adolescents Think and Feel about Sharenting on Social Network Sites," *Children and Youth Services Review* 104 (September 1, 2019): 104401, doi.org/10.1016/j.childyouth.2019.104401.

28. Gaëlle Ouvrein and Karen Verswijvel, "Sharenting: Parental Adoration or Public Humiliation? A Focus Group Study on Adolescents' Experiences with Sharenting against the Background of Their Own Impression Management," *Children and Youth Services Review* 99 (2019): 319–327, doi.org/10.1016/j.childyouth.2019.02.011.

Chapter 7: Love, Relationships, and Sexual Identity

1. TeenHealthFX, "Who We Are, " accessed November 5, 2024, teenhealthfx.com/about.html.

2. Antonella Juline von Rosen, Frederik Tilmann von Rosen, Peter Tinnemann, and Falk Müller-Riemenschneider, "Sexual Health and the Internet: Cross-Sectional Study of Online Preferences Among Adolescents," *Journal of Medical Internet Research* 19, no. 11 (November 8, 2017): e379, doi.org/10.2196/jmir.7068.

3. Common Sense Media, Hopelab, and Center for Digital Thriving, "Teen and Young Adult Perspectives on Generative AI: Patterns of Use, Excitements, and Concerns" (Common Sense Media, 2024), commonsensemedia.org/sites/default/files/research/report/teen-and-young-adult-perspectives-on-generative-ai.pdf, 27.

4. Anna Kågesten and Miranda van Reeuwijk, "Healthy Sexuality Development in Adolescence: Proposing a Competency-Based Framework to Inform Programmes and Research," *Sexual and Reproductive Health Matters* 29, no. 1 (2021): 1996116, doi.org/10.1080/26410397.2021.1996116.

5. American Psychological Association, "Understanding Sexual Orientation and Homosexuality," October 29, 2008, apa.org/topics/lgbtq/orientation.

6. Cara Natterson and Vanessa Kroll Bennett, *This Is So Awkward: Modern Puberty Explained* (Rodale Books, 2023), 212.

7. Centers for Disease Control and Prevention, "Youth Risk Behavior Surveillance System (YRBSS)," October 4, 2023, cdc.gov/healthyyouth/data/yrbs/index.htm.

8. Laura D. Lindberg and Leslie M. Kantor, "Adolescents' Receipt of Sex Education in a Nationally Representative Sample, 2011–2019," *Journal of Adolescent Health* 70, no. 2 (February 1, 2022): 290–297, doi.org/10.1016/j.jadohealth.2021.08.027.

9. Namrata Garg and Anna Volerman, "A National Analysis of State Policies on Lesbian, Gay, Bisexual, Transgender, and Questioning/Queer Inclusive Sex Education," *Journal of School Health* 91, no. 2 (February 2021): 164–175, doi.org/10.1111/josh.12987.

10. Laura Widman, Hannah Javidi, Anne J. Maheux, Reina Evans, Jacqueline Nesi, and Sophia Choukas-Bradley, "Sexual Communication in the Digital Age: Adolescent Sexual Communication with Parents and Friends About Sexting, Pornography, and Starting Relationships Online," *Sexuality & Culture* 25, no. 6 (December 1, 2021): 2092–2109, doi.org/10.1007/s12119-021-09866-1.

11. Ariella R. Tabaac, Eric G. Benotsch, Madina Agénor, S. Bryn Austin, and Brittany M. Charlton, "Use of Media Sources in Seeking and Receiving Sexual Health Information during Adolescence among Adults of Diverse Sexual Orientations in a US Cohort," *Sex Education* 21, no. 6 (2021): 723–731, doi.org/10.1080/14681811.2021.1873122.

12. Nazeema Isaacs, Xolani Ntinga, Thabo Keetsi, Lindelwa Bhembe, Bongumenzi Mthembu, Allanise Cloete, and Candice Groenewald, "Are mHealth Interventions Effective in Improving the Uptake of Sexual and Reproductive Health Services among Adolescents? A Scoping Review," *International Journal of Environmental Research and Public Health* 21, no. 2 (February 2024): 165, doi.org/10.3390/ijerph21020165.

13. Geoffrey A. Fowler, "Perspective | Snapchat Tried to Make a Safe AI. It Chats with Me About Booze and Sex," *Washington Post*, April 14, 2023, washingtonpost.com/technology/2023/03/14/snapchat-myai/.

14. Emily J. Pfender and M. Marie Devlin, "What Do Social Media Influencers Say About Birth Control? A Content Analysis of YouTube Vlogs About Birth Control," *Health Communication* 38, no. 14 (December 6, 2023): 3336–3345, doi.org/10.1080/10410236.2022.2149091.

15. Richard Weissbourd with Trisha Ross Anderson, Alison Cashin, and Joe McIntyre, "The Talk: How Adults Can Promote Healthy Relationships and Prevent Misogyny and Sexual Harassment," Making Caring Common Project, Harvard Graduate School of Education, May 2017, mcc.gse.harvard.edu/reports/the-talk.

16. Emily Weinstein, Interview by Erin Walsh, Riverside, June 10, 2024.

17. Laura Widman, Sophia Choukas-Bradley, Seth M. Noar, Jacqueline Nesi, and Kyla Garrett, "Parent-Adolescent Sexual Communication and Adolescent Safer Sex Behavior: A Meta-Analysis," *JAMA Pediatrics* 170, no. 1 (January 1, 2016): 52–61, doi.org/10.1001/jamapediatrics.2015.2731.

18. Weissbourd, Anderson, Cashin, and McIntyre, "The Talk," 2.

19. Amie M. Ashcraft and Pamela J. Murray, "Talking to Parents About Adolescent Sexuality," *Pediatric Clinics of North America* 64, no. 2 (April 2017): 305–320, doi.org/10.1016/j.pcl.2016.11.002.

20. Michael B. Robb and Supreet Mann, "Teens and Pornography" (Common Sense Media, 2023), commonsensemedia.org/research/teens-and-pornography.

21. Robb and Mann, "Teens and Pornography."

22. Robb and Mann, "Teens and Pornography," 27.

23. Robb and Mann, "Teens and Pornography."

24. Megan Maas, Interview by Erin Walsh, Riverside, May 15, 2024.

25. Paul J. Wright, Debby Herbenick, Bryant Paul, and Robert S. Tokunaga "Exploratory Findings on U.S. Adolescents' Pornography Use, Dominant Behavior, and Sexual Satisfaction," *International Journal of Sexual Health* 33, no. 2 (April 3, 2021): 222–228, doi.org/10.1080/19317611.2021.1888170.

26. Andrea Waling, Adrian Farrugia, and Suzanne Fraser, "Embarrassment, Shame, and Reassurance: Emotion and Young People's Access to Online Sexual Health Information," *Sexuality Research & Social Policy* 20, no. 1 (2023): 45–57, doi.org/10.1007/s13178-021-00668-6.

27. Robb and Mann, "Teens and Pornography."

28. Robb and Mann, "Teens and Pornography," 24.

29. AMAZE, "The #AskableParent Porn Guide," accessed November 5, 2024, amaze.org/parents/guides/porn.

30. Sanna Spišák, "'Everywhere They Say That It's Harmful but They Don't Say How, so I'm Asking Here': Young People, Pornography and Negotiations with Notions of Risk and Harm," *Sex Education* 16, no. 2 (March 3, 2016): 130–142, doi.org/10.1080/14681811.2015.1080158, 130.

31. Maas, Interview by Erin Walsh.

32. Sheri Madigan, Anh Ly, Christina L. Rash, Joris Van Ouytsel, and Jeff R. Temple, "Prevalence of Multiple Forms of Sexting Behavior Among Youth: A Systematic Review and Meta-Analysis," *JAMA Pediatrics* 172, no. 4 (April 2018): 327–335, doi.org/10.1001/jamapediatrics.2017.5314.

33. Yu Lu, Elizabeth Baumler, and Jeff R. Temple, "Multiple Forms of Sexting and Associations with Psychosocial Health in Early Adolescents," *International Journal of Environmental Research and Public Health* 18, no. 5 (March 9, 2021): 2760, doi.org/10.3390/ijerph18052760.

34. Caoimhe Doyle, Ellen Douglas, and Gary O'Reilly, "The Outcomes of

Sexting for Children and Adolescents: A Systematic Review of the Literature," *Journal of Adolescence* 92, no. 1 (October 1, 2021): 86–113, doi.org/10.1016/j.adolescence.2021.08.009.

35. Camille Mori, Jeff R. Temple, Dillon Browne, and Sheri Madigan, "Association of Sexting with Sexual Behaviors and Mental Health Among Adolescents: A Systematic Review and Meta-Analysis," *JAMA Pediatrics* 173, no. 8 (August 1, 2019): 770–779, doi.org/10.1001/jamapediatrics.2019.1658.

36. Camille Mori, Hye Jeong Choi, Jeff R. Temple, and Sheri Madigan, "Patterns of Sexting and Sexual Behaviors in Youth: A Latent Class Analysis," *Journal of Adolescence* 88, no. 1 (March 5, 2021): 97–106, doi.org/10.1016/j.adolescence.2021.01.010.

37. Lu, Baumler, and Temple, "Multiple Forms of Sexting."

38. Emily Weinstein and Carrie James, *Behind Their Screens: What Teens Are Facing (And Adults Are Missing)* (The MIT Press, 2022).

39. Joris Van Ouytsel, Michel Walrave, and Koen Ponnet, "An Exploratory Study of Sexting Behaviors Among Heterosexual and Sexual Minority Early Adolescents," *Journal of Adolescent Health* 65, no. 5 (November 1, 2019): 621–626, doi.org/10.1016/j.jadohealth.2019.06.003.

40. Devorah Heitner, *Growing Up in Public: Coming of Age in a Digital World* (TarcherPerigee, 2023), 184.

41. Lauren A. Reed, Margaret P. Boyer, Haley Meskunas, Richard M. Tolman, and L. Monique Ward, "How Do Adolescents Experience Sexting in Dating Relationships? Motivations to Sext and Responses to Sexting Requests from Dating Partners," *Children and Youth Services Review* 109 (February 2020): 104696, doi.org/10.1016/j.childyouth.2019.104696.

42. Julia R. Lippman and Scott W. Campbell, "Damned If You Do, Damned If You Don't…If You're a Girl: Relational and Normative Contexts of Adolescent Sexting in the United States," *Journal of Children and Media* 8, no. 4 (October 2, 2014): 371–386, doi.org/10.1080/17482798.2014.923009, 371.

43. PBS Learning Media, "What Is Mentionable Is Manageable: Mister Rogers," *Meet the Helpers*, video, 0:35, accessed November 5, 2024, pbslearningmedia.org/resource/mentionable-manageable-mister-rogers-video/meet-the-helpers.

Chapter 8: Belonging with Friends

1. Hanke Korpershoek, Esther T. Canrinus, Marjon Fokkens-Bruinsma, and H. de Boer, "The Relationships between School Belonging and Students' Motivational, Social-Emotional, Behavioural, and Academic Outcomes in Secondary Education: A Meta-Analytic Review," *Research Papers in Education* 35, no. 6 (November 1, 2020): 641–680, doi.org/10.1080/02671522.2019.1615116.

2. Ethan Kross, Marc G. Berman, Walter Mischel, Edward E. Smith, and Tor D. Wager, "Social Rejection Shares Somatosensory Representations with Physical Pain," *Proceedings of the National Academy of Sciences of the United States of America* 108, no. 15 (April 12, 2011): 6270–6275, doi.org/10.1073/pnas.1102693108.

3. Office of the Surgeon General, "Our Epidemic of Loneliness and Isolation: The U.S. Surgeon General's Advisory on the Healing Effects of Social Connection and Community" (US Department of Health and Human Services, 2023), hhs.gov/sites/default/files/surgeon-general-social-connection-advisory.pdf.

4. Livia Tomova, Jack L. Andrews, and Sarah-Jayne Blakemore, "The Importance of Belonging and the Avoidance of Social Risk Taking in Adolescence," *Developmental Review* 61 (September 1, 2021): 100981, doi.org/10.1016/j.dr.2021.100981.

5. David Elkind, "Egocentrism in Adolescence," *Child Development* 38, no. 4 (1967): 1025–1034, doi.org/10.2307/1127100.

6. Leah H. Somerville, Rebecca M. Jones, Erika J. Ruberry, Jonathan P. Dyke, and B. J. Casey, "Medial Prefrontal Cortex and the Emergence of Self-Conscious Emotion in Adolescence," *Psychological Science* 24, no. 8 (August 1, 2013): 1554–1562, doi. org/10.1177/0956797613475633.

7. Stefania A. Barzeva, Jennifer S. Richards, René Veenstra, Wim H. J. Meeus, and Albertine J. Oldehinkel, "Quality over Quantity: A Transactional Model of Social Withdrawal and Friendship Development in Late Adolescence," *Social Development (Oxford, England)* 31, no. 1 (February 2022): 126–146, doi. org/10.1111/sode.12530.

8. Sherry Turkle, *Alone Together: Why We Expect More from Technology and Less from Each Other* (Basic Books, 2012), 1.

9. Chia-chen Yang and Kaia Christofferson, "On the Phone When We're Hanging Out: Digital Social Multitasking (DSMT) and Its Socioemotional Implications," *Journal of Youth and Adolescence* 49, no. 6 (June 1, 2020): 1209–1224, doi.org/10.1007/ s10964-020-01230-0.

10. Yang and Christofferson, "On the Phone."

11. Chia-chen Yang, "(Dis)Connected? Relationships in the Digital Age," Children and Screens Ask The Experts Webinar Series, Zoom, November 9, 2022, childrenandscreens.org/learn-explore/research/relationships-and-tech/.

12. Chia-Chen Yang, Christina Smith, Thomas Pham, and Jati Ariati, "Digital Social Multitasking (DSMT), Digital Stress, and Socioemotional Wellbeing Among Adolescents," *Cyberpsychology: Journal of Psychosocial Research on Cyberspace* 17, no. 1 (January 30, 2023), doi.org/10.5817/CP2023-1-6.

13. Chia-chen Yang, Thomas Pham, Jati Ariati, Christina Smith, and Misti D. Foster, "Digital Social Multitasking (DSMT), Friendship Quality, and Basic Psychological Needs Satisfaction Among Adolescents: Perceptions as Mediators," *Journal of Youth and Adolescence* 50, no. 12 (December 1, 2021): 2456–2471, doi. org/10.1007/s10964-021-01442-y.

14. Yang, "(Dis)Connected?"

15. Office of the Surgeon General, "Our Epidemic of Loneliness and Isolation."

16. Brené Brown, *Daring Greatly: How the Courage to Be Vulnerable Transforms the Way We Live, Love, Parent, and Lead* (Avery, 2015), 231.

17. Louise Chapman, Kieran Rose, Laura Hull, and William Mandy, "'I Want to Fit In…but I Don't Want to Change Myself Fundamentally': A Qualitative Exploration of the Relationship between Masking and Mental Health for Autistic Teenagers," *Research in Autism Spectrum Disorders* 99 (November 1, 2022): 102069, doi.org/10.1016/j.rasd.2022.102069.

18. Common Sense Media, Hopelab, and Center for Digital Thriving, "Teen and Young Adult Perspectives on Generative AI: Patterns of Use, Excitements, and Concerns" (Common Sense Media, 2024), commonsensemedia.org/sites/ default/files/research/report/teen-and-young-adult-perspectives-on-generative-ai.pdf, 27.

19. Southern Poverty Law Center, "Building Resilience & Confronting Risk: A Parents and Caregivers Guide to Online Radicalization," Southern Poverty Law Center and Polarization & Extremism Research & Innovation Lab (PERIL), January 31, 2022, splcenter.org/peril-guide-online-youth-radicalization.

20. Southern Poverty Law Center, "Building Resilience."

21. Nelson Reed and Katie Joseff, "Kids and the Metaverse: What Parents, Policymakers, and Companies Need to Know" (Common Sense Media, 2022), commonsensemedia.org/sites/default/ files/featured-content/files/metaverse-white-paper.pdf, 9.

22. Southern Poverty Law Center, "Building Resilience."

23. Elizabeth K. Englander, *25 Myths About Bullying and Cyberbullying* (Wiley-Blackwell, 2020).

24. Dylan Marron, "The Most Loving Story," *The Redemption of Jar Jar Binks* (podcast),

TED Audio Collective, 33:00, July 25, 2023, ted.com/podcasts/the-redemption-of-jar-jar-binks.

25. Dieter Wolke and Suzet Tanya Lereya, "Long-Term Effects of Bullying," *Archives of Disease in Childhood* 100, no. 9 (September 2015): 879–885, doi.org/10.1136/archdischild-2014-306667.

26. Ann John et al., "Self-Harm, Suicidal Behaviours, and Cyberbullying in Children and Young People: Systematic Review," *Journal of Medical Internet Research* 20, no. 4 (April 19, 2018): e9044, doi.org/10.2196/jmir.9044.

27. Sameer Hinduja and Justin W. Patchin, *Bullying Beyond the Schoolyard: Preventing and Responding to Cyberbullying*, third edition (Corwin, 2023).

28. Englander, *25 Myths About Bullying and Cyberbullying*.

29. Hinduja and Patchin, *Bullying Beyond the Schoolyard*.

30. Hinduja and Patchin, *Bullying Beyond the Schoolyard*.

31. Centers for Disease Control and Prevention, "Youth Risk Behavior Survey Data Summary & Trends Report: 2011–2021" (Centers for Disease Control and Prevention, 2023), cdc.gov/healthyyouth/data/yrbs/pdf/YRBS_Data-Summary-Trends_Report2023_508.pdf.

32. Emily A. Vogels, "Teens and Cyberbullying 2022," Pew Research Center, December 15, 2022, pewresearch.org/internet/2022/12/15/teens-and-cyberbullying-2022.

33. Hinduja and Patchin, *Bullying Beyond the Schoolyard*.

34. Jacqueline Nesi, Sophia Choukas-Bradley, and Mitchell J. Prinstein, "Transformation of Adolescent Peer Relations in the Social Media Context: Part 1—A Theoretical Framework and Application to Dyadic Peer Relationships," *Clinical Child and Family Psychology Review* 21, no. 3 (September 2018): 267–294, doi.org/10.1007/s10567-018-0261-x.

35. John Suler, "The Online Disinhibition Effect," *Cyberpsychology & Behavior* 7, no. 3 (June 2004): 321–326, doi.org/10.1089/1094931041291295.

36. Englander, *25 Myths About Bullying and Cyberbullying*.

37. Englander, *25 Myths About Bullying and Cyberbullying*.

38. Englander, *25 Myths About Bullying and Cyberbullying*.

39. Elizabeth Englander, Interview by Erin Walsh, Riverside, April 10, 2024.

40. Englander, *25 Myths About Bullying and Cyberbullying*.

41. Englander, Interview by Erin Walsh.

42. H. Wesley Perkins, David W. Craig, and Jessica M. Perkins, "Using Social Norms to Reduce Bullying: A Research Intervention Among Adolescents in Five Middle Schools," *Group Processes & Intergroup Relations* 14, no. 5 (September 1, 2011): 703–722, doi.org/10.1177/1368430210398004.

43. Mitch Prinstein, *Popular: The Power of Likability in a Status-Obsessed World* (Viking, 2017).

44. Naomi I. Eisenberger, Matthew D. Lieberman, and Kipling D. Williams, "Does Rejection Hurt? An FMRI Study of Social Exclusion," *Science* 302, no. 5643 (October 10, 2003): 290–292, doi.org/10.1126/science.1089134.

45. Jason Chein, Dustin Albert, Lia O'Brien, Kaitlyn Uckert, and Laurence Steinberg, "Peers Increase Adolescent Risk Taking by Enhancing Activity in the Brain's Reward Circuitry," *Developmental Science* 14, no. 2 (March 2011): F1–F10, doi.org/10.1111/j.1467-7687.2010.01035.x.

46. Kathy T. Do, João F. Guassi Moreira, and Eva H. Telzer, "But Is Helping You Worth the Risk? Defining Prosocial Risk Taking in Adolescence," *Developmental Cognitive Neuroscience* 25 (June 2017): 260–271, doi.org/10.1016/j.dcn.2016.11.008.

47. Do, Guassi Moreira, and Telzer, "But Is Helping You Worth the Risk?"

48. Englander, *25 Myths About Bullying and Cyberbullying*.

49. Englander, Interview by Erin Walsh.

50. Justin W. Patchin and Sameer Hinduja, *Words Wound: Delete Cyberbullying and Make Kindness Go Viral* (Free Spirit Publishing, 2013), 85.

51. Emily Weinstein and Carrie James, *Behind Their Screens: What Teens Are Facing (And Adults Are Missing)* (The MIT Press, 2022), 91.

Chapter 9: Self-Worth

1. William James, *The Principles of Psychology, Vol I.* (Henry Holt and Co, 1890), doi.org/10.1037/10538-000.

2. Linda Charmaraman, Horacio Hojman, Jenni Quichimbo Auqui, and Zhamilya Bilyalova, "Understanding Adolescent Self-Esteem and Self-Image Through Social Media Behaviors," *Pediatric Clinics of North America*, in press, September 4, 2024, doi.org/10.1016/j.pcl.2024.07.034.

3. Jacqueline Nesi, Supreet Mann, and Michael B. Robb, "Teens and Mental Health: How Girls Really Feel About Social Media" (Common Sense Media, 2023), commonsensemedia.org/sites/default/files/research/report/how-girls-really-feel-about-social-media-researchreport_web_final_2.pdf.

4. David Elkind and Robert Bowen, "Imaginary Audience Behavior in Children and Adolescents," *Developmental Psychology* 15, no. 1 (1979): 38–44, doi.org/10.1037/0012-1649.15.1.38.

5. Lauren E. Sherman, Ashley A. Payton, Leanna M. Hernandez, Patricia M. Greenfield, and Mirella Dapretto, "The Power of the Like in Adolescence: Effects of Peer Influence on Neural and Behavioral Responses to Social Media," *Psychological Science* 27, no. 7 (2016): 1027–1035, doi.org/10.1177/0956797616645673.

6. Jacqueline Nesi and Mitchell J. Prinstein, "In Search of Likes: Longitudinal Associations Between Adolescents' Digital Status Seeking and Health Risk Behaviors," *Journal of Clinical Child and Adolescent Psychology* 48, no. 5 (2019): 740–748, doi.org/10.1080/15374416.2018.1437733.

7. Victoria J. Rideout and Susannah Fox, "Digital Health Practices, Social Media Use, and Mental Well-Being Among Teens and Young Adults in the U.S.," 2018, semanticscholar.org/paper/Digital-Health-Practices%2C-Social-Media-Use-and-and-Rideout-Fox/3c1a46299ab2f7e902d881e1b5ba557c409968ca.

8. Hae Yeon Lee et al., "Getting Fewer 'Likes' Than Others on Social Media Elicits Emotional Distress Among Victimized Adolescents," *Child Development* 91, no. 6 (2020): 2141–2159, doi.org/10.1111/cdev.13422.

9. Emily Weinstein, Interview by Erin Walsh, Riverside, June 10, 2024.

10. Center for Digital Thriving, "Thinking Traps," accessed June 5, 2024, digitalthriving.gse.harvard.edu/resources/thinking-traps/.

11. Savannah R. Roberts, Anne J. Maheux, Rowan A. Hunt, Brianna A. Ladd, and Sophia Choukas-Bradley, "Incorporating Social Media and Muscular Ideal Internalization into the Tripartite Influence Model of Body Image: Towards a Modern Understanding of Adolescent Girls' Body Dissatisfaction," *Body Image* 41 (June 1, 2022): 239–247, doi.org/10.1016/j.bodyim.2022.03.002.

12. Brianna A. Ladd, Anne J. Maheux, Savannah R. Roberts, and Sophia Choukas-Bradley, "Black Adolescents' Appearance Concerns, Depressive Symptoms, and Self-Objectification: Exploring the Roles of Gender and Ethnic-Racial Identity Commitment," *Body Image* 43 (December 1, 2022): 314–325, doi.org/10.1016/j.bodyim.2022.09.008.

13. C. S. Mott Children's Hospital, "Parents' Perception of Their Child's Body Image," *Mott Poll Report* 41, no. 5 (September 19, 2022), mottpoll.org/reports/parents-perception-their-childs-body-image.

14. Jacqueline Nesi, Sophia Choukas-Bradley, and Mitchell J. Prinstein, "Transformation of Adolescent Peer Relations in the Social Media Context: Part 1—A Theoretical Framework and Application to Dyadic Peer Relationships," *Clinical Child and Family Psychology Review* 21, no. 3 (September 2018): 267–294, doi.org/10.1007/s10567-018-0261-x.

15. Miao Li and Sarah Mustillo, "Linking Mother and Offspring Depressive Symptoms: The Mediating Role of Child Appearance Contingent Self-Worth," *Journal of Affective Disorders* 273 (August 1, 2020): 113–121, doi.org/10.1016/j.jad.2020.03.117.

16. Sophia Choukas-Bradley, Savannah R. Roberts, Anne J. Maheux, and Jacqueline Nesi, "The Perfect Storm: A Developmental-Sociocultural Framework for the Role of Social Media in Adolescent Girls' Body Image Concerns and Mental Health," *Clinical Child and Family Psychology Review* 25, no. 4 (December 2022): 681–701, doi.org/10.1007/s10567-022-00404-5.

17. Alyssa N. Saiphoo and Zahra Vahedi, "A Meta-Analytic Review of the Relationship Between Social Media Use and Body Image Disturbance," *Computers in Human Behavior* 101 (December 1, 2019): 259–275, doi.org/10.1016/j.chb.2019.07.028.

18. Marisa Minadeo and Lizzy Pope, "Weight-Normative Messaging Predominates on TikTok—A Qualitative Content Analysis," *PLOS ONE* 17, no. 11 (November 1, 2022): e0267997, doi.org/10.1371/journal.pone.0267997.

19. José Francisco López-Gil et al., "Global Proportion of Disordered Eating in Children and Adolescents: A Systematic Review and Meta-Analysis," *JAMA Pediatrics* 177, no. 4 (April 1, 2023): 363–372, doi.org/10.1001/jamapediatrics.2022.5848.

20. Maria Pastore, Flavia Indrio, Donjeta Bali, Mehmet Vural, Ida Giardino, and Massimo Pettoello-Mantovani, "Alarming Increase of Eating Disorders in Children and Adolescents," *The Journal of Pediatrics* 263 (December 1, 2023): 113733, doi.org/10.1016/j.jpeds.2023.113733.

21. Dianne Neumark-Sztainer, Melanie Wall, Nicole I. Larson, Marla E. Eisenberg, and Katie Loth, "Dieting and Disordered Eating Behaviors from Adolescence to Young Adulthood: Findings from a 10-Year Longitudinal Study," *Journal of the American Dietetic Association* 111, no. 7 (July 1, 2011): 1004–1011, doi.org/10.1016/j.jada.2011.04.012.

22. Lacie L. Parker and Jennifer A. Harriger, "Eating Disorders and Disordered Eating Behaviors in the LGBT Population: A Review of the Literature," *Journal of Eating Disorders* 8, no. 1 (October 16, 2020): 51, doi.org/10.1186/s40337-020-00327-y.

23. The Trevor Project, "Research Brief: LGBTQ Youth and Body Dissatisfaction" (The Trevor Project, January 2023), thetrevorproject.org/wp-content/uploads/2023/01/January_2023_Research_Brief_Final.pdf.

24. American Psychological Association, "APA Guidelines for Psychological Practice with Boys and Men," August 2018, apa.org/about/policy/boys-men-practice-guidelines.pdf.

25. Jason M. Nagata, Interview by Erin Walsh, Riverside, March 28, 2024.

26. Jason M. Nagata, Kirsten Bibbins-Domingo, Andrea K. Garber, Scott Griffiths, Eric Vittinghoff, and Stuart B. Murray, "Boys, Bulk, and Body Ideals: Sex Differences in Weight-Gain Attempts Among Adolescents in the United States," *Journal of Adolescent Health* 64, no. 4 (April 1, 2019): 450–453, doi.org/10.1016/j.jadohealth.2018.09.002.

27. Thomas Gültzow, Jeanine P. D. Guidry, Francine Schneider, and Hoving, "Male Body Image Portrayals on Instagram," *Cyberpsychology, Behavior, and Social Networking* 23, no. 5 (May 2020): 281–289, doi.org/10.1089/cyber.2019.0368.

28. Nagata et al., "Boys, Bulk, and Body Ideals."

29. Jason M. Nagata, Tiffany A. Brown, Jason M. Lavender, and Stuart B. Murray,

"Emerging Trends in Eating Disorders Among Adolescent Boys: Muscles, Macronutrients, and Biohacking," *The Lancet Child & Adolescent Health* 3, no. 7 (July 1, 2019): 444–445, doi.org/10.1016/S2352-4642(19)30147-6.

30. Nagata, Interview by Erin Walsh.

31. Sophia Choukas-Bradley, Jacqueline Nesi, Laura Widman, and Mary Higgins Neyland, "Camera-Ready: Young Women's Appearance-Related Social Media Consciousness," *Psychology of Popular Media Culture* 8, no. 4 (October 2019): 473–481, doi.org/10.1037/ppm0000196, 473.

32. Sophia Choukas-Bradley, Jacqueline Nesi, Laura Widman, and Brian M. Galla, "The Appearance-Related Social Media Consciousness Scale: Development and Validation with Adolescents," *Body Image* 33 (June 1, 2020): 164–174, doi.org/10.1016/j.bodyim.2020.02.017.

33. Jasmine Fardouly, Amy Slater, Jade Parnell, and Phillippa C. Diedrichs, "Can Following Body Positive or Appearance Neutral Facebook Pages Improve Young Women's Body Image and Mood? Testing Novel Social Media Micro-Interventions," *Body Image* 44 (March 1, 2023): 136–147, doi.org/10.1016/j.bodyim.2022.12.008.

34. Rachel F. Rodgers, Susan J. Paxton, and Eleanor H. Wertheim, "#Take Idealized Bodies out of the Picture: A Scoping Review of Social Media Content Aiming to Protect and Promote Positive Body Image," *Body Image* 38 (2021): 10–36, doi.org/10.1016/j.bodyim.2021.03.009.

35. Kristin Neff and Christopher Germer, *The Mindful Self-Compassion Workbook: A Proven Way to Accept Yourself, Build Inner Strength, and Thrive* (The Guilford Press, 2018), 9.

36. Neff and Germer, *The Mindful Self-Compassion Workbook*.

37. Neff and Germer, *The Mindful Self-Compassion Workbook*, 10.

38. Christina Ewert, Annika Vater, and Michela Schröder-Abé, "Self-Compassion and Coping: A Meta-Analysis," *Mindfulness* 12 (May 1, 2021): 1063–1077, doi.org/10.1007/s12671-020-01563-8.

39. Kristin Neff, "Self-Compassion" accessed November 5, 2024, self-compassion.org.

40. Mister Rogers' Neighborhood, "It's You I Like," video, 1:31, 1984, music and lyrics by Fred M. Rogers, misterrogers.org/videos/its-you-i-like.

41. Alex Shevrin Venet, *Equity-Centered Trauma-Informed Education: Transforming Classrooms, Shifting Systems* (W. W. Norton & Co, 2021).

42. Venet, *Equity-Centered Trauma-Informed Education*, 98.

43. Alex Shevrin Venet and Matthew Portell, "Trauma-Informed Education," *The Learning Spring* (podcast), Pegasus Spings Education Collective, 1:03:28, June 15, 2023, pegasussprings.org/learning-spring-education-podcast/episode-2-shevrin-venet-portell.

44. Jennifer Breheny Wallace, *Never Enough: When Achievement Culture Becomes Toxic—and What We Can Do About It* (Portfolio, 2023).

Chapter 10: The Power of Purpose

1. Matthias J. Gruber, Bernard D. Gelman, and Charan Ranganath, "States of Curiosity Modulate Hippocampus-Dependent Learning via the Dopaminergic Circuit," *Neuron* 84, no. 2 (October 22, 2014): 486–496, doi.org/10.1016/j.neuron.2014.08.060.

2. Seydi Ahmet Satici, Emine Gocet Tekin, M. Engin Deniz, and Begum Satici, "Doomscrolling Scale: Its Association with Personality Traits, Psychological Distress, Social Media Use, and Wellbeing," *Applied Research in Quality of Life* 18, no. 2 (2023): 833–847, doi.org/10.1007/s11482-022-10110-7.

3. Ellen Galinsky, *The Breakthrough Years: A New Scientific Framework for Raising Thriving Teens* (Flatiron Books, 2024).

4. Mary Helen Immordino-Yang and Douglas R. Knecht, "Building Meaning Builds Teens' Brains," *Educational Leadership* 77 (May 1, 2020): 36–43, semanticscholar.org/paper/Building-Meaning-Builds-Teens'-Brains.-

Immordino%E2%80%90Yang-Knecht/5b6ab8eed71179f83f049ee4f7c5c2046d46ffb6.

5. William Damon, Jenni Menon, and Kendall Cotton Bronk, "The Development of Purpose During Adolescence," *Applied Developmental Science* 7, no. 3 (July 1, 2003): 119–128, doi.org/10.1207/S1532480XADS0703_2.

6. David S. Yeager et al., "Boring but Important: A Self-Transcendent Purpose for Learning Fosters Academic Self-Regulation," *Journal of Personality and Social Psychology* 107, no. 4 (2014): 559–580, doi.org/10.1037/a0037637.

7. Kaylin Ratner, Qingyi, Gaoxia Zhu, Melody Estevez, and Anthony L. Burrow, "Daily Adolescent Purposefulness, Daily Subjective Well-Being, and Individual Differences in Autistic Traits," *Journal of Happiness Studies* 24, no. 3 (March 1, 2023): 967–989, doi.org/10.1007/s10902-023-00625-7; Patrick E. McKnight and Todd B. Kashdan, "Purpose in Life as a System That Creates and Sustains Health and Well-Being: An Integrative, Testable Theory," *Review of General Psychology* 13, no. 3 (September 1, 2009): 242–251, doi.org/10.1037/a0017152; Randy Cohen, Chirag Bavishi, and Alan Rozanski, "Purpose in Life and Its Relationship to All-Cause Mortality and Cardiovascular Events: A Meta-Analysis," *Psychosomatic Medicine* 78, no. 2 (2016): 122–133, doi.org/10.1097/PSY.0000000000000274.

8. Anthony L. Burrow and Nicolette Rainone, "How Many Likes Did I Get?: Purpose Moderates Links between Positive Social Media Feedback and Self-Esteem.," *Journal of Experimental Social Psychology* 69 (March 1, 2017): 232–236, doi.org/10.1016/j.jesp.2016.09.005.

9. National Scientific Council on Adolescence, "Cultivating Purpose in Adolescence" (UCLA Center for the Developing Adolescent, 2023), developingadolescent.semel.ucla.edu/assets/uploads/research/resources/CR3_PurposeReport_2023_FINAL.pdf, 8.

10. Patrick L. Hill, Rachel Sumner, and Anthony L. Burrow, "Understanding the Pathways to Purpose: Examining Personality and Well-Being Correlates Across Adulthood," *The Journal of Positive Psychology* 9, no. 3 (2014): 227–234, doi.org/10.1080/17439760.2014.888584.

11. Kendall Cotton Bronk, "Five Ways to Foster Purpose in Adolescents," *Greater Good Magazine*, December 21, 2017, greatergood.berkeley.edu/article/item/five_ways_to_foster_purpose_in_adolescents.

12. National Scientific Council on Adolescence, "Cultivating Purpose in Adolescence."

13. Judy H. Hong, David C. Talavera, Mary O. Odafe, Christopher D. Barr, and Rheeda L. Walker, "Does Purpose in Life or Ethnic Identity Moderate the Association for Racial Discrimination and Suicide Ideation in Racial/Ethnic Minority Emerging Adults?," *Cultural Diversity and Ethnic Minority Psychology* 30, no. 1 (2024): 1–10, doi.org/10.1037/cdp0000245.

14. Ellen Middaugh, Lynn Schofield Clark, and Parissa J. Ballard, "Digital Media, Participatory Politics, and Positive Youth Development," *Pediatrics* 140, no. Supplement_2 (November 1, 2017): S127–S131, doi.org/10.1542/peds.2016-1758Q.

15. Joseph Kahne, Nam-Jin Lee, and Jessica T. Feezell, "The Civic and Political Significance of Online Participatory Cultures Among Youth Transitioning to Adulthood," *Journal of Information Technology & Politics* 10, no. 1 (January 1, 2013): 1–20, doi.org/10.1080/19331681.2012.701109.

16. Emily Weinstein and Carrie James, *Behind Their Screens: What Teens Are Facing (And Adults Are Missing)* (The MIT Press, 2022), 129.

17. Henry Jenkins, moderator, "Young Voices Online: An Exploration of Teens' and Tweens' Civic Engagement," Children and Screens Expert Webinar Series, video, 1:22:22, May 12, 2021, youtube.com/watch?v=u_59_GDZKtE.

18. Mizuko Ito et al., *Hanging Out, Messing Around, and Geeking Out: Kids Living and Learning with New Media* (The MIT Press, 2013).

19. Kelly Hoffman, Mega Subramaniam, Saba Kawas, Ligaya Scaff, and Katie Davis, "Connected Libraries: Surveying the Current Landscape and Charting a Path to the Future" (The ConnectedLib Project, June 8, 2017), papers.ssrn.com/sol3/papers.cfm?abstract_id=2982532.

20. Mizuko Ito et al., "The Connected Learning Research Network: Reflections on a Decade of Engaged Scholarship" (Connected Learning Alliance, 2020), clalliance.org/publications/the-connected-learning-research-network-reflections-on-a-decade-of-engaged-scholarship.

21. Ito et al., "The Connected Learning Research Network."

22. Nashville Public Library, "Studio NPL," accessed November 5, 2024, nashvillepubliclibrary.org/events/studio-npl.

23. Hartford Public Library, "YOUmedia Hartford," accessed November 5, 2024, youmedia.org/locations/hartford-ct-youmedia-hartford.

24. Kiley Larson, Mizuko Ito, Eric Brown, Mike Hawkins, Nichole Pinkard, and Penny Sebring, "Safe Space and Shared Interests: YOUmedia Chicago as a Laboratory for Connected Learning" (Connected Learning Alliance, 2013), clalliance.org/publications/safe-space-and-shared-interests-youmedia-chicago-as-a-laboratory-for-connected-learning/.

Chapter 11: The Power of Voice

1. Felix Warneken, "Precocious Prosociality: Why Do Young Children Help?," *Child Development Perspectives* 9, no. 1 (March 2015): 1–6, doi.org/10.1111/cdep.12101.

2. Making Caring Common Project, "The Children We Mean to Raise: The Real Messages Adults Are Sending About Values" (Harvard Graduate School of Education, 2014), mcc.gse.harvard.edu/reports/children-mean-raise.

3. Andrew J. Fuligni, "The Need to Contribute During Adolescence," *Perspectives on Psychological Science* 14, no. 3 (May 2019): 331–343, doi.org/10.1177/1745691618805437.

4. Andrew J. Fuligni, "Adolescents Have a Fundamental Need to Contribute," *The Conversation*, February 15, 2019, theconversation.com/adolescents-have-a-fundamental-need-to-contribute-110424.

5. Kathryn R. Wentzel, "Prosocial Behavior and Peer Relations in Adolescence," in *Prosocial Development: A Multidimensional Approach* (Oxford University Press, 2014), 178–200, doi.org/10.1093/acprof:oso/9780199964772.003.0009.

6. Frank Martela and Richard M. Ryan, "The Benefits of Benevolence: Basic Psychological Needs, Beneficence and the Enhancement of Well-Being," *Journal of Personality* 84, no. 6 (August 6, 2015): 750–764, doi.org/10.1111/jopy.12215.

7. Hannah L. Schacter and Gayla Margolin, "When It Feels Good to Give: Depressive Symptoms, Daily Prosocial Behavior, and Adolescent Mood," *Emotion* 19, no. 5 (2019): 923–927, doi.org/10.1037/emo0000494.

8. Eva H. Telzer and Andrew J. Fuligni, "Daily Family Assistance and the Psychological Well-Being of Adolescents from Latin American, Asian, and European Backgrounds," *Developmental Psychology* 45, no. 4 (2009): 1177–1189, doi.org/10.1037/a0014728.

9. Meghan Lynch Forder, "What Teens Gain When They Contribute to Their Social Groups," *Greater Good Magazine*, July 22, 2019, greatergood.berkeley.edu/article/item/what_teens_gain_when_they_contribute_to_their_social_groups.

10. United Nations, "Convention on the Rights of the Child," General Assembly resolution 44/25, OHCHR, November 20, 1989, ohchr.org/en/instruments-mechanisms/instruments/convention-rights-child.

11. Julia Callahan, "Who Has The Solutions For Thriving In A Digital World? Young

People," Connected Learning Alliance, December 6, 2022, clalliance.org/blog/who-has-the-solutions-for-thriving-in-a-digital-world-young-people.

12. Thriving Youth in a Digital World, "The Why: Technology, Digital Media, and Virtual Communications Are Ubiquitous," Susan Crown Exchange, accessed November 5, 2024, youthdigitalwellbeing.org/about.

13. Emily Weinstein, Beck Tench, and Sophia Choukas-Bradley, "Teaching Digital Well-Being: Evidence-Based Resources to Help Youth Thrive" (Center for Digital Thriving, 2023), https://drive.google.com/file/d/1isY8MKWP_xYt--VnXcpcv19B0RSLjJ9f/view?usp=embed_facebook.

14. #HalftheStory, accessed November 5, 2024, halfthestoryproject.com.

Afterword: Do Parents Still Matter?

1. Robyn Fivush et al., "Family Narratives and the Development of Children's Emotional Well-Being," in *Family Stories and the Life Course: Across Time and Generations*, edited by Michael W. Pratt and Barbara H. Fiese (Lawrence Erlbaum Associates Publishers, 2004).

2. Emily Weinstein, Beck Tench, and Sophia Choukas-Bradley, "Teaching Digital Well-Being: Evidence-Based Resources to Help Youth Thrive" (Center for Digital Thriving, 2023), https://drive.google.com/file/d/1isY8MKWP_xYt--VnXcpcv19B0RSLjJ9f/view?usp=embed_facebook.

3. Linda Charmaraman, Interviewed by Erin Walsh, Riverside, January 9, 2024.

4. Megan A. Moreno and Jenny Radesky, "Putting Forward a New Narrative for Adolescent Media: The American Academy of Pediatrics Center of Excellence on Social Media and Youth Mental Health," *Journal of Adolescent Health* 73, no. 2 (August 1, 2023): 227–229, doi.org/10.1016/j.jadohealth.2023.04.027, 4.

5. Renee E. Sieving et al., "Youth–Adult Connectedness," *American Journal of Preventive Medicine* 52, no. 3 Supplement 3 (March 2017): S275–S278, doi.org/10.1016/j.amepre.2016.07.037.

6. Yang Qu, Andrew J. Fuligni, Adriana Galvan, and Eva H. Telzer, "Buffering Effect of Positive Parent-Child Relationships on Adolescent Risk Taking: A Longitudinal Neuroimaging Investigation," *Developmental Cognitive Neuroscience* 15 (October 2015): 26–34, doi.org/10.1016/j.dcn.2015.08.005.

Index

A

addiction, internet, 41

ADHD (attention deficit hyperactivity disorder), 15, 35, 40

adolescence, 1–2. *See also* brain, the
definition, 4
falling in love, 129–130
independence during, 94–95
risk-taking during. *See* risks and risk-taking
search for purpose in, 190–191
separation-individuation phase during, 78–79
sexuality and relationships during, 129–130
teens describing, 12
as a window of opportunity, 13–14

adults. *See also* parent(s)
partnering with young people to solve digital challenges, 209–210
responding to emotional expressions, 57–58
teens talking about online cruelty to, 59
using media with teens, 19

AI (artificial intelligence) chatbot, 5
information about sex/sexuality on, 129, 131
lonely kids turning to, 152–153
online cruelty and, 159

Alper, Meryl, 68, 119

Alter, Adam, 37

American Academy of Pediatrics, 49, 96, 206

American Psychiatric Association (APA), 41

American Psychological Association, 61, 100, 213

anxiety, 49, 50, 64–65. *See also* mental health

app(s)
deleting an, 47–48
for tracking, 92–94

appearance-related content, 65, 173–177

appearance-related social media consciousness (ASMC) scale, 178

artificial intelligence (AI). *See* AI (artificial intelligence) chatbot

Asian Americans, 120, 156–157

attention
focused, 15, 40, 44–45
multitasking and, 39–40

attention systems, 34–35

autism, 26–27, 35, 119

B

Barnum effect, 69

beauty ideals, 177. *See also* Appearance-related content

belonging, sense of, 152, 153, 154–155, 164–166

Bennett, Vanessa Kroll, 130

Black Twitter, 120

Black youth, 58, 173

blossoming (developmental process in the brain), 13

body image, 173–177, 178–179

both/and parenting, 70–72, 143

boundaries
autonomy-supportive parenting and, 107
being clear about purpose of, 108–109
devices away from sleeping areas, 37
family media agreements, 102, 205–206
guidelines for autonomy-supportive, 107
guidelines on setting, 109–110
for managing digital distractions, 37
monitoring tools and, 101–102
reflecting on, 112
restrictive strategies, problems with, 19–21
study on parental use of, 22

boyd, danah, 103

boys, body image concerns among teen, 175–177

brain-derived neurotropic factor (BDNF), 51

brain development, child, 12–13

brain, the
abstract thinking and, 191
attention systems, 34–35
as built for discovery and learning, 17–19
development from childhood to adolescence, 12–13
development processes in, 13
dopamine and, 29
emotions of teens and, 57
environmental/experiential influences and, 14–16
executive function skills, 14, 17, 56, 96
idea of a "broken," 11–12
looking-out and looking-in networks in, 112
memories and, 18
peer influence and, 163
prefrontal cortex, 12, 14, 17, 28, 34, 51, 53, 56, 111, 129–130, 140
rapid development of, 12–13
restrictive strategies to screen use and, 20
reward sensitivity and the teenage, 28–31
rewards from social feedback and, 171
risk-taking and, 17
sex, relationships, and the, 129–130
stress and the, 50–51, 53

Bronk, Kendall Cotton, 193

Brown, Brené, 152

bullying, offline, 156

bullying, online. *See* Cyberbullying

bystanders, 162–164

C

cellphones. *See* phone(s)
Center for Digital Thriving, Harvard School of Education, 173, 204–205
Centers for Disease Control and Prevention (CDC), 49
Charmaraman, Linda, 213
Choukas-Bradley, Sophia, 174, 178
civic engagement, 194
cognitive distortions, 172–173
Common Sense Media, 98, 135, 155, 171
comparisons, social, 170, 174, 180, 181
connected learning, 197–198
Connected Learning Lab, University of California, 30
connection/connectedness. *See also* belonging, sense of
  importance of parent-child, 80–82
  parent-child, changing as children get older, 89–90
  parents reflecting on a mindset for, 90–91
  with people at school, 146–147
  prioritizing personal connection over phones and, 83–85
  prioritizing when setting boundaries, 109–110
  relationships with other adults and, 88–89
  screen-free containers for, 85–87
  self-compassion and, 181
  through digital interests, 197, 198
  through technology, 87–88
  through warmth and support, 82
  without devices, 79–80
context collapse, 103
contributing, by teens, 200–210
conversations
  about mental health, 66–67, 70
  about online belonging and exclusion, 155
  about phones and friends, 151–152
  about porn, 136–137
  about role of technology in your child's life, 62–64
  about sex and relationships, 130–131, 132–134, 143–144
  about sexting and nudes, 142–143
  about sharing things online, 123–124
  about social media, 70
  after seeing something on your child's phone, 104–105
  questions to ask your teen about technology, 62–64
  using values-aligned messaging, 37–39
  when setting boundaries, 108–109
COVID-19 pandemic, 49, 215
cyberbullying, 154–158, 160, 161–162

D

Damon, William, 191
Damour, Lisa, 1, 57, 82
dark patterns, 35–36
Davis, Katie, 33, 116
decision-making
  rewards of risk-taking and, 29–30
  young people's contributions to, 203–204, 205–206
dendrites, 13
depression. *See also* mental health
  experienced by parents, 50
  online relationships and, 64–65
  rise in, 49
devices. *See also* phone(s)
  mealtimes without, 79–80
  notifications from, 36
  placed away from sleeping areas, 37
  used by parents, 42–43
digital activity/use
  benefit of self-directed experiences, 33
  boundaries for. *See* boundaries
  brain development and, 14–16
  co-creation of family media agreements for, 205–206
  connecting with your teen through, 87–88
  conversations about. *see* conversations
  doomscrolling, 189
  mindful, 40
  multitasking and, 39–40
  as not designed for healthy risk-taking, 30–31
  by parents, 38–39, 42–43, 45–46
  parent's both/and approach to, 70–72
  parent's responses to what they see from their child's, 102–105
  as a portal to purpose, 194–195
  problematic overuse, 41–42
  questions about mental health and, 64–66
  teens being in control of their, 31–33
  that are self-directed and community supported, 33
digital challenges
  adults partnering with young people to solve, 209–210, 214–215
  boundaries for. *See* boundaries
  conversations about. *See* conversations
  online conflict and cruelty. *See* online cruelty and conflicts
  overuse, 41–42
  responding with agency and respect, 108
  young people contributing to solutions for, 205–207
digital footprint, 122–123
digital interests/skills, 196–198
digital media. *See also* internet; social media (use)

dark patterns in, 35–36
eight characteristics of, 116–117
narratives of, 212–215
remaining engaged with your child's, 215–216
self-directed media experiences, 43–44
digital social multitasking, 148–151
digital status seeking, 172
Discord, 17, 58, 59, 154
distractions, 34–35, 36–37, 40
doomscrolling, 189, 195
dopamine, 29, 30, 36, 111, 129
Dosomething.org, 204
dysgraphia, 35

E

early adolescence
delaying social media use beyond, 64, 100
digital distractions and, 150
use of term, 4
early childhood, brain development in, 12–13
eating disorders, 175–177
emotional regulation, 12, 51, 53, 55, 56, 57–59
emotions
bewildering adolescent behavior and, 14
stress and, 55–56
Englander, Elizabeth, 59, 157, 160, 161, 164
entertainment media
average number of hours spent on, 6
impact on adolescent brain development, 14–15
Erikson, Erik, 114
ethnic identity, 120–121, 173
exercise/movement, prioritizing, 111
exploration, 95–98, 114–115. See also identity formation
extremist groups, 154–155

F

family decision-making, contributions by young people for, 205–206, 207
family media agreements, 102, 205–206
fitting in, 146, 152, 153
focused attention, 15, 34–35, 39, 40, 44–45
Forder, Meghan Lynch, 203
friends/friendship
AI chatbots and, 153
avoiding making new, 54–55
experiencing belonging with, 164–166
finding, 146–147
phones and, 148–152
phone use and connecting with/supporting, 71–72, 110
social sensitivity and, 147–148
Fuligni, Andrew, 202

G

Galinsky, Ellen, 11, 14
Galván, Adriana, 29
gaming
overuse of, 41–42
as a way of maintaining old friends and avoiding make new friends, 54–55
gaming disorder, 41
Gearity, Anne, 207
gender
attention paid to physical appearance and, 174
eating disorders and, 175–176
emotional responses and, 57–58
sexting and, 141–142
gender identity, 129
genetics, brain development and, 15
geotracking, 93
Germer, Christopher, 181
green time, prioritizing, 111
group chats, 16, 17
group texts, 162–163

H

Harrison, Kristen, 71
Heitner, Devorah, 93, 104, 118–119, 141
Hinduja, Sameer, 156, 157
HOMAGO (Hanging Out, Messing Around, and Geeking Out), 196
hormones, 28, 51, 129

I

identity formation, 114–127
as different from past generations, 117
digital footprint and, 122–123
online playgrounds for, 115–116
parental involvement and, 127
sharenting and, 125–127
sharing personal information online and, 118–122, 124
imaginary audience ideation, 147–148
imaginary audiences, 166, 171, 174
Immordino-Yang, Mary Helen, 112, 191
In Action tools, 7
independence, 92–113
age to start using social media and, 100–101
autonomy-supportive parenting and, 107
boundaries and, 109–112
first devices and, 100–101
importance of roaming and, 95–97
monitoring tools and, 101–102, 104
online platforms and, 98
phone ownership and, 98–99
push and pull of, 94–95
responses by parents and, 102–104, 108–109
teen's need for respect and, 105–108
of toddlers, 94

tracking teens and, 92–94, 104
inevitability, narrative of, 212–213
influencers, online, 118, 174, 176
Instagram, 100, 120–121, 123, 174, 176
internet. *See also* online cruelty and conflicts;
    social media (use)
  finding a sense of belonging on, 152,
      154–155
  harmful content on, 65
  is not ideal environment for roaming and
      independence, 98
  offline personas aligned with online
      personas on, 116
  overuse of, 41–42, 65
  pornography on, 134–139
  safety and ethical issues when using, 16
  sexual health information on, 128, 131–132
  teens navigating life stressors through the,
      48–49
internet gaming disorder, 41
inventory, for identifying internet overuse,
    41–42
Ito, Mizuko (Mimi), 119, 196, 197

J

James, Carrie, 116, 121, 141, 195
James, William, 169
Jha, Amishi, 40

K

Knecht, Douglas R., 191

L

Lenhart, Amanda, 31
LGBTQ+ youth, 120, 131, 156–157, 175
listening to adolescents and teens, 32, 207–208
loneliness, 146, 147, 148–149, 152–153, 154,
    164
love
  child's self-worth and, 184, 185
  self-compassion and, 181
Lythcott-Haims, Julie, 96

M

Marron, Dylan, 155
mealtimes without devices, 79–80
media agreements, 102, 205–206
media sensory curation, 71–72
mental health
  body image concerns and, 175
  complicated relationship between
      technology and, 49
  cyberbullying and, 156
  diagnosed through social media, 67, 69
  digital platforms for, 30–31
  doomscrolling and, 189
  importance of independence for, 96–97
  learning about on social media, 67–69

of parents, 49–50
prevalence of anxiety and depression, 49
questions about screen use and your child's,
    64–66
self-compassion and, 182
social media and, 60–62
talking to teens about, 66–67, 70
toll of being camera ready on, 178
vulnerability to extremist groups and, 154
young people receiving information on,
    67–69
metacognition, 43–44
Middaugh, Ellen, 195
mindful digital use, 45
mindfulness, 40, 59, 111–112
mind wandering, 111–112
Minecraft, 83–84, 115–116, 215
monitoring digital use, 101–105. *See also*
    tracking apps
Morales, Ricardo Levins, 211
Moreno, Megan, 213
multitasking, 39–40
Murthy, Vivek, 50, 61
myelination (developmental process in the
    brain), 13

N

Nagata, Jason, 175–176, 177
National Scientific Council on Adolescence,
    43, 192
Natterson, Cara, 130
Neff, Kristin, 181, 182
Nesi, Jacqueline, 62, 69, 109, 171–172
neurodiversity/neurodivergent youth, 15, 35,
    67, 71, 152
neurotransmitters, 28–29
news, reading online, 189
notifications, 36, 110

O

older adolescence. *See also* teens
  civic expressions posted by, 123
  restrictive strategies towards screen time
      during, 20
  study on outcome of lower social media use
      during, 100–101
  use of term, 4
online cruelty and conflicts
  compared with experiencing cruelty in
      person, 158–159
  cyberbullying, 154–158, 160, 161–162
  digital design features and, 159
  emotional regulation and, 51, 58
  in group chat, 16
  monitoring and, 101
  offline behaviors and, 159–160
  parents responding to, 160–162

peer influence and, 162–164
practicing skills for, 165
teens talking to adults about, 59
online feedback. *See* social feedback
online pornography, 134–139
Owens, Kellie, 31

P

parent(s). *See also* conversations; reflection
    exercises
  asking their teen open-ended and curious
      questions, 76–77
  awareness of their tech habits, 45–46
  bolstering their child's self-worth, 180–181
  child's self-esteem and, 169–170
  communicating to teens they are on the
      same team, 23–24
  connection to child, 80–82, 89–90
  digital use by, 38–39, 42–43, 45–46
  helping kids deal with challenges, 52–53
  impact of screen use by, 22
  impact on child's self-worth, 184–185
  importance of involvement by, 21–22
  listening by, 207–208
  as mattering to young people, 216–218
  modeling self-compassion, 182–183
  monitoring digital use, 101–105
  prioritizing personal connections *versus*
      devices, 83–85
  questions to ask your adolescent, 62–63
  reflecting on their approach to risks and
      rewards, 44–45
  remaining engaged with child's digital life,
      215–216
  responding to child's desire for an video
      game online account, 25
  responding to cyberbullying and online
      cruelty, 160–162
  responding to what they see on their child's
      phone, 101–105
  restrictive approach to screen time by,
      19–21
  separation-individuation phase of teens and,
      78–79
  sharing positive stories on risk-taking, 27
  staying connected with their teens, 80–82
  stress experienced by, 49–50
  study on approach to screen use by, 21–22
  supporting child experiencing stress, 56,
      58, 59
  tracking their teens, 92–94
  use of term, 4
parental controls, 5, 101, 102, 214
parenthood, 1–2
parenting style, identifying your, 24–25
Patchin, Justin W., 156, 157
Pediatrics, 95, 97

peer influences
    peer cruelty/cyberbullying and, 162–164
    social feedback online and, 170–173
perfectionism, 56
Perry, Bruce, 52, 81
personal solutions to collective problems,
    narrative of, 214–215
phone(s). *See also* devices
  feelings when child gets a new, 5
  friendships and, 148–152
  nude photos on, 139–141, 142–143
  parents responding to what they see on their
      child's, 102–105
  when to introduce to children, 98–100
photos
  appearance-related concerns and, 178–179
  of children, sharing online, 126–127
  nude, 139–141
political activity, online, 194–195
political identities and opinions, 121–122, 123
pornography, 130, 134–139
presence, self-compassion and, 181
privacy, 123
pruning (developmental process in the brain),
    13
purpose, 188–199
  in adolescent development, 191
  benefits of, 192
  civic engagement and, 194–195
  digital interests and, 196–198
  importance of opportunities cultivating,
      193–194
  pathways to, 192–193
  providing opportunities to explore, 198–199
  three key criteria defining, 191

Q

queer adolescents, 130. *See also* LGBTQ+
    youth

R

racial identity, 120–121, 173
Radesky, Jenny, 35, 213
Ratey, John, 111
reactive attention system, 34, 36
reflection exercises, 7
  on a connection mindset, 90–91
  on cultivating purpose, 198–199
  on cyberbullying and online cruelty,
      161–162
  on digital social multitasking, 150–151
  digital stress check-in, 72–73
  on giving your child their first device, 99
  inventory on online activities, 41–42
  on responding to teen's stress, 60
  on risks, rewards, and digital-age parenting,
      44–45

on screen-free containers, 87
on screen time boundaries, 112
on self-worth and social media, 180
on sharenting, 126
on stories you inherited about sex and
    relationships, 132–133
on talking about sexting and nudes,
    142–143
on unconditional positive regard, 184
on your parenting style, 24–25
relationships. *See also* friends/friendship
    characteristic of digital, 159
    falling in love, 129–130
    fitting in *versus* belonging in, 152, 153
    having conversations about, 132–134
    as key to facilitating healthy self-
        exploration, 115
    mental health and online, 64–65
    online, 64–65
    phones and quality of, 148–150
respect, 105–107
restrictive mediation strategies, 19
reward(s)
    digital design features and, 35–37
    risk-taking and, 27–28
    from social feedback, 171
    teen brain and sensitivity to, 28–31
risks and risk-taking, 17
    dopamine and, 29
    emotional rewards of, 29–30
    opportunities for skill development and,
        20–21
    parents' self-reflection on how they
        approach, 44
    positive stories about, 26–27
    rewards and, 27–28
    social media use and, 30
roaming, 95, 97, 99

S

scratch, 119
screen-free time, 85–87
screen time. *See also* Digital activity/use
    average time spent on by teens, 6
    boundaries on. *See* Boundaries
    "digital playgrounds" for young children, 19
    parents using, 21–22
    problems with restrictive strategies for,
        19–21
    recommendations on, 61–62
    talking to your adolescent about, 62–64
seeking brain, 36
self-compassion, 180–183
self-expression. *See* Identity formation
self-worth and self-esteem, 168–185
    appraisal from others on social media and,
        168–169

body image and, 173–177
    efforts by parents to boost child's, 169–170
    parent's impact on, 185
    related to your online physical appearance,
        177–180
    self-compassion and, 180–183
    as set of opinions about oneself, 169
    social feedback online and, 170–173
    unconditional positive regard, 183–184
separation-individuation phase, 78–79
sex, sexuality, and sexual health
    adolescent bodies/brains and, 129–130
    having conversations about, 130–131,
        132–134, 143–144
    information from the internet on, 131–132
    online porn and, 134–139
    questions by adolescents on, 128–129
sex education, 130, 132, 134–135
sexting, 130, 139–143
sextortion, 140–141
sexual identity, 120, 130
shame, narrative of, 213–214
sharenting, 125–127
skill development, restrictive strategies not
        promoting, 20–21
slacktivism, 195
sleep, influence of technology on, 110–111
sleeping areas, devices placed away from, 37
Snapchat, 32, 33, 100, 174
social comparison, 170, 174, 180, 181
social conflict. *See* online cruelty and conflicts
social feedback, 64, 147–148, 168–169,
        170–173, 180, 184
social media (use). *See also* digital activity/use
    body image concerns and, 174–175
    creating rewards loops for risky behavior, 30
    diagnosing and learning about mental
        health issues on, 67–69
    mental health issues and, 60–62
    motivating teens to control use of, 37–38
    parents sharing information about their
        children on, 125–127
    personal lives of actors, musicians, and
        athletes on, 118
    self-esteem and appraisal from others on,
        168–169
    sharing personal things on, 118–122, 124
    study on outcomes of low *versus* high use of,
        100–101
    toll of being camera ready on, 177–179
    values-alignment messaging about, 37–38
    when to start using, 100
Steinberg, Laurence, 18
Stone, Elizabeth, 93
stress and distress
    the brain and, 50–51, 53
    deleting an app because of, 47–48

digital stress check-in, 72–73
experienced by parents, 49–50
how people respond to, 55–56
kids learning to navigate, 52–53
learning to cope with, 53
looking for signs of, 65–67
managing emotions and, 53, 57–59
responding to a teen's, 59
signs of, 65–66
situations leading to toxic, 52
stress toolkit, 60
suicide/suicide attempts, 49, 156
Susan Crown Exchange, 204
Szalavitz, Maia, 52, 81

T

tech companies
business priorities of, 35–36, 98
manipulative design features by, 214
parent's concerns about, 93
questions motivating adolescents to control
digital use about, 37–38
recommendation algorithms of, 179
treated like Big Tobacco, 62
values-alignment messaging about social
media use and, 37
technoconference, 83–85
technology. *See also* devices; digital activity/
use; internet; phone(s); social media
(use)
connection/connectedness through, 87–88
keeping up with changes in, 5
parents on benefits of, 92–93
research on risks and benefits of, 21–22
teen ambivalence about, 48
what to prioritize over, 109–112
teens
average time spent on screen media, 6
boundaries for. *See* boundaries
consistency of offline and online personas
of, 116
conversations with. *See* Conversations
describing adolescence, 12
desire to contribute, 200–210
developmental questions of, 6
digital activities of. *See* Digital activity/use
feeling disrespected, 105–107
friendships of. *See* Friends(hips)
identity formation in. *See* Identity formation
independence of. *See* Independence
managing emotions, 57–59
parents staying connected with their, 80–82
self-worth in. *See* Self-worth and self-esteem
sensitive to social feedback, 147–148
social media use. *See* Social media (use)
stress in. *See* Stress and distress
tracking, 92–93

Tench, Beck, 132
TikTok, 33, 68, 69, 120–121, 174, 176
time limits, for young children, 19
Tourette syndrome, 35
toxic stress, 51, 52
tracking apps, 92–93
trans youth, 156–157, 175
traumatic experiences, 52, 121, 156
Turkle, Sherry, 148
2020 Native Youth Health Tech Survey, 120

U

UCLA Center for the Developing Adolescent,
17
unconditional positive regard, 183–184
US Surgeon General, 49, 50, 61, 147

V

values-aligned messaging, 37–38
Venet, Shevrin, 183
video games
overuse of, 41–42
parent's response to challenges with, 108
teen wanting an online account for, 25
voice, giving young people a, 200–210

W

Wallace, Jennifer Breheny, 184
Walsh, David, 41
Weinstein, Emily, 71–72, 116, 121, 132, 141,
173, 195
Weissbourd, Richard, 49–50
Williams, Joanna Lee, 121
Willis, Henry, 121
World Health Organization (WHO), 41

Y

Yang, Chia-chen, 149, 150
Youth Voice in the Digital Age Challenge, 204
YouTube, 36, 108, 131, 195–196

Reading Guide

1. You likely started this book with a set of beliefs, assumptions, and concerns related to your child's tech habits and activities. Has reading this book shifted your perspective in any way? How?

2. This book asks you to turn away from news headlines and toward your teenager. Have you found ways to do this? What have you learned about their digital world? What has been surprising? Confusing? Concerning? Inspiring?

3. Your teen may not be eager to discuss challenging topics, but talking with you about sexting, porn, cyberbullying, body image, and online hate increases the likelihood that your teen will navigate these issues safely. What helps you gather courage to have these conversations? What barriers do you face? Are some topics easier to address than others are?

4. This book shares that young people learn through trial and error, and they benefit from exploring new terrain to discover what they are capable of. In your own family, how do you balance the need for safety online with your teen's developmental drive to explore and discover? What about offline?

5. Try as you might to create "safe enough" places to explore, your teen will encounter digital risks and challenges. What is it like for you when your teenager hits a tech-related challenge? How do you tend to respond? While you read this book, were there moments when you felt encouraged to reframe how you approach online challenges? How might you adjust your approach?

6. Learning how to use technology in healthy ways is a shared struggle. Did this book inspire you to reflect on your own relationship with technology? What struggles came up for you? How might you communicate this awareness to your teen or other members of your family?

7. While staying connected and communicating with your teen is key, this book explains that your teenager may temporarily pull away from you to figure out who they are and where they belong. What does that look like for your teen? How does it feel to you?

8. This book encourages you to think of creative ways to stay connected during the sometimes-rocky adolescent development process. What's going well for you and your teen? What do you want to change or try?

9. Teens need both warm connection and structured boundaries to thrive. Setting boundaries with teens is not always easy. After reading this book, have you either affirmed or changed where, when, or how you set technology boundaries? If so, in what ways?

10. Learning about adolescent brain development can help parents take things less personally. It can also help parents cultivate empathy for young people's experiences. Can you identify any aha moments you had while reading this book when you better understood your teen's behavior, perspective, or experience? Did this new understanding shift the way you respond to your teen when it comes to technology? How?

11. In the conclusion, the author notes that screen-time shame doesn't serve parents (or teens) well. Do you ever feel screen-time shame? What would it feel like to let that go?

12. This book reminds you that as a parent of a teenager, you are growing and learning alongside your kid. What a powerful model for your teen! Which specific tools, exercises, or resources mentioned in the book would you like to explore further?

13. If your teen were to write you a letter thanking you for stepping meaningfully into their digital life, what do you think it would say? If you were to write a letter to your teen expressing your love for them, your commitment to them, and your confidence in their ability to navigate the digital world, what would it say? Consider writing this letter. Consider giving it to them. Don't expect a thank-you. That part might come later.

About the Author

Erin Walsh is a parent, speaker, and author. She has worked with communities across the United States and Canada who want to better understand child and adolescent development and cut through conflicting information about kids and technology. She is committed to bringing an equity lens and asset-based approach to our understanding of, and response to, youth and media. Her signature down-to-earth approach and sense of humor help families and educators engage in complicated topics and leave feeling capable and motivated.

Erin has enjoyed bringing science and strategies to families and educators alongside her father, Dr. David Walsh, for nearly twenty years. They started working together at the National Institute on Media and the Family before creating Spark & Stitch Institute in 2019. In addition to writing articles for several publications, including *Psychology Today*, she coauthored the tenth anniversary edition of the national bestseller *Why Do They Act That Way? A Survival Guide to the Adolescent Brain for You and Your Teen.*

Before the creation of Spark & Stitch Institute, Erin taught undergraduate students for nine years with the Higher Education Consortium for Urban Affairs and was a lead program facilitator for Youth Frontiers. Her work has been featured in local publications across the country as well as the *Washington Post, Parents.com,* and *Yahoo News.* Erin has served several community organizations, including as a professional mentor for NextGen Connect at Fairplay, an intergenerational mentoring program for youth digital wellness leaders, and as board chair of YMCA Camp Widjiwagan, a wilderness-based youth development program. She has worked with schools, school districts, parent groups, and other youth-serving organizations throughout North America on issues related to digital media, children, and youth.

Erin lives in Minneapolis, Minnesota, with her wife, two kids, and husky dog. In her free time, she is likely skijoring, singing her heart out, gathering community, or exploring outdoors.